Praise for *The Roots of Resistance*

"If you loved Starhawk's *Fifth Sacred Thing*, if you loved recently-departed Ursula K. LeGuin's *The Dispossessed*, if you admire the spirit of the Standing Rock Water Protectors, you will drink in this must-read page-turner . . . an epic story that will move your spirit, bringing tears to your eyes and healing to your soul." - Rosa Zubizarreta, Author of *From Conflict to Creative Collaboration*

"A tale of revolution, resistance and the indomitable power of love . . . skims tantalizingly close to the surface of what could be political reality in these United States in just a few short years. Recommended for wanderers, whistleblowers, and anyone curious about the question of violence vs. nonviolence." - Elizabeth Murray, former Deputy National Intelligence Office for the Near East, National Intelligence Council and Member in Residence, Ground Zero Center for Nonviolent Action

"*The Roots of Resistance* is a compelling page-turner about the inner workings of a nonviolent movement and how it deals with forces that try to sabotage it. I loved this book!" - Judy Olson, Backbone Campaign

"This book is a treasure of a resource; it's a repertoire of nonviolence techniques disguised as a novel." - Michael Nagler, Founder and President, The Metta Center for Nonviolence

"A must-read, written by the talented Rivera Sun! Resistance is essential, as nonviolent actions will save humanity. Amazingly inspirational!" - Robin Wildman, Nonviolent Schools

"Billed as 'Book Two of the Dandelion Trilogy,' this one makes me hope Sun is punching out Book Three soon and perhaps, like Douglas Adams, will give us, someday, Books Four and Five of the Trilogy." - Tom H. Hastings, Conflict Resolution Assistant Professor, Portland State University

"In times of despair, we need hope. In times of frustration, we need inspiration. In times of confusion, we need clarity. Rivera brings us all of these and more."
- Stephen Zunes, University of San Francisco

"Excellent sequel and continuation of the Dandelion Trilogy, can't wait for #3! Meanwhile, there is much to digest and to share. Rivera is a true visionary." - Joni LeViness

"Once again Rivera Sun weaves a captivating story of change and shows us a path forward out of the fear and control of our current chaotic world and toward a world whose foundation is Love. This is just the story we need to inform, inspire and call us forth into action." - Cindy Reinhardt, the Success Zone

"Rivera paints a gritty story. . . *Pero, asi es la vida. The Roots* characters unapologetically show us that the change we want won't be easy. Buckle up for a bumpy, triumphant ride!" - Elyssa Marie Serrilli

"*The Roots of Resistance* is an exciting read. I am always entertained, educated and inspired by Rivera Sun's writing! I am grateful to her." - Kathryn Morse

"This novel represents Rivera Sun at her best - plenty of action, a gripping story-line, really interesting and conscious characters (at least the good guys!), and all in the service of a non-violent, yet wholly believable revolution that could just transform these United States." - Jim Dreaver, author, *End Your Story, Begin Your Life*

Other Works

by

Rivera Sun

Novels, Books & Poetry

The Dandelion Insurrection

The Way Between

Billionaire Buddha

Steam Drills, Treadmills, and Shooting Stars

The Dandelion Insurrection Study Guide

Skylandia: Farm Poetry From Maine

Freedom Stories: volume one

The Imagine-a-nation of Lala Child

RISING SUN

PRESS WORKS

The Roots of Resistance

by

Rivera Sun

The Roots of Resistance

Copyright © 2018 by Rivera Sun

Rising Sun Press Works
P.O. Box 1751, El Prado, NM 87529
www.riverasun.com

Library of Congress Control Number:
2017956035
ISBN 978-1-948016-99-5
Sun, Rivera 1982-
The Roots of Resistance

Cover design by Asch Phoenix Design.
www.aschphoenixdesign.com

A Community Published Book Supported By:

Anna Schoon
Sue Carroll
Burt Kempner
Donna Lynn Price
Rene and Alex Jalbert
Claire Maitre
Cindy Reinhardt
Brian Cummings
Kathryn Morse
Ken Kailing and Gail Nickel-Kailing
Dolly, Adam, Wyatt, Austyn, and Xyler Vogal
Nigel Jones
Nim Batchelor
Judith Detert-Moriarty
Helen Zuman
Thom & Joan Madden
Tom Atlee
Sunny Dawn Freeman
Robin Wildman
Sunshine Jones
Glenn Cratty LiCSW
Martin Dahlborg
Ashley Olson
Romaldo, Carol, and Luigi Ranellone
Nancy Audette
Karen Lane
Elyssa Marie Serrilli
Ellen Friedman
Steph Mulholland
Tania Chavez
Elizabeth Cooper
Karen "MamaTree" LaGoo
Andrew S. Oliver
Maia Duerr
Stanley Taylor

Joni LeViness
Carol Jussaume, RSM
Laura Clark
Galynne & Mark Riggenbach
Ken Butigan — Cynthia Okayama Dopke, our daughter
Leah Butigan, my nephew Brian Butigan
Leslie Warnick
Leslie A. Donovan
Gloria Switzer
Mary Ryan-Hotchkiss
Bob Banner, HopeDance.org
David Soumis
Bill Warters
Hilda J. Richey
Caroline C.
Christine Kosonen
Judith & Gino Schiavone
Caitlin Waddick, Ursula, Anika, Rustum, and Asim Zia
Mary Pendergast, RSM
Lars Prip, Veterans for Peace
Casey Dorman
Marirose NightSong and Daniel Podgurski
Stephen Zunes, University of San Francisco
Beverly Campbell
Christine JG Upton
Jeri Costa
Starr C. Gilmartin
Alice C. McCain
Rosa Zubizarreta
Saki & Breeze
Lori Frazer
Chris Brickley
Dena Patrick
Lynne A. Dews
Jamie Guerin
Julia Diana Woods

Dedicated to
my three miracles:
being alive,
my healers and doctors,
and the readers who make this book possible!

Table of Contents

The Roots of Resistance

Storm winds of change swept over the country. Victories turned bitter with losses. Forked tongues and deception spread doubt and confusion. Enemies lurked in the guises of friends. Facing threats on all sides, the Dandelion Insurrection dug deep, and held fast to the roots of resistance.

CHAPTER ONE

· · · · ·

Charlie Rider

He shivered. Once again, the dream thundered through him as he slept. The surge of voices soared. Millions rose in song, in love, in hope. The spirit of revolution loomed closer than the next heartbeat. The press of bodies flooded the streets. The inexorable tides of change swept humanity through the capital. The taste of salt hung on his lips. Tears streamed down his cheeks.

And then, the terror. Dream crashed into nightmare. A breath of a moan escaped. He twitched. His arms and legs clenched to run. The reverberations of the drone shuddered down the length of his muscles in spasms. His eyelids jerked; the drone struck. Beautiful living bodies blasted into pieces. Songs turned into screams of horror. His body flailed as he dove for cover. The crowd ran and slammed up against each other.

"Charlie!"

The voice cracked through the nightmare. His blue eyes flew open. He bolted upright and reeled at the sight of strangers. His heart pounded.

"You dozed off," someone told him. "It's time."

Sweat beaded cold on his forehead. A gray sky stretched endlessly overhead. His body ached from the cold metal of the folding chair he had sprawled across. The ceaseless exhaustion of the week sagged into his limbs as the shocked adrenaline left his veins. His mind ran like a frantic rat on a wheel through the

1

list of meetings, tasks, and appointments, trying to remember where he was - and why.

"You'll need this," the stranger said, handing him a black umbrella.

At the sight of the color, the world lurched nauseatingly into focus.

His name was Charlie Rider. He was twenty-six years old. He had won a revolution. He had come to bury his friends.

CHAPTER TWO

. . . . .

The Bitter World

The sharp inhale of death sucked the color from the world. In blacks and grays, the gathered people lined the streets for miles. A child's laugh was abruptly silenced. Muffled sobs rose from the crowd of bowed heads. Charlie Rider staggered to his weary feet, out of the cold chair, away from his nightmare.

For days, clouds had skulked the skyline as the Dandelion Insurrection stumbled through the shock of victory and loss. As if to taunt them, a sliver of light escaped. A small boy broke loose from his aunt's grip and angrily hurled a stone at the burning glare of the sun. A shriek of grief and outrage tore from his lips. At the sound, heads turned. The hot tears in the boy's reddened eyes scalded their hearts. Charlie steeled his body against the urge to join the boy in flinging impotent rocks at a sun that rose and set implacably on the bitter irony of the world.

"*Es un mundo amargo lleno de dolores,*" Inez Hernandez murmured to her nephew as he threw the wires of his arms around her waist. He wept in the embrace of his aunt, and so did not see his mother's coffin passing in the long line of caskets between the two sides of the mourning crowd.

A bitter world full of sorrows, Charlie thought. A world that robbed the thrill of victory from them with a single hand. A world where the joy of the people was stolen by one finger on a trigger in a room far away. A world where the motion of a drone operator poured bitter grief onto a moment of triumph and denied them the sweetness of celebration.

3

Charlie's thoughts broke off as his fury turned white-hot in his chest. Silently, he railed against the gray sky, at the drones no longer overhead, at the throbbing presence that would not leave his nightmares, at the wanton act of destruction that sent a missile screaming into the edge of the crowd and reduced whole people into dismembered parts. And for what? The song of victory was already roaring in the people's throats. The corrupt politicians had fled. The other drones had turned back to the base.

One man. One finger. The world of the Dandelion Insurrection exploded.

Charlie forced himself to name the coffins as they passed: Lupe Hernandez in the first casket. His eyes darted to her husband, children, sister, and mother, standing huddled together with tears streaming down their faces. Charlie's cousin Matt came next, the mischievous dreamer crushed by hurtling concrete. His eyes blurred with tears for the companion of his childhood. The next coffins contained people he had barely known - a journalist, an organizer from New York, a woman taking action for the first time in her life, and a young man who had survived the prison camp along with Matt only to meet death in the District of Columbia. Each twisted his gut with the unique loss of a stranger and the unquenchable yearning to know them. His breath caught in his chest.

Count the living, he commanded himself as the coffins passed. So many lived: the lawyer Tansy Beaulisle, his grandfather Valier, his mother Natalie, Bill Gray, Tucker Jones, Inez Hernandez . . . millions in the crowd had survived. The missile had struck the far edge of the teeming masses; if it had landed in the middle of the protestors, many more would have died. *We are lucky to be alive*, Charlie forced himself to remember. *We took the risk when we defied the drones and walked*

4

toward the Capitol Building in the midst of chaos and political upheaval.

The Devil's luck, he cursed and his eyes fell on the coffin that would haunt him all his life, the woman he had seen just before the blast ripped a gaping hole in the crowd; a woman tall and thin and beautiful.

"Mom," Zadie whispered.

Charlie drew her close, folding his arms around the sorrow etched into Zadie Byrd Gray's thin limbs. A ghost memory flashed in his muscles - throwing his arms frantically around Zadie as she spun toward the strike, hauling her back from running straight into danger, holding her as she fought to break free, his heart pounding in terror at the chance of a second attack, the screams erupting around them.

Charlie pressed his face into the softness of Zadie's black curls and shook with relief that they still lived, that she was not in the coffin behind her mother, that he was not, like Zadie's father, lying in the hospital about to awaken to the greatest tragedy of his life. Together, he and Zadie stood alive, shaking as the line of coffins triggered memories of the attack. They had seen the explosion tear through Ellen Byrd. The scene haunted their nightmares.

As the white dome of the capitol had risen into view, he had glanced back at the swelling masses of millions marching for democracy, for justice. Ellen and Bill had been far back in the crowd. From the looming shadow of a drone, a missile had come searing down. Ellen was tossed like a ragdoll, her husband Bill thrown backwards and buried under her long limbs, their tangled bodies flung among the others. The pandemonium of fear broke out, but Charlie knew that Ellen had saved a thousand lives that day with the disciplined training she had instilled in the movement. Even as her body fell, her spirit rose

5

in frightened hearts and stopped panicked demonstrators from trampling each other.

But none of that would bring her back. Zadie's hands clenched his fingers tight enough to bruise. Her eyes fixed on her mother's coffin. Charlie felt the gazes of the crowd upon them and swallowed with difficulty.

"I'm glad Dad's not here," she choked out.

Charlie nodded in agreement. The fiery man lay in critical condition with numerous broken bones and deep wounds. *Just as well*, Charlie thought. The black mourning clothes, the caskets, the priests, the inevitable presence of officials, the whole spectacle of the funeral would have sent the man into a seething storm of fury. Inside Ellen's casket was an urn of ashes; her will requested cremation. She would not lie in the National Cemetery - hardly any of the Dandelion Insurrectionists would. The officials had offered them a place next to all the fallen heroes, but they had families and homes and came from all corners of the country. Zadie, Bill, and Charlie would bring Ellen's ashes back to her beloved farm up north where the tractor still sat in the field from the day when her heart had said enough. She had turned off the engine and marched away from the farmlands, her husband locked in prison, her daughter forced into hiding, the nation controlled by a hidden corporate dictatorship. She had marched to the nation's capital with millions of people to oust the regime from power as a nationwide general strike ground business-as-usual to a complete halt.

And they had won.

A hastily formed Interim Government of the remaining public officials scrambled to make order out of chaos. A clearinghouse of politicians implicated in the stolen elections had resigned or faced imminent impeachment; a bevy of bureaucrats fled the country to avoid arrest. The entire nation hung in the shocked suspense of change, uncertain how the next moment would unfold. The mass surveillance system of the empire held its breath. The repressive police hunkered down and eyed the capital nervously. The propaganda machine of the media cautiously issued non-statements, trying to discern which of the new power holders would come out on top. The people breathed a sigh of relief. The wealthy hyperventilated. The nation gaped at the strangeness of success. The Dandelion Insurrection reeled in victory and mourning, a pair of storm winds that battered their hearts.

Charlie glanced at the somber group of officials wearing appropriately downcast expressions as the crowd filed behind the last of the coffins into the cemetery.

"Come on," he said quietly to Zadie.

"Do we have to?" she muttered.

Charlie sighed. Propriety hemmed their lives. The arc of revolution had thrust them into fame. Notoriety locked them into public figures. They longed to rest, retreat, hide and weep and heal, but they were chained to a schedule of expectations . . . including attending this spectacle of a state funeral that brought them no solace.

"I'm supposed to speak," he reminded her.

They turned among the black-clad mourners and walked slowly toward the graves. *Just take one step after another,* Charlie repeated silently as he had every day since the drone strike. One moment after another, a revolution is a wheel turning inexorably toward change. *Just keep going,* he repeated as he slogged through meetings, negotiations, press conferences, and the staggeringly overwhelming load of questions flung at him from all sides. Everyone wanted answers he didn't have; each

7

day required an extra year of time to accomplish all that had to be done.

His feet dragged on the damp pavement. The clouds pressed down on his hunched shoulders. Along the edge of the low hill, he could see the silhouettes of armed security officers. The crowd was thick with agents. They filed past the military section of the cemetery. The long, precise rows of white tombstones sent a shiver down Charlie's spine. The Dandelion Insurrection had suffered losses - their hearts grieved heavily - yet, despite facing snipers, thugs, drones, police, and other dangers unarmed, their losses were small compared to the wars and revolutions that picked up weapons. Had they chosen to launch a second civil war, they would need whole new cemeteries to honor their dead.

Another irony, Charlie conceded. The politicians could make a great fuss over the fallen nonviolent activists because they had lost so few. Meanwhile, the soldiers killed in the politicians' endless wars could not be counted, and for years had been relegated to statistics the government suppressed.

Charlie's mouth twisted. Each gravestone stamped uniformity on a human soul, compressed the glorious chaos of a once-living being into the final box and form of a regulated soldier. The government had wanted to do the same to the Dandelion Insurrectionists, but the relatives had rebelled. There would be a shared memorial marker in the corner of the section allotted to them, but each grave would have a unique tombstone - some flat to the ground, others tall and ornate. A slight smile crossed Charlie's face. They had become a small patch of unruliness in the orderly cemetery. Even in death, they stood for life.

They reached the graves, a sobering area of open pits and mounds of fresh-dug dirt. Charlie gripped Zadie's hand as they walked toward the officials. He forced himself to see beyond the day's grimness and into the future. Far from now, when time healed all wounds, a small meadow would emerge in this corner of the mowed cemetery lawn. The graves of dead presidents would be poisoned to keep out the dandelions, but on the day Lupe's kids came to pay their respects to their mother, they would be able to gather the golden flowers that had been allowed to grow.

"Ready, Charlie?"

The tenor voice of the new president pro tempore of the Senate interrupted his thoughts. The forced sympathetic expression on the middle-aged man's face did nothing to raise him in Charlie's estimation. John C. Friend would speak after Charlie, offering condolences prepared by a well-paid speechwriter.

Charlie's speech lay crumpled in his pocket. He already knew he would not glance at it. The words he had to say had been seared into his soul. He would tell the families only the truth: he loved them. He mourned with them. And the lives of their loved ones were carried in all of their hearts, now, forever, and for always.

"Charlie?" the question came again. "Are you ready?"

"We're never ready," he answered.

Then he took another step toward life.

CHAPTER THREE

. . . . .

President Pro Tempore

Thunder shook the building. Lightning cracked across the capital. John C. Friend lifted his eyes from the dossiers on the four insurrectionists coming to the next meeting and stared out the window. His salt-and-pepper eyebrows drew together as he blinked at the gloom of the churlish clouds. He snapped on the desk lamp and rubbed the tension out of his face. Rain splattered against the glass panes.

The District of Columbia hunkered under black and gray umbrellas and scurried through the downpour. Friend thought fleetingly of the funeral - had it only been three days? A year's worth of meetings seemed to have transpired in a mere seventy-two hours. He had moved mountains by the minute as time raced by. Already, a hint of autumn gnashed its teeth in the edges of the storm. September loomed just a few days away. The extraordinary essence of summer had fled; school, work, cold, and normalcy summoned the citizenry back to regular life after a season of unparalleled upheaval.

Scurry along, John C. Friend urged the people silently. A nation could only sustain the heat of revolution for so long.

He was not the sort of man who inspired strong confidence. He lacked the type of bold charisma that was required of great leaders. He was a man of average height, graying hair, nice teeth, and unremarkable features. He carried a comforting paunch and an adequately firm grip. People found him generally unobjectionable at a time when politicians evoked curses that would make a sailor blush.

11

As the politicians implicated in the stolen elections fled, the more astute Congress members decided that something out of the ordinary needed to occur. The chain of succession for the Oval Office held a golden opportunity . . . they scanned the room to see who would stick his neck out and risk his career. John C. Friend smiled back and nodded amiably. He was exactly the type of public servant to reassure a nation caught in tumultuous upheaval. He gave the impression of solidity and boring sincerity. The people expected general incompetence; the powerful business class required blandness - not boldness - during the transitional period.

And that was precisely what John C. Friend appeared ready to deliver.

Scheming members of Congress pulled strings, bribed, bullied, threatened, and cajoled the rest of their colleagues into line. Before the smoke of the tear gas had cleared, John C. Friend, an unremarkable senator from Iowa, was elected president pro tempore of the Senate, third in line for the Oval Office. With the former vice president hiding in the Cayman Islands and the current speaker of the house suffering from a stress-induced heart attack, that left Friend - a politician everyone on Capitol Hill owed and no one in the rest of the country remembered - with a clear path to the presidency. He would be sworn into office in three days.

As long as those Dandelion Insurrectionists didn't cause an uproar.

Friend's chest fluttered in a fit of nerves. Every human had the seed of rebellion hardwired into their heart. Squeeze the shell of conformity hard enough and it cracks, allowing the spirit of resistance to burst forth. The previous administration had put the masses under the unbearable pressures of poverty, incarceration, surveillance, repression, authoritarian control, and

12

propaganda. The vice tightened, the shell split, and the Dandelion Insurrection burst into existence.

Ignited by the incendiary essays of Charlie Rider, the Man From the North, the movement had leapt out of rumor and legend into a roiling sea of resistance. The sleeping giant of the people woke up with a roar. Long standing injustices toppled like dominoes. The tables turned on the corporate powers. Politicians scattered like rats off a sinking ship. Not even the tragedy of the drone strike would keep those indomitable dandelions down for long.

John C. Friend sensed the gathering breath of tsunami growing in the movement. As the remaining politicians floundered in the exposed mudflats of corruption, Friend stayed calm, avoided the muck of scandal, and swiftly repositioned himself on moral high ground as a supporter of the movement. The charging surge of the people would soon rush into action again . . . and he intended to surf this tidal wave to the top.

The Interim Government had already bent over backward to appease the masses. An Elections Commission had been appointed to overhaul the voting system and guarantee that the numerous special elections - covering everything from local dogcatchers to city councilors to state governors to federal legislators - would be fair. The odious Freedom of Defense Act had been repealed, the Food Assistance Program was on track to be reinstated, and campaign finance reform legislation would be passed once the remaining Congress members quit arguing over which of their favorite loopholes to leave in place. And, though it gave a number of politicians acid reflux and heart palpitations thinking about it, the Interim Government had jumped swiftly to draft several bills that at least gave the appearance of addressing the rest of the demands of the Dandelion Insurrection. The people had broken free of the chains of control and fences of fear. The times called for concessions, appeasement, and soothing promises.

Friend frowned. These upstarts were accustomed to flashy slogans and brilliant speeches, but they'd have to get used to the dreary teeth-pulling negotiations by which all bureaucracies function. Governments lived on pragmatism and inside deals, not miracles and dreams. The insurrectionists would simply have to come down from the heights of noble idealism to the hard concrete of reality.

Friend glanced at the time and rose to standing. Tucking in his white, collared shirt and straightening his tie, he stepped out to greet the insurrectionists as they arrived. Friend wanted their support as he was sworn into office . . . even a man on track to become president would be wise to meet the Dandelion Insurrection halfway. They held the nation in the palm of their hand. They could bring down dictators and presidents alike. No business could withstand their organized opposition. Entire industries crumbled under the weight of their boycotts and strikes. The military and police stood down at their request. By their word, the people rose up and resisted.

They were, arguably, the most powerful group in the world.

Shoulder-to-shoulder, they came. Strides matched, hearts united, paces measured. The four insurrectionists walked quietly through the halls of power. Together, they had done the impossible. Through the shadows of fear, the death grip of greed, the stranglehold of tyranny, the weight of despair, the movement had risen like a song in the hearts of the people, and emerged like the answer to their prayers. More than a revolution, the true change of the Dandelion Insurrection took root in each person. It was the insurrection of love against hate, hope against despair, courage over fear, and kindness over cruelty. The Dandelion Insurrection was as simple as feeding a hungry child and as complex as caring for the whole Earth. It was older than time and as eternal as love. It came to life in the present and gave rise to the future. It endured in the hearts of the people.

The bustling building of congressional offices grew still. The corridor fell silent. Interns flattened to the walls. Staff gathered in doorways. Smiles widened on faces. Cheers rose up in throats. An irrepressible round of applause burst loose.

Charlie Rider turned red around the ears. Zadie Byrd Gray's grin curved across her cheeks. Inez Hernandez gave a small wave with a laugh. Tansy Beaulisle clamped down on her pride, but a hint of a strut crept into her stride.

John C. Friend met them in front of his suite and stretched out his hand with an affable smile. He posed for the cameras and cellphones of staff. Then he waved them away and gestured the four insurrectionists inside, masking his twinge of annoyance at the presence of the three women. Young Charlie Rider had been appointed liaison for the movement, but he insisted on bringing the others with him, explaining that they made their decisions collectively.

"Come in, come in," Friend urged them, closing the door on prying eyes, drawing them past his secretary, and leading them into his office.

"Congratulations on the presidency," Charlie began in a cautious tone as they sat down in the empty chairs on the far side of his desk.

Friend waved the words away.

"It is a mere formality," he blustered. "*Someone* had to step up to the duty, and you know as well as I that we can't have the old cabinet members taking charge right now. Can you imagine

15

the former Secretary of Defense handling our national situation?"

The youth shook his head and raised his eyebrows. The cabinet members of the old regime were all corporate cronies of the former president. Putting one of them in the Oval Office was backsliding toward corporate dictatorship.

"My service is only temporary," Friend told them. "Until we have a full Congress, and a fresh presidential election cycle, we've all agreed to think of ourselves as the Interim Government. Keeps us in our place!" Charlie looked unconvinced, so Friend added in a generously confiding tone, "I wasn't even going to move offices, but Secret Service insists."

He looked around at his congressional office with mournful regret, as if he hated to leave its familiar rooms. He ran an affectionate hand over the edge of his desk.

"Let's get started," he said, briskly. "There is much to discuss - "

"First off," Tansy Beaulisle cut in with a business-like tone, "let's talk about our demands. When're you going to meet 'em?"

Friend forced a laugh.

"There are a few other things we ought to look at - "

"Not so far as we're concerned," Tansy warned him. She had no intention of being derailed. Born in Louisiana, Black, poor, and bold as brass, Tansy Beaulisle had clawed her long-red-finger-nailed way up the ladder of challenges to become one of the brightest - and most colorful - legal powerhouses defending justice and equality for all. Known for taking on lost and noble causes - as well as for her shocking litany of outrageous phrases and unrepentant irreverence - Tansy stood tall even without her three-inch heels and took no nonsense no matter how rich, powerful, or dangerous her adversary.

"Now, come," Friend entreated, "let's not start out at claws and daggers. I'm on your side . . . don't you want to cooperate with the Interim Government?"

"That depends," Charlie shot back boldly. "Does the Interim Government want to cooperate with us?"

Friend regarded the young man with the gentle look of understanding he used on upset constituents. Ah, to be young again! Full of bravado and confidence, blithely unaware of the mundane cruelty of the world. It was not the blatant evil that broke the soul. No, in the face of utter darkness, the human spirit often rose to soaring heights. It was the shades of gray, the nuances and subtleties that wore people down. It was dealing with sellouts and side deals, small injustices and petty grievances that turned heroes into stoop-shouldered, weary old men. That was how they crumbled, idealists like this young man. They tripped on the garbage heap of miserly greed and fearful half-measures. *They'll get you someday, m'boy,* he warned Charlie Rider silently.

"Mr. Rider, the Interim Government wants to move with the full cooperation of the people, and therefore, the Dandelion Insurrection," he replied. "We have a tough job ahead of us, but you can be assured that I will do everything in my power to serve the people. My staff has prepared a preliminary timeline and feasibility report for addressing your demands."

Friend proffered printed copies of the document.

Charlie frowned as Friend beamed. The phrase *everything in my power* snagged in his mind. The uncharted depths of the man's power made Charlie uneasy . . . even if those powers were ostensibly employed toward the goals of the Dandelion Insurrection. Flashes of memory pounded him: brutalities, prison camps, drones, snipers.

17

"What are your powers, exactly?" he challenged Friend. "The old president greatly expanded the powers of the executive office. Will you go back to regular constitutional limits?"

"Ah, the million dollar question!" Friend exclaimed. "The Interim Government is still sorting out the details, but we're working on correcting the excesses of the previous administration."

As Tansy followed up with a series of legal questions, Zadie impatiently tapped her fingers on the armrest of the chair. The hopes and dreams of the nation sizzled like bottled lightning in her heart. The thousand cries for change reverberated in her bones. She had vowed to serve as the midwife to the coming world, to pull the emerging change out of people's hearts and send it leaping into life. The Dandelion Insurrection had risen up like a tidal wave of love, riding the demand for justice that swelled into the flashflood of the movement.

Be kind, be connected, be unafraid, they had chanted, even as the drone's shadow loomed overhead. As Friend's words garbled into a mush of budgets, commissions, elections, and legislation, Zadie realized with the clarity of a seasoned midwife that the Interim Government stood coiled around the neck of their newborn world, an umbilical cord of constitutional law that gave form to democracy, but was also positioned to strangle the people's hopes and dreams. Zadie drew a breath, rolled up her sleeves, and got to work. She refused to be thwarted by politicians who could not utter the word love without choking on their tongues or gagging on hypocrisy.

"What will you do to help the people right now?" she asked abruptly, thinking of the homeless shivering in the rain, the poor children going hungry, and the debt prisoners still locked in cells.

Friend looked like he had swallowed a toad, but he managed to croak out something about a Relief Bill, pointing to the timeline Inez held. As she examined the notes, John C. Friend eyed Zadie Byrd Gray balefully, understanding, at last, why his colleagues had labeled her a domestic terrorist. When charisma and intelligence joined hands with compassion, the result was dangerous to greed, destruction, and cruelty. Business-as-usual acquired a serious foe in Zadie Byrd Gray. She stuffed all three qualities into a disarmingly lovely bundle of long legs and wild curls.

Don't be fooled by hoop earrings or knee-high boots, Friend warned himself sternly, *that girl is more trouble than three guerrilla generals put together.*

Inez studied the section of the timeline that included passing a bill for poverty and debt relief then shook her head as she flipped through the rest of the pages.

"Everything to your satisfaction, Ms. Hernandez?" Friend asked solicitously.

"Mmm," she assented, privately reflecting that Washington, DC, was where the lifeblood of democracy came to die a slow and agonizing death of calcification and fossilization. In the neighborhoods and sidewalks of the communities she worked with, on the poorer outskirts of New York City, democracy crackled with electricity, pulsing with vitality and spirit. It strutted in high heels and swaggered in sneakers. Democracy wasn't a set of dry documents nicely laid out on office stationary - it brimmed in the lips of thousands of souls and debated in dozens of accents as it crossed the street from one neighborhood to the next. It was the smell of stale coffee and bodies packed into an old community center. It was the typos in the fliers. It was exasperation, realization, illumination - a knockdown, drag out, sweaty, tearful, impassioned process of people making decisions together.

She gave John C. Friend a skeptical look.

"The timeline is very ambitious," she warned him. "If you pull it off, it would be a miracle."

"Well, given recent events, and what *you* have accomplished," Friend replied with an approving tone, "a bit of miracle-working from our end is called for."

"Is this public information?" Charlie asked, holding up the document.

"Yes, by all means, and I must say, if you would write about this timeline, it would certainly help me accomplish it."

"How so?" Charlie asked suspiciously.

Friend waved his hand airily.

"Keep my colleagues' noses to the grindstone, Charlie. Force them to stick to the plan. They're here to serve the people, after all."

"So are we," Charlie cut in.

"Exactly," Friend replied smoothly, "and we should work together."

As the two stared at each other in a silent weighing of character, Charlie's gut surged with unreasonable dislike. *Calm down*, he ordered himself, swallowing back the bile and bristle of animosity.

Friend cleared his throat and glanced at Zadie.

"Now, there is another item . . . the Interim Government would like to make a gesture of contrition, apology, and mourning for the lost lives and the injustices created by our predecessors. We feel some public, visible sign of atonement is important to send a clear message to those who would seize power for personal gain. We want to know if you mind if we take such action?"

Inez, Charlie, and Zadie exchanged surprised glances.

"Mind?" Tansy said, voicing their shared thought. "Knock yourselves out."

The meeting dragged on for hours as the rain pounded the building and ran waterfalls down the windows. At quarter to five, Friend opened the door. A flash of lightning struck. His office intern shrieked and dropped her stack of files, apologizing on the next breath as she recognized Friend in the doorway.

"Jane - " he began, then broke off. "Who're you?"

He scowled at the unknown person handling the main office computer as his prim, purse-lipped assistant stood watching. The thin . . . man? Woman? Friend's eyebrows furrowed in confusion at the figure - slender as a boy, short cropped hair, flat chested, and yet . . . he shrugged.

"Alex Kelley," the person said; half-rising with an extended hand that Friend dutifully shook. "Congressional Data Management and Interdepartmental IT Specialist. I was sent over to upgrade your staff's security access and integrate databases - "

He waved his hand to cut off the technical details.

"Jane, I'm going to need copies of the budget proposal before the insurrectionists leave."

"Yes, sir. Which draft?"

"Don't be daft," he snapped. "The one with the Relief Bill."

She blanched and apologized. He retreated to his office. The technician turned to the secretary with interest.

"He seemed grumpy - what's got him so riled?" Alex asked curiously.

"Those Dandelion people," Jane frowned disapprovingly and sniffed. "They're probably giving him grief over those demands."

"They seemed reasonable enough," Alex Kelley answered in a safe, noncommittal tone intended to draw out the woman's opinion.

"Oh," Jane huffed superiorly, "some are doable - fair elections, of course, but revising the tax code and passing new legislation on environment and debt reform? That's just going to have to wait."

Alex's eyes narrowed, but she seemed absorbed in her work. Almost absently, she mentioned, "I suppose this Interim Government operates in a bit of a no man's land, right? Who knows what it can or can't do?"

"Well, it can't authorize the kind of money those activists want for poverty relief," Jane sighed. "We ran the numbers. We just can't afford it."

Not without taxing the rich or slashing the military budget, Alex added silently, certain that the Interim Government had no intention of doing either.

"So, he's got one draft to show the activists, and another one for . . . ?"

"Campaign donors, the corporate lobby, you know, the usual suspects."

Alex nodded sagely. She did know. She thought for a moment, took a risk, and quickly keyed in an extra line of code before straightening up in satisfaction and changing the subject back to the task at hand.

"There, that ought to take care of the glitch, but if it gives you more trouble, I'll come over. These integrations can be a headache."

"I don't know how you deal with it."

"Just doing my job."

"It doesn't help that those insurrectionists crashed the Internet last week," Jane complained.

A smile teased the thin lips of the technician. Brown eyes crinkled in the corners.

"Oh, that didn't cause me hardly a hiccup. Nice piece of programming, that. The way their Alternet replaced the Internet when the former president ordered the Internet shutdown was a masterstroke."

"The security guys weren't so thrilled," Jane pointed out.

"They lost all their backdoor access to places they shouldn't have had entry to in the first place," Alex commented reprovingly. "My programs have been running on similar protocols to the Alternet for years - more protection, less risks."

Quickly, Alex rose and left the office before the laughter bubbling in her throat burst loose. The truth of the matter was that she had helped design the Alternet's security functions . . . and Alex Kelley hoped that she'd one day meet the mastermind who had put together the design team, a brilliant programmer who went by the screen name Cybermonk; someday, she was determined to shake that genius' hand!

Dandelion Insurrection supporters abounded within these halls. The difficulty was spotting them. Unlike their bold counterparts in the streets, civil servants and federal employees tended toward subtlety and discretion, taking action in the machinery of bureaucracy in ways most people never noticed. They lost files and stalled paperwork. They sank bills and delayed orders. When the Dandelion Insurrection marched on the capital, people like Alex Kelley did not race out into the streets. They held their posts, securing their piece of the massive state apparatus in support of the popular movement. Alex had crashed several networks of administrative computers, effectively halting access to funds. Even now, in the wake of the bittersweet victory, she preferred not to flaunt her support of the movement. Not until democracy resurrected from the ashes of this upheaval. The people needed loyal public servants like her in place . . . just in case the struggle was far from over.

Alex shook her head. She hoped the insurrectionists would be careful. While John C. Friend gave the impression of being a well-intentioned rube, his record showed a different story. He maintained a popular image by introducing people's legislation, sticking up for the common man, and appearing to be a last bastion of decency left on Capitol Hill. There was always someone like Friend hanging around. It was how the avaricious kept the people from revolting. Over the years, Friend had grown very rich and powerful by providing an outlet for public outrage. Like a pressure release valve, he blew off a lot of steam and decompressed people's frustrations. He promised hope, fought the good fights, lost nobly . . . but nothing ever changed.

Where you did see Friend was on the roster of every handout to the wealthy passed by Congress. He stuck his little band-aid and public relations clauses into bills, handed out scholarships to kids, and never got too far into the limelight or the muck. No one associated him with the big, multi-billion dollar deals, but his portfolio increased year after year. He was the worst sort of enemy of the people because everyone thought he was a good guy. Friend would have them all signing their own death warrants and thanking him for it.

Alex surreptitiously watched the four insurrectionists leaving Friend's office. If he wasn't going to show them the real version of his budget proposal, she'd have to get ahold of it and leak it back to them . . . along with a stern warning to keep a close watch on John C. Friend.

CHAPTER FOUR

. . . . .

The Roots

Midnight gripped the hospital windows and squatted down over the lights of the city like a hulking night predator, watchful and wary. The underbellies of the clouds bore the stains of the streetlights, turning a queasy pinkish-orange. The buildings glinted, damp with rain. Charlie rubbed his reddened eyes. Zadie sat vigil next to Bill Gray, waiting for him to awaken from the day's torment of surgeries to repair the broken pieces of his body.

Charlie went down the hall to the lobby to work, leaving Zadie and Bill in peace as he returned phone calls, checked emails, and tried to catch up on the constant barrage of messages hurled in his direction. Overhead, the waiting room television screen flickered with a replay of Friend's speech at the funeral. Charlie watched the man's flaccid face bend around hollow words.

"Let this be known as a day of mourning and commemoration. As your friend, as I have always been, I swear to make right the wrongs and to bring those that fired the drone to justice."

The restless family members of patients studied the figure standing to the left of John C. Friend and compared his features to the youth sprawled across the nearby chair. Charlie slouched low, strategizing an escape route from the curious stares. His feet perched on the edge of the coffee table, partially obscuring the newspaper headline that read: *Movement Buries Losses,*

Nation Mourns. In smaller typeface, it added: *Friend Vows Full Investigation of Attack.*

"I vow to give tyranny no compromise. Blood was spilled tragically and I, John C. Friend, take up the vow that Zadie Byrd Gray spoke just moments before the attack. As she said, *we will hound these perpetrators at every turn, resist them, strip them of power and position, and bring them to justice!*"

Clever move, using Zadie's words from the courthouse steps, Charlie thought silently. His weary eyes turned back to the screen as the crowd roared in approval and Zadie's miserable, black-clad figure burst into fresh tears. *Too bad he probably didn't mean a word of it,* Charlie brooded cynically. Platitudes and false promises came as quick as breath in this city. Charlie trusted none of the remaining politicians, least of all John. C. Friend. Something irked him about the man. Inez and Tansy were surprised and pleased to hear that the chain of succession would put him in the White House. Charlie couldn't shake his niggling sense of unease . . . but he'd had that since the drone strike, as the others reminded him, so he nursed his suspicions silently.

Coffee, he decided as his figure stepped toward the microphone on the screen, *I need more coffee.* He rose and stepped around the knees of a teenager and over a toddler napping on the floor at his exhausted mother's feet. On the television, Charlie heard his voice say,

"It was love that called us into action, and our love that brings us here today."

He bolted toward the room where Bill Gray lay in critical condition and Zadie sat vigil, waiting for him to wake up.

"Zadie?" he murmured softly, sticking his head in the door.

She had dozed off with her elbow resting awkwardly on the window ledge, the exhaustion in her face etched in the shadows.

Charlie leaned against the doorframe and traced her fine bones with his eyes, caressing the black curls that tumbled wildly over the back of the chair. Zadie had always been slender, but sorrow thinned her, stripping the curves he loved down to bones. She curled easily in the chair, like a bird tucking under her wing, sheltered in the fragility of a moment's rest. Charlie sighed. They had been through unimaginable challenges together, fomented a revolution, evaded the government, scraped through close calls, revealed the evidence of the stolen elections, marched on DC, and used a general strike to cripple the regime economically and politically until finally ousting the corrupt politicians from power.

We'll get through this, he promised her.

He shut the door softly and paced down the hall.

"Will you let her know I've gone for coffee?" Charlie asked the receptionist, tilting his head toward the ICU room.

"Sure," the woman said, giving him a sympathetic look. He turned and she called out, "The maternity ward on the fifth floor makes the best brew. I'm sure they wouldn't begrudge you - of all people - a cup."

Charlie stammered thanks as the receptionist smiled indulgently. He bolted for the open elevator and hit the number five button.

"Hold the door!" a voice called.

Charlie jammed his foot between the closing doors and they sprung apart.

"Thanks," a young man panted. He was tall and muscular with shoulders that seemed to loom somewhere around Charlie's ear. His features were a blend of backgrounds: black hair shorn close to scalp in a pattern that indicated tight curls, chestnut skin tone, a strong nose bent slightly in the middle -

whether from birth or break, Charlie couldn't tell. A whisper of unease ran through him.

"Will Sharp," the fellow offered.

"Charlie - "

"I know."

Charlie sighed, resigned to notoriety.

"What floor do you want?" he asked the newcomer.

"Five."

Charlie startled.

"Heard a rumor there's some good coffee in the maternity ward," Will mentioned with a wink.

Charlie nodded, strangely nervous despite Will's disarming grin. The elevator jolted downward. He glanced at the man.

"Do I know you from somewhere?" he asked with a frown of thought. The back of his neck was prickling again.

"You'll have seen me here and there," Will acknowledged, staring at the wall panel that indicated the floors as they descended.

"Waiting for someone in the ICU?" Charlie asked gently.

Will shrugged.

"Actually, I've been waiting for you."

Charlie's body clenched. His heart hammered in his chest and alarm bells sounded in his ears. *Assassin*, his adrenals warned him. His eyes scoured the elevator buttons - no, not emergency, stopping mid-floor wouldn't save him.

"Aren't you going to ask me why I've been waiting?" Will suggested softly.

"Alright, why?" Charlie retorted. *Keep him talking, distract him, break through the mental pattern of killer-victim,* his mind commented frantically.

The elevator bumped to a halt at the fifth floor. The doors slid open. Will gestured.

"After you."

He's not going to kill me in a maternity ward, Charlie reasoned, stepping nervously into the waiting area. The families of expectant mothers glanced up from magazines. Will pointed to the coffee dispenser in the corner.

"Can I help you, gentlemen?" a nurse asked solicitously.

"Uh, we just wanted a cup of coffee," Charlie began.

"Are you an expectant father, young man?" the nurse replied with an irritated tone.

"No," Will answered. "He's Charlie Rider. Zadie Byrd Gray is upstairs waiting to see if her father will survive the drone attack."

"Oh!" the nurse exclaimed, recognizing Charlie. Then she turned back to Will with a frown. "And you are?"

"Bodyguard."

Charlie choked.

"Grab a cuppa, Charlie," Will commented dryly, "and let's go look at newborns. You don't mind do you?" he asked the nurse. "So much death . . . "

The nurse nearly fell over the magazine rack trying to be helpful and in a few moments, Charlie found himself staring through the glass window at the incubators of newborn babies, clutching a Styrofoam cup of what was, indeed, excellent coffee. Will Sharp stood at his shoulder, calmly sipping his black, unadulterated brew.

"I love babies," he said, causing Charlie to nearly spit out his mouthful of cream and sugar laced coffee. "So innocent, trusting, helpless. Somebody's got to look out for them. That's what I like about you and Zadie. You're just like babes in the woods. God, the times you nearly kicked it - so many close calls."

"What on earth are you talking about?" Charlie exploded.

Will turned to look at him.

"I'm your protection, Charlie, have been for most of this year, except when Zadie was on the road - then I was assigned to her."

Charlie didn't know whether to laugh, cry, or throw his coffee on the smug stranger.

"What do you mean assigned? Who assigned you?"

"Let's just say you have friends in powerful places who have been looking out for you, Charlie Rider. Friends who appreciate your particular blend of stupidity and daring, and wished to ensure that your crazy, visionary, idealistic Dandelion Insurrection actually stood a chance at succeeding. It would have been most unfortunate if the movement's best writer bit the untimely dust. Isn't that cute?"

He pointed to a tiny child shaking her fist and crying soundlessly on the other side of the glass. Charlie refused to be diverted.

"So, you're not an assassin?"

"I'm special ops and Secret Service rolled into one - or rather, one team."

"There are more of you?" he spluttered.

"There's only one Will Sharp," the man replied with a touch of disdainful arrogance, "but there are thirteen members of the Roots."

"The what?!" Charlie exclaimed, scowling at Will.

"The Roots. We're an underground cell of the Dandelion Insurrection. Our mission is to protect the key leaders, namely you and Zadie, and take care of a few other tasks related to ensuring the success of the movement."

"In the elevator, you said you were waiting for me. Why?"

"It was time to reveal myself," Will answered, his face inscrutable.

"Because the struggle's over?" Charlie scoffed. The guy was a lunatic.

"No," Will said soberly, "because it is far from over . . . and Charlie, you're not in the cornfields now. This is DC, and you're messing with the big league - powerful interests, huge money - and let me tell you, you are persona non gratis no matter what your smirking Friend says."

Charlie felt a chill run down his back. Perhaps this Will Sharp was serious.

"Why didn't you come forward before?"

"Secrecy was one of our best protections," Will replied with a shrug, "but when we get back upstairs, ask Zadie. She knows me."

Charlie's stomach dropped.

"How?" he demanded.

"Who did you think got her out of New York City when they branded her a terrorist? Who kept the wraps on Zadie and Inez before that? Like I said, you are babes in the woods playing a dangerous game you don't know anything about. You have no security, no protection, no sense of defense."

Charlie couldn't argue with that.

"Look," Will pointed out, "you go for a cup of coffee. You hold the door for a stranger. I could have murdered you on the ninth floor, stepped off on the seventh, and let the nice nurses on the fifth floor scream over your body as I disappeared down the other elevator. You didn't think about that until we were locked inside together."

Charlie said nothing. A baby yawned.

"Zadie didn't tell you because she knew you'd reject the protection," Will added softly.

Every fiber in Charlie's body wanted to punch the other man. He was right . . . and Charlie resented it. His hackles rose like an old dog, possessive and territorial. Irritated that Zadie had never mentioned Will to him, Charlie pushed away from the glass.

"I'm going upstairs," he announced in disgust. "Get your own elevator. If I'm not dead by the twelfth floor, we can talk about it with Zadie."

He stormed off, leaving Will shaking his head over the defenseless babies cradled and protected behind glass.

CHAPTER FIVE

. . . . .

Gray Atonement

"A bodyguard, Zadie?"

"Shhh," she admonished, glaring.

They huddled over the coffee maker at Tansy's house. The echoes of last night's truncated argument at the hospital scorched their voices. Bill had woken up in the middle of their heated exchange about Will Sharp and the Roots, delaying the rest of the confrontation until this morning. As the stream of coffee flooded the pot, the first streaks of pale yellow pierced the gray light of dawn.

The house hunkered down comfortably in the shade of old elms on a quiet side street that was slowly being swallowed up by modern architecture. After ditching her second husband, Tansy rented the old house from her former law professor, Myles Horowitz, and offered up a way station for students, interns, impassioned lawyers, activists, and most recently, Dandelion Insurrectionists.

"What'll your old neighbors think, Myles?" Tansy had asked when she began harboring insurrectionists under her roof.

"Oh, they'll be properly appalled, no doubt, just as they were in the fifties when they learned I was a conscientious objector on top of my flat feet; as they were in the sixties when they saw card-carrying communists coming over for dinner; as they were in the seventies when they figured out my housemate was more than just a fellow professor; and as they have been ever since at some shocking new idea that's older than time."

The living room sported an odd collection of armchairs with personalities - paisley and plump, grouchy old leather, a faded maroon velour with tassels, a striped loveseat with carved wooden feet, and a pair of seductively comfortable couches that had been salvaged from street corners. Behind the living room was a small study lined floor-to-ceiling with books. Across the narrow hall, the kitchen welcomed them with skewed cupboards painted butter yellow and a sturdy, wooden dining table with matching chairs. A staircase led up to the landing on the second floor. Four small, but sunny rooms opened off the central corridor. A bathroom at the end of the hall squeezed all the necessary fixtures into a marvel of architecture. It was a house of authenticity and humility, alive with stories. The back porch overlooked a scraggly lawn. A patch of dandelions winked by the listing fence.

"Best stay at my place," Tansy had advised Charlie, Zadie, and Inez. "Y'all's gonna have to set up shop here for a while to keep an eye on them crooks, 'cuz sure as day breaks, they're not gonna go quietly into the dark night of political obscurity."

"They weren't implicated in the elections fraud, Tansy," Zadie reminded her.

"They're politicians," Tansy harrumphed. "Just 'cuz you ain't caught them in the act don't mean they're not wheeling and dealing. Most of 'em would just as soon steal as breathe. Like it or not, you're gonna have to be here for the duration."

"How long is that?" Zadie sighed.

"Longer than a month and shorter than a lifetime . . . hopefully," Tansy declared.

Inez settled into the room next to Tansy's, and Charlie and Zadie took over the empty east gable. Tansy's hospitality offered a refuge for their battered hearts amidst their frantic schedule. This morning, as the coffee pot gurgled to a finish,

Zadie poured two cups and tilted her head toward the back porch. Yesterday's rain hung in fat drops on the leaves. A few birds bravely sucked in the damp air, fluffed their chest feathers, and warbled. Zadie shivered. She and Charlie sat close on the swinging bench. Despite the arguing, he reached his arm around her shoulders and pressed the warmth of his side into her ribs.

"Will said the Roots have been following us for months," Charlie stated.

"I didn't know about the Roots," she replied, her dark eyebrows drawing together as her blue-gray eyes clouded with worry. "Will handled security for Inez and I while we were organizing. We would have been arrested - or worse - several times without his help. He's respected by a lot of Inez' organizers."

"Who is he?" Charlie demanded, fighting a surge of jealousy. "Where did he come from?"

"The Bronx," she answered with a wry expression.

In a low murmur, she told Charlie what she knew about Will Sharp. His rough childhood led into a dangerous adolescence until the survival skills of his youth were tapped by the military. He entered special ops training, but left when his time expired, preferring private security work. He had attended a few meetings and wound up warning Inez about her lax security. One night, after Will's careful alertness and quick thinking saved them all during a government raid, Inez took him up on his offer to help them.

"He got Inez and I out of some tight spots," Zadie admitted, squeezing Charlie's hand to remind him of the weeks she had disappeared while the government launched a witch-hunt to find her.

"He's armed," Charlie commented shortly. "And so are his Roots, I assume."

"For self-defense," Zadie explained.

"Zadie! We're a nonviolent movement. We can't be running around with bodyguards armed with guns."

"Another reason why the Roots might have elected for secrecy," Zadie reflected quietly.

"We have to fire him," Charlie objected.

"*We* didn't hire him in the first place," Zadie countered.

Charlie threw his head back and blew a breath of frustration at the porch roof.

"Look, Zadie - "

A sound cut him off.

Charlie swiveled on the swinging bench and saw Tansy through the glass window in the back door. Her hair was crammed under a scarf and her day-glow jogging sneaker flashed as she kicked the front door shut. She disappeared into the kitchen to drop off a gallon of milk and bags of groceries. Then she poked her head out the back door, slapping the rolled-up daily paper in her palm.

"Y'all been out yet this morning?" she queried.

"No, we've been discussing our so-called bodyguards," Charlie remarked caustically, taking a huge gulp of coffee so his eyes could wake up to the hot pink glare of Tansy's jogging shorts. Steam rose off her goose pimpled legs as she harrumphed in reply.

"Yeah, I got *approached* on the way to the corner store - scared the bejeezus out of me - nearly drop-kicked the lout - what's his name? Will," she grunted the word out with dislike. "I told him, don't you ever sneak up on a forty-five year old Black woman out jogging in the morning or I'll mace your eyes before you can explain your business. You wanna talk to me, you come into my law office between nine and five like a civilized person."

Tansy leaned against the porch column with her hand over her bosom as if still feeling the base drum of her heart pounding in her chest.

"Had the gall to tell me I wasn't safe jogging around my own house alone. I said to him, the doctor ordered cardiovascular and so far as I'm concerned, it ain't safe sitting at my desk all day with a ticking time bomb in my heart. He claimed I needed protection and one of his Roots would discreetly follow me in the mornings - and I said, *hell no!* I got St. Peter and a host of lesser angels looking over me and ain't no mortal watching my wiggles and jiggles at this hour of the morning. Then I gave him the ninth degree about his Roots and followed that up by reading him the legal riot act."

Tansy mopped the cooling sweat off her brow and shook her head with worry. The last thing her overworked legal team needed was a bunch of self-appointed, armed vigilantes showing up to *protect* Dandelion Insurrectionists. Every single one of them was an assault or murder trial loaded and waiting to fire. One trigger-happy paranoid shooting at the wrong person represented a migraine of a case she'd rather avoid.

"He ain't sic'ing a pair of his watchdogs on me, that's for darn sure. I'll haul 'em up for stalking . . . but we're gonna hafta deal with these Roots somehow. They're making my hair stand up on end."

Tansy pushed off the porch column and winced at sore muscles growing cold. She eyed their coffee mugs enviously and mumbled about a long, hot shower. As she reached for the door, she suddenly smacked her forehead.

"Nearly forgot! Come on with me and let's walk down to the end of the block," Tansy urged grimly. "There's something you outta see."

The quiet residential neighborhood spilled out onto a commercial corridor with a corner market at the intersection. A thoroughfare full of shopping plazas stretched in one direction; boutiques and restaurants lined the other. Up and down the street, crews of city workers were hanging gray banners from the streetlights. One tall building after another unfurled huge rolls of fabric from the rooftop to the ground. The post office and bank had decked their front entryways with gray fabric.

"Are those gray-toned American flags?" Charlie asked with a frown.

"Uh-huh," Tansy confirmed. "Remember how Friend said the Interim Government wanted to make a public gesture of atonement?"

A quick whip of wind punched the gray-toned stars and stripes. The crews scrambled to catch the unsecured fabric as it billowed. Bits of street grit flung up into their eyes. A shiver darted through Tansy. Charlie and Zadie gaped. The overcast sky snatched the sun into hiding. Color vanished. Drab grays remained. Charlie's heart sank like a stone. Wordlessly, Tansy steered them to the corner market's racks of daily newspapers and tabloids.

Interim Government Unveils Gray Atonement
Friend Issues Public Apology for Losses

Charlie flipped the paper over, ignoring the glare from the cashier. The lead story reported that a gray flag of contrition and regret was being hoisted across the capital to symbolize the Interim Government's commitment to the people and repudiation of the terrible actions of the previous administration.

"As if he wasn't part of that regime," Charlie muttered under his breath. "All of them had a hand in the policies of the past."

"Yeah, well, they're covering their butts," Tansy pointed out.

"Friend has called for a period of public mourning nationwide," Zadie read over Charlie's shoulder. "Government buildings will display the gray flag, businesses are encouraged to hang gray banners on their buildings, and people are invited to wear gray - dark or light - to join in this symbol of national unity."

"In Hitler's time, the flags were red," Charlie commented acerbically.

Zadie frowned at him.

"I think it's a moving gesture," she countered, her eyes moist. "There have been losses."

"Of course there have," Charlie argued, "but this? This is ridiculous."

"Why?" she challenged.

"Because . . . because," he struggled for the words, "it's sheer propaganda and empty gestures."

"Not to those of us who lost someone," she snapped back.

"Then how about yellow for dandelions? For life, for the things we believe in," he bickered. "Not the color of ashes and death."

"You're such a control freak," Zadie hissed, lowering her voice. "You just can't stand that you're not in charge anymore, that people are making decisions without approval of the Man From the North."

Charlie stared at her in disbelief. All he'd ever used his Man From the North alias for was to tell the stories of resistance and write what everyone thought, but no one dared to say. The firebrand essays stirred up courage and held out hope. He'd ignited the smoldering pile of frustration into a blaze of revolution . . . but he was no more in charge of the movement than he was in control of an earthquake. He followed the lead of the thousand sparks of resistance, amplifying the rising chorus of dissent. Zadie's accusation hurt. He turned away in irritation.

Zadie ignored him and asked the cashier where she had gotten the gray flag hung in the window.

The woman shrugged.

"Some government worker came around handing them out. Supervisor thought it'd be best to hang it up. It's official."

She shot Zadie a significant look. The past ten years had taught people to be cautious about questioning the government. Not even the burst of the Dandelion Insurrection could counter all the instinctive head ducking and hunching of shoulders. Charlie watched the exchange sadly. Tyranny and fear left deep scars on the psyche of a nation. Healing would take time.

"You can buy one of the new flags," the cashier suggested pointedly. "We got some for homes and individuals. 'Course, we'll be outsold by the Boy Scouts and cheer teams. Interim Government's gonna let them sell 'em as fundraisers as a way to give back to the people."

"And mass market the new propaganda," Charlie muttered under his breath.

Zadie overheard and elbowed his ribs. Tansy grabbed them by the shoulders, thanked the cashier, and steered the pair out the door before a lovers' quarrel erupted.

Charlie itched to write a ferocious denouncement of the campaign, but the fire in Zadie's eyes stopped him cold. He scuffed the concrete moodily on the way back to the house feeling boxed into an uneasy corner of silence and implied consent. Zadie's accusation stung . . . he wasn't a control freak, why couldn't she see through this despicable ploy?

Half-hearted sprinkles splattered the sidewalks as they returned to the house. The day dragged. Charlie waved distractedly as Zadie left to visit Bill then plunged back into his work. That evening, as he scrubbed the dinner dishes, he thought he spotted Will Sharp lurking in the rainy gloom. The soapy pot in his hand slipped out of his grip with a crash and splashed him. When he looked back out the window, the figure had vanished.

Later, as he looked over Friend's proposed Relief Bill with Zadie and Inez, a message popped into his inbox.

"Whoa, hold on," he told the others. "Look at this."

They crowded over his shoulders. A whistleblower using a moniker of the Mouse claimed that Friend was pulling the wool over their eyes with a fake Relief Bill draft. There were two versions in circulation, said the Mouse, warning them not to bite into the rosy red apple of the draft Friend had given them. The second version showed the poisonous truth behind the politician's intentions.

> *Beneath the forked tongues and double speak,*
> *there's no relief in this budget.*
> *Here's the numbers.*
> *- The Mouse*

Attached was a budget proposal that made Charlie gag.

"This definitely isn't what Friend gave us," Inez complained, studying the two versions side-by-side.

In the leaked document, the unholy fat cow of the bloated military budget continued to devour seventy percent of the funds. The document contained notes indicating that Oil Subsidies would be renamed *Clean Fuel Program,* and the mass surveillance system would receive funding under the

Department of Education. Footnotes and attached documents explained that a program called *Poverty Relief* would be a corporate give-away, offering deals in which the government would buy surplus at high prices, and resell it to distributors for pennies. The *Affordable Housing Plan* turned out to be a set of development schemes for high-rise, expensive condominiums. The budget included funding for abolishing debt prisons, but it replaced them with mandatory work programs for parolees - all of the slave labor, but with none of the expense of housing inmates.

"This is a nightmare," Zadie groaned.

"No," Inez countered, "it's worse."

It was politics and business-as-usual, the exact political maneuvers that had led them to organize a revolution in the first place. It was the old corporate regime trying to steal more money. If the people wanted justice, they were going to have to push for it.

The next day, when Charlie confronted Friend about the second version of the budget, the politician pretended to be horrified and protested that draft was not the real budget. He claimed to have rejected the leaked version, appalled at the duplicity of the numbers.

"We're on your side," Friend professed.

Charlie told him he'd have to prove it through actions, not empty promises and hollow words.

"Charlie, if your people come up with a new draft of the Relief Bill, I'll make sure it passes," Friend vowed.

Inez had been watching Friend like a hawk searching for a chance to swoop down and snatch change up in her talons. Whoever this Mouse was, he or she had done the movement a great turn. Friend's challenge of drafting a new Relief Bill opened a chink in the Interim Government's bureaucratic armor, and she knew exactly how to exploit it.

CHAPTER SIX

. . . . .

Heart Matters

The next day, Inez cornered Zadie on the back porch of the old house, hopping up on the railing as her friend stretched her long legs from the swinging bench to the wooden rail. The time had come to stride briskly into action, to stir heat into the veins, and shake off the grip of sorrow. *Rise*, the wind hissed in the branches, *resist*. Inez could hear the clatter of the leaves urging her to stir up change before the season turned.

"Remember that list of demands compiled by the organizers in New York City?" Inez asked.

Zadie shook her curls out of her eyes thoughtfully and tugged the edges of her jean jacket tighter around her chest.

"The crowd sourced one that started as a workshop exercise on participatory democracy?" she guessed.

Inez nodded vigorously. Under the oppressive shadows of the corporate dictatorship, Inez and Zadie had found dandelions willing to shine boldly against the smothering gloom. In the most unlikely and inhospitable places, they had launched community self-governance projects, building participatory democracy in poor neighborhoods abandoned by everyone else.

In these neighborhoods, the police prowled like hyenas, searching for prey. The flesh of people walking down the street was slapped in handcuffs to fulfill monthly quotas. A call for help brought gunshots and death to the door. Mothers' sons bore the targets of racism on their young skin. Police practiced their aim with impunity. The bodies fell. The officers lied. The

45

court records took down the version spouted by authority, backed up by the police chief. The outrage of witnesses and the wails of mothers were ignored.

Inez came from the places where people died of heart attacks on concrete sidewalks because the privatized ambulances refused to enter the dangerous neighborhoods. Ignored by the nation, these blacked-out zones embodied the inherent cruelties of the massive systems of inequality and injustice. The politicians had feasted after closing the doors of the Food Assistance Program, but the children had wept from hunger. Addicts turned violent and desperate because recovery programs were slashed. Diabetic veterans wrestled failing wheelchairs up unrepaired sidewalks; one leg sacrificed in war, the other sacrificed to the greed of an extortionist healthcare industry.

In the run-down apartments with thin walls and leaky pipes lived the flesh-and-blood people the corporate media portrayed as depraved and dangerous, lazy and stupid. They were not saints, but neither were they monsters. They were humans squeezed under the steel press of unjust systems, their lifeblood oozing out so rich people could swig the wines of luxury.

They came to Inez' meetings for coffee and donuts, and stayed for the soup and bread she fed to their children. Inez never bothered to preach about eternal salvation or the Kingdom of Heaven. She told the truth: they burned in the living hell of massive injustice, and none would save them . . . but them. She and Zadie brought tools and skills of self-organization. They supported mothers in forming childcare coops. They helped gang members launch trainings in de-escalation tactics and violence intervention skills. They aided families in starting neighborhood conflict resolution and restorative justice circles to keep loved ones out of jail so that the bail and legal fees stayed in the community to feed people, turn the heat on in the winter, and keep roofs over heads. Each of Inez' strategies saved lives, souls, hearts, families, and money. All were needed for survival in a world where the odds stacked high against the poor. Desperation cracked open the door of radical possibility. People showed up, wracked with skepticism, but grasping for straws of something - anything - that could break through the meat grinder of poverty that was pulverizing the bodies of their children, family, and friends.

At the crux of everything stood democracy - real democracy, not the once-a-year voting for smiling liars - the participatory decision-making practices that engaged hundreds of people in solving problems that ranged from keeping the streets safe to checking on old people to resolving arguments over harms done to confronting greedy rent-spiking landlords.

For practice in early gatherings, Inez and Zadie would challenge the group to create a list of shared demands for the Dandelion Insurrection using small group discussions, report backs, debates, and negotiation skills. The task grabbed the imagination, engaged problem-solving, let grievances be aired, and required intense conversations about priorities.

"This is democracy," Inez insisted. "It's not about voting on which other people are going to rule over our lives. Democracy is finding ways to solve our problems, together."

As the local group generated demands, Zadie and Inez would share the lists compiled by other people in neighborhoods nationwide. A second round of discussions would then unfold to identify what the local group would add or subtract from the list. At the end of the session, Inez would invite everyone back for a second workshop: how the Dandelion Insurrection - including them - could get those demands met. Thus far, much of the list remained visionary and hypothetical, an exercise in democracy and strategic planning, but Inez sensed a shift in the swirling winds of change.

"It's time to put plans into action," she told Zadie as they sat on the back porch of Tansy's house.

Zadie laughed, her eyes suddenly illuminating with understanding.

"Inez," she asked bluntly, "are you bored?"

Inez grinned.

"Maybe . . . but mostly, I'm homesick. I want *los chiles rellenos de mi madre.* I'm sick of meetings with suits. I want to stick my hands in the soil of my community garden and work with the roots of this resistance where they're grounded in real people, real neighborhoods, real change. All they do around here is talk, talk, talk."

Inez longed to pace the stubborn sidewalks and argue with people in multiple languages. She wanted to repair rundown churches and paint murals on community centers. She yearned to leap into the fray of pushing for change, up to her elbows in the muck of life. She missed her sister Guadalupe like a vital organ and ached for the clang of humanity.

"I'm going back home to stir up trouble. You want to come?"

Zadie considered the idea as she swung the bench back and forth. Her eyes fixed on the patches of dandelions in the grass. She chewed her lip pensively. Dark circles hung under her eyes and she ached from sleeplessness. Bill's idea of recuperation involved snarling at the doctor's cautionary urges and trying to walk before he could stand. Yesterday's visit had been fraught with his unbearable irascibility. Father and daughter both longed to fling the weight of grief into action, to churn sorrow into hard and sweaty tasks like breaking concrete or pounding nails. After an hour together, Bill Gray had growled at his daughter.

"Get out of here. Just because I have to be tied to this bed doesn't mean you do."

In truth, he couldn't bear to see her sadness. They draped their hanging clouds of loss over one another and sank into depression. Bill would try to be strong for Zadie, and she would pull a stiff upper lip for him, until their mutual charade drove Bill wild-eyed with emotional cycles he didn't know how to break. He wanted space to cry and not see that pain strike his daughter. He wanted time alone with his thoughts to curse and swear and not worry Zadie over his outrage. He wanted her to go pace the groomed parks or sob on Charlie's shoulder or something more cathartic than slouching in grief on that uncomfortable hospital armchair by his bed.

Zadie could not guess the complexity of her father's thoughts, but his growling injunction struck her like a bell. She grabbed her jacket, alternating between relief and guilt, and squeezed Bill's good hand before bolting out the door.

"Someone's got to look in on Bill," she murmured to Inez, torn between her sense of obligation and the sudden, fierce yearning to drive as fast and far away from this sad nightmare as possible.

"Ask Charlie to," Inez suggested with a knowing glint in her eye.

"Maybe he wants to come," Zadie sighed.

"He can't," Inez pointed out. "He's got meetings with Friend and the Interim Government members all week, and mountains of writing to do. Has he even stopped scribbling except for meals?"

Zadie shook her head. The torrent of words pounded through Charlie again, rattling the nation and stirring up awareness that they could not wait for further government inaction.

We must shift our energy from the incredible burst of strength that toppled the old regime into the sustained pressure that ensures our revolution results in actual change, he had written recently. *The clearinghouse of politicians swept the puppets from the stage, but the same old puppet masters lurk in the wings, readying new pawns to tie to their strings of wealth. This is the moment when all our hard work could either come to fruition or to nothing.*

Privately, Zadie sometimes wondered if Charlie continued to agitate because he couldn't give up his role as a rabble-rouser . . . or if writing was his way of avoiding his aching heart. He hadn't spoken much about the drone attack, but she knew his nightmares woke him up as often as her own. She rubbed her eyes; they were both exhausted. Charlie had written about it in his last essay.

I know you are tired. We all are. We long to let down our guard, to rest, to return home, to breathe. And yet, we cannot lose focus now.

Zadie had seen him staring northward. His mother and grandfather had departed after the funeral, leaving him reluctantly, but longing for the familiar contours of their French Acadian community in Maine. In the valley, way up by the border of Canada, the changing seasons turned dramatically. The potato harvests were being brought in from the field. Zadie thought of her mother's tractor, stilled and idled, halted in a row of potatoes she did not live to harvest. She envied Charlie the total concentration with which he could drown his sorrow in the river of language.

"You're right," Zadie told Inez. "If I don't tell Charlie I'm going, he might not even notice that I'm gone."

Inez caught the note of worry under Zadie's joking tone.

"That's not true, *querida*, and you know it," she chastised her young friend. "That boy lives and breathes for you."

Zadie sighed.

Later, over supper, Charlie responded to the proposal with surprise.

"But, we need you here," he said to Inez.

"*Madre de Dios*," Inez complained, "I can't stomach another boring meeting with politicians. I want to work with people who haven't sold their souls to the Devil."

"But Friend respects you - "

"Friend's afraid of me," Inez laughed. "He sees a street-savvy Latina with hard grit and utter determination. He knows I'll hold his heels to the fire of hell if he doesn't meet those demands and pass a real Relief Act."

"So, why leave?" Charlie argued.

"Because, I have to go stoke the fire of the people to make him squirm."

Charlie stewed on a thought and finally spit it out.

"What about the special elections? Maybe we should stay focused on winning seats state by state. Then we can pass all the legislation we want."

"The people need relief now, Charlie," she pointed out. "And we're a movement, not a political party. We have to stay in shape for action, not become couch potatoes waiting for politicians to fix everything."

Charlie nodded at that.

"Besides," Zadie chimed in, "Inez and I can encourage people to run for seats while we're working on the Relief Bill."

"You want to go, too?" he asked Zadie.

"Just for a few days," she inserted quickly, seeing the anxiety in his eyes. "I need a break, Charlie. I keep seeing . . . " she trailed off with a haunted expression.

Charlie nodded. They all longed to escape the city's nightmares and ghosts.

The wind poured through the car window and danced across her scalp. Zadie's black curls whipped and tangled as she drummed her hands on the steering wheel, singing along with the blaring radio. Barreling up the freeway toward New York, she felt the oppressive weight of the nation's capital lifting by the mile.

That city was cursed, she decided, *built on swamplands and rotten with corruption from the founding days of the country.* If she never saw the white buildings of federal power again it would be too soon. She threaded her fingers through the wind's caress. If only she could live like this - in motion, hung in the decision-less liminal space between destinations, her mind empty of hard-edged thoughts.

Inez snapped off the radio.

"I want to talk to you."

Zadie flinched at the steely hint in the small woman's tone. Inez had spent the last two hours of the drive staring pensively out the window. Zadie had tried to shake her out of her mood, but ultimately decided to ignore the gathering storm in the passenger seat.

"I'd rather not," Zadie replied, switching hands on the wheel and reaching for the radio dial. "Can't we just drive along and enjoy life for once?"

"You don't even know what I want to talk about," Inez retorted in a grumpy tone. Her dark eyes flashed with sudden irritation.

Zadie snorted knowingly.

"Let me guess: politics, the movement, or death," she sighed. "That's all we ever talk about these days."

She turned on the radio.

Inez shut it off.

"Fine. Let's talk about life, liberty, and love," she said to Zadie. "Remember those? You used to believe in them."

Zadie let out a dry laugh.

"We wanted life and found death waiting. We dreamed of liberty, but where is our freedom, Inez? We're tied to this movement whether we like it or not. We can't just haul off and leave. And love?" Zadie groaned. "Everyone on Capitol Hill is laughing at our naive faith in love. Makes me want to crawl into a corner and cry."

Inez grabbed the steering wheel.

"Pull over," she ordered, pointing to the looming exit and yanking the wheel.

"Are you trying to get us killed?" Zadie screeched.

"There," Inez said shortly, indicating a place to stop. "Pull up on the side of the road. It doesn't matter where."

The car lurched as one side bumped over the loose gravel. A stand of highway trees rustled beside them. Vehicles shook the car as they thundered past, headed for gas stations and take-out burger joints. The vacancy of sound hung between them for a moment, comforting yet lonely. Then Inez took a deep breath and began to speak.

"You are not the only person holding in her silent tears," she reminded Zadie. "Guadalupe Dolores was connected to me like my own limbs and that drone snapped her out of my life. I am choking full of sorrow, yet hollow all at once. She is - was - my baby sister. I was there at her wedding, the births of her children, and now her funeral. I wanted to fall in love someday and live through her merciless teasing. I wanted her to give me annoying advice. I wanted to nag her to lose weight when we got as old and fat as Mama. I wanted to cry on her shoulder as we lit candles for our old *bruja* of a mother."

Tears welled in her eyes as she stared out the windshield.

"I want to curl up in a ball, but we have responsibilities that are bigger than us, larger than our sorrow and grief. They can be a balm to our hearts. Purpose goes a long way when the journey seems unbearable."

"What if I don't believe in that purpose anymore?" Zadie asked in a very quiet voice. Her lips trembled as she spoke her fear. "What if I don't believe in our slogans and catch phrases? What if that's not enough?"

"It was never enough for some of us," Inez replied, tempering her impulse to laugh at Zadie's plaintive tone. "Do you think *mi madre* is doing this for one of Charlie's convenient slogans?"

Zadie had to smile at the thought.

"No," Inez continued emphatically. "The old *bruja* is doing it for something deeper. Oh, I know if you asked her she'd say she's doing it for the money - *el pinche* government is making it hard to make a living on the black market."

Zadie laughed at Inez' perfect imitation of Pilar Maria's scowl.

"But, you have not seen the look on my mother's face as she tucks Lupe's children into bed. You did not see her when she broke through the blockades of the city to start the people's evacuations. You did not grow up with her; you do not know the comfort of her arms in your darkest hour of despair."

Inez turned in her seat to catch Zadie's eyes.

"*Mi madre* is driven by love. A love so fierce and intense it frightens her. She jokes and spits and hides it under that toughness, but don't be fooled. She says it's all survival in this dog-eat-dog world, but she would throw herself in front of bullets for me - she would have thrown herself in front of Lupe if she could. That's not just survival; that's love. And Mama feels it for her neighbors in the city. She feels it for the youths making trouble in the alley that she harasses to break up their fights. She feels it for the homeless she pretends to curse while slipping money and warm socks to them when she thinks no one is looking. Mama was taught to believe that love makes us vulnerable, and so she hides it."

Inez' eyes turned bright.

"But your mother? Your mother had unwavering faith that our love makes us strong and that our vulnerability gives us grace under pressure." Inez had trained thousands of people along with Ellen Byrd. They had marched side-by-side for miles. "My mama is tough," she said, "but your mother was fearless."

"Yes, but your mother is alive, and mine is not," Zadie said bluntly.

Inez sighed.

Watch out for that bitterness, Zadie Byrd Gray, she thought quietly, *or you'll grow up like my mama, not yours.*

"What's the point of fighting this struggle . . . if not for love?" Inez argued. "Love for the children, for the earth, for the people. You lose your love, Zadie Byrd Gray, and they've won. You've got nothing. But if you hold fast to love, you can walk into their offices with your head held high. You'll look at that Capitol Building and the White House and see that they're just wood and white paint and pointless greed. You'll laugh at that whole corrupt city because they are missing the point of life. And you'll be able to march - like your mother, fearless, humble, dignified, and strong - straight into the heart of darkness blazing with love."

Inez paused thoughtfully.

"Don't lose your faith in love, Zadie. It's stalking you . . . and if you turn your back, love will pounce. If you run away, love will chase you. If you shut it out, love will break down all of your defenses."

"You sound like Charlie," Zadie commented softly.

Inez snorted.

"Well, listen to him. Don't bite his head off."

"I don't!"

"You do."

"You're hardly one to give out relationship advice," Zadie said pointedly to Inez.

"Haven't I blown enough chances to know when you're screwing something up?" Inez shot back.

Zadie hid a smile. She leaned across the awkward constraints of seatbelts and cup holders to hug her in forgiveness.

"*Ai, chica,*" Inez murmured to her. "It's not easy, *la vida.* Let's not make it harder on each other, okay?"

"Yeah," Zadie agreed.

"And let's find something to eat. You're all sticks and bones."

"Says the ninety-pound heavyweight," Zadie replied, rolling her eyes.

"I'm not the one who stands as tall as your mother," Inez commented in a tone that softened gently at the end. "She's in you, Zadie, never far from your heart. You have her eyes, height, build . . . and her heart. Remember to love, and that beautiful heart of hers beats inside you, too."

She placed her hand over Zadie's heart. Tears came to the young woman's eyes. She nodded and clasped Inez' small, weathered hand. Inez breathed deeply. Now they could continue northward. They were ready for the challenges ahead.

CHAPTER SEVEN

. . . . .

The City

The city throbbed around them, ten million microcosms strong; every alley, subway, and street corner pulsed with a story. The weather of a different social barometer gusted through every intersection. The political temperature shifted by the block. Zadie and Inez wound through the congested city traffic, windows rolled down, soaking in the urban energy, watching expressions for the fleeting signs of hope and despair.

Upscale districts broiled in suppressed fury and palpable anxiety. The Dandelion Insurrection had delivered a blow to the guts of obscene wealth. The legendary Greenback Street no longer stuck the nose of its exclusivity in the air. The winds of change had turned the playgrounds of the wealthy topsy-turvy. Caution marked their well-heeled footsteps. Gone were the flashy displays of wealth, the ostentation, the wild extravagance. Haute couture proclaimed discretion to be the better part of valor.

Zadie pointed silently to a building-length billboard - a shared advertisement from a diamond company and a large bank - that featured a model draped in diamonds and nothing else, except one of Friend's gray atonement flags, upside down, a symbol of a nation in distress. Her tears were diamonds.

"Clever," Inez scoffed. "Almost patriotic, if you didn't know better."

Zadie nodded in agreement. The advertisement sneered straight at her, jabbing back at her for being the woman who had crippled the diamond industry and excoriated the wealthy with a single sentence:

When the children go to bed hungry, she had boldly said, *the diamonds of the rich become the emblems of their shame.*

The diamonds had vanished, languishing in lockboxes and jewelry cases, gathering dust as people donned dandelion pins and posies collected by their children. The wrath of the wealthy had quickly attacked Zadie Byrd Gray, labeling her a domestic terrorist and launching a witch-hunt unparalleled even by the search for Charlie Rider, the Man From the North. Even now, Zadie's spine tingled as she and Inez passed through the moneyed end of the city.

"Let's get out of here," Zadie suggested with a shudder of unease.

Gray atonement flags sprouted from storefronts as they entered the next class of city blocks. Storeowners and restaurateurs quickly cooperated with the Interim Government, hoping political stability would return sales and profits. They somberly complied with the new authorities, just as they had submitted to the old.

"Do you think those flags represent support for us or just for the Interim Government?" Inez wondered thoughtfully.

Zadie shrugged. She knew what Charlie would say; all the flags were a charade of insincerity to him. She preferred to imagine that people genuinely mourned the loss of life and the tragedy that struck at the moment of triumph.

As they turned into the poorer neighborhoods, the flags vanished and shrines to lost friends began to dot the chain-linked fences of abandoned commercial lots.

"These are the real memorials," Inez commented, pointing out a large one.

From these neighborhoods, some of the most ardent supporters of the Dandelion Insurrection had sprung, propelled by the utter necessity of change. Decades of betrayal kept people wary of authorities' tricks. The storm of political change would not subside until justice became tangible in these blocks. Here, the tensions remained electric, sparking in alternating currents of the organized and energized, and the wild fissions of the frustrated and desperate. Inez savored the metallic sting of the streets on the tip of her tongue. Her veins hissed with the insistence of survival. In these blocks, the Dandelion Insurrection burned brighter than ever. Until change reached the pockets and tables of the poor, the Dandelion Insurrection would not - could not - diminish.

Here, Inez knew, her soul had come home.

"What good is a revolution if we have no bread?" Inez' voice called out to the murmuring organizers in the church basement. "If we have to go into debt to keep the heat on in the winter? If the landlord keeps spiking our rents?"

The meeting had already started when Will slid in the door. His quick, cautious scan sighted Zadie and Inez in the midst of the group crammed tightly together under the low ceiling. The steam of living breaths whitened the windows. Will shook the chill out of his jacket and leaned quietly against the wall.

He'd left two other Roots stationed in the District of Columbia and followed the women to New York. The city was his turf, his home territory. He knew these neighborhoods like the lifelines running across his palm. He'd gotten Zadie and Inez out of several no exit corners before, and he'd do it again if he had to. The Interim Government swore it would rein in the mass surveillance system, but at the moment, it still churned forward by the sheer weight of its past operations. Crackdowns and arrests could still happen.

"The Relief Bill we're calling for is not just about the money," Zadie chimed in, standing on a metal folding chair next to Inez. "It's about justice. We need support programs that shift the massive stockpiles of wealth back to the people. In the past decade, under corporate rule, the rich have grown richer, gorged fat as ticks on the backs of the poor."

No one could argue with that - except the wealthy. A tiny one percent of the citizenry held over sixty percent of the nation's wealth. The second tier of rich people held most of what remained. The rest of the country had fallen into poverty. The poor had no assets, no houses, no bank accounts, no trust funds, no investment portfolios, nothing. They had debt, overdue bills, and worries. With every housing crisis, banks seized mortgages and sold the homes to the few management companies that had the capital to buy them. Families were evicted by the thousands and cast out into the tempest of a rental market where the tightening fist of a massive monopoly squeezed them into paying obscene rates and inflated prices.

To eat, to live, to communicate, to learn, to get to work: all of it cost money the poor didn't have. So, they were forced to borrow against their future wages, shackled to the threat of debt prison, and enslaved to a lifetime of endless work.

"Friend's budget contains bailouts for the corporations that we struck hard during the general strike," Zadie pointed out. "It includes bonus subsidies to the fossil fuel companies we blockaded last year. It offers relief to rich people for stock market plunges caused by national unrest ... but it does nothing for the rest of us."

"Friend told us to come up with a Relief Bill," Inez told the organizers. "Zadie and I think that the list of our demands can be worked into a powerful piece of legislation, but if we want it to pass, we're going to have to push and push hard."

Zadie smiled at her friend's passionate intensity. One fist curled against her open palm; she pressed them together like a laboring mother striving with all her might to bring the hope of new life into the world. She and Inez had worked as midwives to the possibility of change, reaching into the darkness of the unknown to grasp the world that was coming. They couldn't do it alone, though. They needed the sweat and effort of all the mothers, fathers, brothers, sisters, grandmothers, friends, and community. It took everyone to bring a world of respect, justice, kindness, and courage into existence.

"Are you willing to do this?" she asked the group.

Smiles and murmured assent broke out. A few heads nodded in agreement. A woman leaned forward and spoke.

"Do we have a plan?"

"Not yet," Inez answered, looking around, "but that's why I wanted to meet with you all. It has to be *our* plan; involving actions you know your people can pull off. If we're in agreement to take some kind of action, then perhaps we can split into breakout groups for strategizing."

Zadie called for a show of hands in favor of pushing the demands forward in the form of a new Relief Bill. A smattering of hands leapt up immediately, followed by a slower dozen supporters. One faith leader shifted thoughtfully and added his hand. Another person excused herself from the vote, saying that she had to weigh in with her cohort before committing. A second man stated that he'd like to wait until after the plans were strategized. Several hesitant participants agreed. One woman suggested proceeding into strategy and checking in again at the end of the evening. Vigorous nods met her idea. The circle broke into small groups. The scuffle of coffee refills, notebook gathering, and rearranging chairs and bodies rose up for a moment then settled.

Will watched from the sidelines, ironically noticing how soldiers and organizers both got caught up in the anticipation of battle. Looming struggles sent humans into a surreal frenzy, an oddly exalted - if insane - state. The organizers had broken into working groups and were strategizing with the primal enthusiasm of warriors rallying before war. He shrugged. Until he heard a better argument than turn the other cheek, he was sticking to his guns, literally. His life story could be crammed into a single slender volume comprised mostly of the dangerous and unpredictable turbulence of a streetwise childhood, followed by a terse description of his monotonous, but intense years of disciplined training. For most of it, he watched and waited, filling whole chapters of his days with the still observance of a wild creature. Even his childhood bore this quality, punctuated with bursts of trouble and calculated maneuvers for power and position in the minor hierarchies of youth.

He picked his role in the Dandelion Insurrection carefully, positioning himself in the odd safety of security; armed, alert, and tasked with keeping core organizers alive - and thus, him - to accomplish the stated goals of the movement. He had one cardinal rule: stay unattached. Do not be drawn in. Attachments led to trouble. Will did not get involved in the worlds of those he watched.

As a child, he had spooked his mother's boyfriends with his silent, aloof ways. *Kid's uncanny*, they'd grumble, but from his mother's string of relationships, he learned how to drink, sweat, gamble, evade authorities, pick pockets, throw darts, and fire a gun. The ex-cop had been the most useful of his mother's partners, though he drank too much hard liquor and eventually got rough. He knew the streets, the gutters, the petty politicians, the legal and illegal, the gray zones, and the fine lines. He was the most corrupt person Will had ever met - and he had seen the Devil's company of scoundrels. The ex-cop liked to boast about his exploits in a growl of grit and cynicism. When he caught on that the weird kid was soaking up his words like a sponge, he got talkative and poured out stories of murder, suicide, rape, drug overdoses, gang rings, pimps and prostitutes. Angeline let her nine-year-old absorb it all. She drew the line, however, at politics in an unshakeable conviction that baffled both boy and man.

"He isn't going into politics," Angeline would state with an uncompromising tone. "You can talk about anything else in my house, 'cept for that."

She spat into the sink in an uncharacteristically venomous gesture.

"Will?"

The voice cracked through his consciousness. Will snapped to the present. Zadie wove through the crowd. A fleeting look of worry crossed her face as she remembered the unfinished argument with Charlie over Will's involvement in the movement. She sighed and made a mental note to call him later.

"What are you doing here, Will?" she asked in a surprised tone.

"I heard a rumor that the poor 'hoods are organizing for some *real* change," he mentioned.

"Wherever did you hear that?" Zadie replied in mock innocence.

"Inez. I spoke with her before you left."

Zadie made a face then grinned.

"Glad you're here. It's like old times."

"Minus the secrecy and assassination attempts," Will noted, though he automatically scanned the room for trouble.

"Well, let's hope. The end of secrecy is a relief. It's nice to have some semblance of democracy again," Zadie enthused happily as the voices rose in the working groups, brainstorming and arguing.

Will resisted the urge to roll his eyes. He never could muster the same idealistic fervor for democracy that the Dandelion Insurrection lived and breathed. Democracy ended at the edge of a bullet, in his experience. That's the way it had always been and he frankly doubted that it would ever change.

"I've got to go," Zadie murmured. "Inez is about to bring everyone back into the full group. Come sit down with us," she invited.

"I'll stand here, thanks."

Zadie lifted an eyebrow, but Will gestured to the window's view of the street.

"I'm working," he said. "I'll leave the democracy to you all."

Truth be told, the circle of chairs gave him shudders. The soft, round bodies of the women triggered ghost memories of his mother, and he craved the safety of his separation from them. Will leaned his back against the wall and looked out at the dark streets below. One ear listened to the strategies and plans of the group. The other stayed alert and wary. If they wanted democracy, someone had to protect them from the forces that didn't. Community self-governance was a fine idea, but you couldn't debate away the dangers in the dark. Will swung his somber gaze to the notes on strategy as Zadie wrote them on the board. He shook his head. The world needed a few wiser heads to rule - people who were smarter than the rest and not afraid to look evil in the eye and use all necessary means to ensure the greater good.

He shrugged. Let the regular people play at democracy. It kept them distracted while the real power games played out around their lives.

CHAPTER EIGHT

· · · · ·

Dandelion Swarm

The poor neighborhoods of the teeming city threw down the gauntlet of the new Relief Bill with a thud that startled the nation. Legislators jolted out of half dozes. Soccer moms slammed on the brakes and turned up the radio. Workers gaped at the news. The rich roared in outrage. The Dandelion Insurrectionists cheered.

Living wages, rent control, debt prison abolition, social support programs, affordable healthcare, and more, the Relief Bill collected the hopes and dreams of the people who had borne the brunt of the injustices of the corporate regime. The wealthy screamed as if the bill heralded the end of their extravagant world. They shuddered in horror at the sight of the four horsemen of their apocalypse: Justice, Equality, Respect, and Dignity.

"Life-as-usual is killing us," Zadie Byrd Gray said in the press conference about the new version of the Relief Bill. "Business-as-usual has been a death sentence for the poor. When we cried *revolution,* we meant it. We want real change, and we want it now."

A new day had dawned and the time for change had come.

Not yet it hasn't, the corporate oligarchs seethed. *Not if we can help it.*

Friend warned the rich not to kick the hornet's nest of the people over this. A few concessions now was better than losing everything. But they ignored him, drunk on decades of unrestrained power and addicted to frequent injections of massive profits. They unleashed their army of lobbyists and uncorked the wine of bribes, laying siege to the remaining members of Congress, demanding the death of the Relief Bill.

Bury it in committee, they ordered. *Slice it to shreds with revisions. That'll teach those impudent upstarts. Change comes where, how, and when we want it . . . and not a moment sooner.*

"I think they're forgetting who they're up against," Zadie said with a slight smile. "Let's remind them."

The Dandelion Insurrection rose into action like a flock of birds thunderously taking wing, blackening the sky with their immense numbers. These were not the early days when the lone voice of the Man From the North wrote to stir the courage of a frightened populace. Now, when the movement rallied, the nation shook.

Dandelions Mobilize Against Interim Government, the headlines claimed.

We're not moving against them, Charlie Rider wrote, *we're helping them do their job.*

Friend read the essay and called Charlie Rider into the Oval Office.

"Apparently, we need to talk," he said, trying to hit a jovial note and missing the mark.

Charlie met his glare steadily, refusing to be intimidated by the newly instated Commander-In-Chief.

"No, Friend, you need to act. That was the point of my essay."

The smile disappeared from Friend's face.

Charlie gave their organizers in DC the nod to deploy the Dandelion Swarm . . . bright as goldfinches, swift and mobile as a flock, armed with Alternet-protected phones and street maps, their task was to hinder, slow, obstruct, disrupt, and block the

Congress members at every turn until they went for the one path open to them: passing the new draft of the Relief Bill.

The Dandelion Swarm's tactics propelled them to national notoriety. New recruits showed up hourly, offering to join the swarm. They held regular trainings in strategy and street tactics. They were to remain respectful, but firm. They studied their talking points, crafted their statements, role-played, and drilled to ensure that each Dandelion Swarm member could maintain focus and calm determination. Tansy employed a whole legal wing devoted to defending the swarm's persistent disruptions. They swooped and circled, evading capture and plaguing officials. The politicians saw yellow everywhere. One by one, they pressured Friend to let them do something about the Relief Bill before they went batty from the pestering flock. Still, Friend stalled and delayed and refused to act.

"We need to turn up the heat," Inez commented to Zadie. "Friend's happily roasting chestnuts over our little blaze."

"Let's call for murmurations in other cities," Zadie replied with a wink. "Anything DC can do, NYC thinks it can do better."

With the skillfulness of hard-won experience, the people burst into motion, using the swarming phenomenon of flocks of starlings. Murmurations crisscrossed New York City, using flash mob style tactics to disrupt daily life and raise awareness about the Relief Bill. Everyone knew the four simple rules to organizing a murmuration: fly forward, the leader changes at every shift in direction, keep equidistant, and don't leave your wing mate out on a limb. Small groups swept the streets, converging in crosswalks, holding up traffic long enough to pass out fliers, dispersing before the cops arrived then gathering again six blocks down the street.

Chicago, not to be outdone by New York, defied their local panhandling laws and occupied the street corners with people holding *Begging for Change* signs, shaking coffee cans with coins to rattle the nerves of the complacent, and passing out fliers about the Relief Bill. In San Francisco, people flocked into the offices of rental companies and city commissioners demanding rent control. In Los Angeles, swarms disrupted fancy restaurants at lunch hour by swooping through the tables. In Dallas, workers staged short, but frequent die-ins to demonstrate that they couldn't live on starvation wages. In Philadelphia, workers organized a series of murmurations that put low-wage businesses in a panic as the employees turned their smoke and bathroom breaks into walkouts and quickie strikes.

People rose up everywhere. The news teemed with stories of short, but effective protest actions. One afternoon, Charlie got a phone call from his grand-père, Valier, and could hear the sound of the television in the background reporting on one of their actions in Boston.

"Charlie!" he cackled in delight. "Tell your people to make more noise. If the politicians won't listen to us, we have to deafen them. The racket should be louder than the *tintamarre!*"

Charlie grinned. While some French-speakers called the loud pots-and-pans banging protests *casseroles* and Spanish-speakers referred to it as a *cacerolazo*, the French Acadians knew it as the *tintamarre*, which meant a din or racket.

"Down there, *la,* on the coast," Valier told his grandson, "there is a marsh - *Tintamarre Marsh*. It is named for the sound of the migrating birds. When something disturbs them, you see, they rise up with a racket. Then they settle down in a new place. It can travel like that for miles. Just like Zadie's flocks, eh?"

Charlie nodded thoughtfully. For his family, the *tintamarre* was more than just a protest. It was a declaration of existence. It celebrated the survival of the French Acadians despite the English and American attempts to round them up, deport them, destroy their culture, deny them the ability to speak French, and strip them of their heritage. When the Acadians burst into cacophony, banging pots and pans, ringing bells, and blowing whistles, they were announcing to the world: *We are here! We are alive! We survived!*

"Just like the poor people," Valier pointed out gently.

They had survived the cruel greed of the corporate dictatorship. They had endured debt oppression and prison. They had managed to raise children against impossible odds. They had endured dangers, repression, and crippling poverty. They were alive and kicking, and rising up to demand justice.

Old Valier Beaulier would not be satisfied until his grandson wrote an essay explaining the story and encouraging the murmurations to bring pots and pans, bells and whistles into the actions, standing up for change loudly and clearly, with vitality and exuberance. Throughout history, people of so many backgrounds had endured and persisted, resisted and rebelled against injustice. Every strand of humanity had stories to share.

Let us remember the past as we strive for our future, Charlie wrote. *Make noise. Celebrate our aliveness. Take flight and soar toward the world we envision.*

The cacophony erupted in cities and towns nationwide. It ground meetings to a halt. It disrupted business. It filled the streets and flooded the stores as the Dandelion Swarms and murmurations flew through buildings and shopping malls, across intersections and down sidewalks. The banging racket migrated like the wing beats of birds, disturbed by the inaction of politicians, refusing to settle down until the Relief Bill was passed. They railed against the wealthy, the corporations, and the politicians who opposed them, seeing those factions as threats to their families' survival.

"Our murmurations - like those of the starlings - have a purpose," Zadie told the skeptical press. "The tiny birds are using collective action to drive hawks away from their nests, protecting their communities without hurting the predators. Wing beat by wing beat, we are driving these wealthy hawks away from our Relief Bill."

In a bland cubicle in a government office, a quiet little mouse of a worker heard Zadie's comment and sat up with a jolt. She suddenly saw the protest actions in a strategic light. *If they want to chase hawks,* she thought, *I can help them target their swarms.*

That evening, Charlie received another message from the Mouse:

Here's who's working against you.
Hit 'em where it counts.
- The Mouse

Attached was a list of the corporations and wealthy individuals lobbying against the Relief Bill and how much they were spending.

Not one penny more should go to these businesses until the Relief Bill is passed, wrote the Man From the North in an essay calling for boycotts. *We have to show them that legislating against the poor while protecting the greed of the rich is bad for business, not to mention the soul.*

Not one penny more! the people cried, picketing storefronts and shopping malls.

Not one penny more! they chanted as they blocked roads in front of corporate headquarters.

Not one penny more! they shouted as they boycotted sports channels and ball games owned by wealthy elites.

The first of October approached. One old lady with a face as wrinkled as the leaves falling off the trees threw down her stack of bills in despair. Her skin clung to her bones. She shivered as the days turned biting with cold. She put on a third sweater, rubbed her arthritic knuckles, and when the landlord came knocking, she shook her head.

"Not one penny more," she said, refusing to pay rent to an extortionist management company that was not only working to block the Relief Bill, but had also spiked her rent three times that year and still refused to fix her leaky faucet.

He threw her out on the street. The neighbors took her in.

Not one penny more! they vowed. *No rents should be paid until the Relief Bill is passed. If greed is worth more than an old lady's life, we refuse to be part of the cruelty.*

The Rent Strike snapped across the country as fast as the hard frost's icy hand slammed down on the continent. The Dandelion Insurrection, far and wide, threw the weight of its efforts behind the strike, urging widespread participation. Citizen anti-eviction squads formed to help people defy landlords and stay in their homes.

Hold fast, Charlie wrote. *One company controls thirty percent of the rental market. They can't evict all of us. We must stand together and seize this day.*

They had to dig into the turning point of change and push in the direction of justice. The momentum had to be kept rolling. When the massive gears of upheaval settled once again, they needed to find themselves in the fertile soil of real change, not in the barren wasteland of empty promises.

The nation's poor, driven by the immediacy of the pinch of hunger and the looming threat of yet another unhoused winter, propelled the movement forward. Unlike their counterparts in the suburbs, they had no comfortable resting spots. From the north, south, east, west, the rumblings in the poor neighborhoods grew louder. Rent strikes erupted in apartment buildings, tenements, and trailer parks. One flash of resistance triggered another. A hint of wild unrest flavored the actions as people took to the street.

The crackle of electric tension grew. Sparks burst out unexpectedly. Zadie rolled with the spontaneity, but Inez worried.

"We don't always know who is organizing these protests or what they'll do in the streets," she fretted.

Zadie shrugged.

"We never did. The Dandelion Insurrection has always been this way, springing up where we least expect. We're a swarm of birds, not a silver bullet," Zadie said. "Our strength is in our diversity and our sheer, dizzying numbers: millions of people, thousands of ideas, hundreds of strategies, dozens of pivot points of change."

The Dandelion Insurrection was not - and never had been - a unified front, but rather, a thousand points of light momentarily united in blazing solidarity with one another, forming cohorts, breaking apart, reforming in new configurations. They responded to nationwide initiatives with autonomy - no orders came down from the top. An idea succeeded or failed because people joined in - or not. It was madness. It was glorious. It was the Dandelion Insurrection.

They were leaderful, colorful, creative, and unruly, hard to control, impossible to stop. The Dandelion Insurrection burst through the nation with a golden indomitability, demonstrating irresistible resilience. They adapted to tough climates. They grappled hard challenges. They shouldered through cracks in the concrete of control. They were as wild as ecosystems, as versatile as evolution, as experimental as Life's vigorous emergence. To the forces of greed, the armies of destruction, the ranks of domination, and those who lusted for control, the Dandelion Insurrection was a nightmare, a headache, a disaster to be stopped. But, like a swooping flock of birds, a buzzing swarm of bees, or a darting school of fish, the movement could not be halted or captured.

The first of the month came and went. The people showed no signs of paying rent. The rental management company owners petitioned the authorities to declare a state of emergency. The resisters retorted that they had been living in a state of emergency for years. Entire blocks faced eviction and when the owner of those buildings called on the police to throw out the tenants, the police reform groups mobilized to blockade the block, declaring autonomous zones and setting up unarmed neighborhood peace teams to de-escalate conflicts, using restorative justice circles to resolve disputes. In San Francisco, a mobilized group conducted a citizen's arrest of a major landlord and brought him to a mediation process in the attempt to renegotiate rents.

The tactic terrified building owners. Pressure mounted. The corporate media screamed about the unrest, the moochers and freeloaders, ingrates and anarchists, communists and terrorists. Every epithet in the book was flung at the poor people mobilizing to demand fairness, justice, and a chance to live with dignity.

The scales of justice teetered. The rich threw more money onto their side. The poor heaved the weight of their desperation onto the other. The Congress members groaned as the tug-of-war split them down the middle. A red-faced, white-knuckled, nerve-strained impasse arose. Neither side of the struggle relented an inch.

Then, unexpectedly, the scales lurched, heaved, and tipped.

CHAPTER NINE

. . . . .

Debt Prison Strike

Hot and humid as a hairy armpit on a southeast afternoon, the debt prison laundry stank of detergents and hissing cotton steam. The incarcerated workers hauled sacks and trolleys of soiled linens from hospitals and hotels, growing more surly and mulish by the minute.

If that break time doesn't come soon, Etta James grumbled silently, *I'm going to snap.*

The back of her green uniform sucked the sweat off the skin of her spine. Trickles ran down her sides and itched as they dried. She watched the clock. Break time came and went without a glance from the manager. A machine malfunction had delayed the day's workload. The prisoners would be kept sweating to make up lost time.

"Is he going to keep us hopping 'til we fall dead today?" Etta muttered to her neighbor.

The other prisoner shook her head blankly, deafened by the thunder of the washers. Etta returned to her own business - unloading a cart into the empty machine by the armload, trying not to think about strangers' semen or infectious diseases rolled up in hospital bed sheets wet with piss. Five years she'd been in here, sweating in the summer, chilled to the bones in the winter, making less money than she would doing the same job on the outside. Debt court sent her here when she fell too far behind - never mind why. Every woman had a *why*: kid got sick, landlord spiked the rent, lost a job just when bills came due. Debt collectors got the police to haul them in. The judge mandated time paying back what they owed by working in one of the debt prison industries.

Etta longed for the clammy cold of the meatpacking plant she'd been sent to once - though she went queasy at the sight of dangling flesh and hunks of meat. Still, it was better than some outfits. She'd heard tales. Chemical factories. Faulty equipment. Injuries. Accidents. Death.

Etta glanced at the clock again, but the heat played tricks on her eyes. She swore the hands had moved backward. She wiped her brow and fanned her neck. The manager glared at her from the observation window of his air-conditioned office. She scowled back as a flush climbed up her veins.

Hot flash. Etta swore a second time. She'd heard rumors that people outside were trying to abolish the debt prisons. *Better hurry the hell up,* Etta thought, *or I'll combust.* There'd been talk of a debt prison strike - all hot air and bluster, not like the one organized when the Dandelion Insurrection hit DC to oust the old president. That was smart. Nobody working, not anywhere in the whole country. Guards just kept 'em in the cells as everyone followed the news.

If they don't call a break, Etta thought furiously, *I'm gonna call a strike. We shouldn't be working for these crooks. Not while people outside are struggling for justice. We're just putting money in rich people's pockets so they can buy politicians and keep us locked up.*

One more minute, she vowed, tugging the sweaty uniform off her stomach and puffing it to circulate some air across her flaming chest. A woman can only take so much. Enough is enough. Etta's lips stretched across her teeth in a grimace of a smile. That's what that woman had said, the one who led the march to DC, Zadie Byrd Gray's momma who died: Revolutions happen when one woman says, enough!

Count to ten, Etta warned her rising temper. *Don't do anything rash.* Her mind raced through all the things they'd do to her - solitary, docked pay, extra work, no meals, beatings - as her temperature shot skyward in a volcano of heat that knocked the strength out of her knees. She sank to the ground, dizzy.

"What are you doing?" her coworker hollered.

"Taking a break," she answered, holding her head.

But the woman misheard her mumbled reply.

Starting a strike.

The other woman read the flush of frustration and frayed nerves in Etta's red face. She turned to the next woman as she, too, slid down to sit on the floor.

"Strike!" she bellowed.

And the Debt Prison Strike began.

Igniting across the half-laid fuses of an actual plan to strike, it spread from one facility to another, setting off chaos and solidarity in its inopportune eruption. By the week's end, hundreds of thousands of debt prisoners had quit working - and flames of alarm spread out of prisons and into industries. Hotels nationwide demanded their fresh laundry and learned - with a shock - why it was not available. Corporate managers tried to hush up the story, but bellhops' and room maids' tongues waggled. Whispers collided like ripples in a rainy pond, crossing and convoluting. Meat shipments were delayed, slaughterhouses ground to a slow trickle of production, and grocery stores posted out-of-stock signs. The stock market lurched, plummeted, had cardiac arrest, staggered back to its feet, and flopped over again.

The Dandelion Insurrection shoved the shoulder of its efforts behind the momentum of the strike and called for everyone to return the prisoners' show of solidarity for the Relief Bill by taking action against the injustice of debt.

Whether we're in prison or not, debt cages us all, Charlie wrote. He called on everyone to strike debt and hit the financial sector where it counts.

Delay your payments, Charlie urged. *For a week, a month, just hold off a little. Make them feel the pinch like a stalling morphine drip. By the time they send the third notice, the finance industry will be screaming in horror. We have their money and they can't have it back unless they stop blocking change.*

Charlie Rider was slapped by the media as a reckless gambler hurtling the nation toward economic crisis. The seething ranks of the rich rolled out thunderous accusations against the folly of the Man From the North, but the populace stood immune. Charlie was always attacked by the wealthy. The outcry against him merely validated his cause. Payments stalled and stopped. From credit cards to mortgages to student loans to medical payments, everyone held a piece of the debt industry.

The rich own us, Charlie wrote, *only until the moment when we realize that by not paying our debts, we own them. We hold their capital hostage in our unpaid debts. They need us to pay this back. But do we need them? We took on these debts to afford the cost of living, and yet, our lives under the burden of massive debt are still unlivable. We must leverage our shared strength for systemic change.*

Inez worked tirelessly to ignite the courage of the poor into determination for action.

"It is better to refuse to pay until this system is overhauled. Better to be sent to debt prison where you can join the work strike inside. Better to risk everything to gain something than to continue to die slowly on the nothing we have now."

In DC, the phones rang nonstop. Pleas, demands, appeals, orders, suggestions, and rants poured in. Police chiefs called Homeland Security for back up. Bankers demanded bailouts from the Treasury Department. Business leaders insisted that the Interim Government do something to quell the unrest. The people asked for help surviving the economic wreckage of the previous regime. Millions of people, in every city, at every turn, harried the Interim Government while the fuel of the economic machine spluttered and choked.

On Wall Street, a meeting of financial behemoths was convened. Business tycoons and the ultra-wealthy gathered in a penthouse conference room brushing the clouds. Their eyes flashed in irritation. They griped over the endless annoyances caused by the Dandelion Insurrection. They swapped notes on political allegiances. They waited impatiently. Friend had been summoned. At ten o'clock sharp, he appeared.

"This is unacceptable," they growled. "Get this situation under control."

Friend listened quietly, waiting for his moment.

"Foreclose on them all and board up their houses," said a man who owned three mansions.

"They're renters, not homeowners," a real estate tycoon answered irritably. His management companies had been unsuccessfully trying to collect rents or evict people across the country. "It's impossible to break a rent strike when no one's looking for an apartment - they're all resisting!"

"Can't evict all of them, anyway," an heiress pointed out with a look of distaste. "Where would they go?"

A disgruntled shifting swept the table. Homeless encampments had swelled from the recent evictions. A nationwide cleanup effort had ousted the unhoused from urban back alleys and abandoned lots, dumping them into the outskirts of the cities and onto the back edges of the wealthy's estates.

"Arrest them all, I say," said the man next to her. "Lock them up."

"Not while they're all striking and refusing to work!" exclaimed the owner of the private prison industry that had taken over the government corrections program. His heart rate elevated dangerously as he testily took a gulp of imported bottled water. His margins were vanishing faster than the last remaining rhinoceros. Suppliers had cut contracts. Accounts had been cancelled. Meanwhile, he was feeding and housing hundreds of thousands of idling ingrates. He glanced at John C. Friend, but saw no hint of relief in the man's noncommittal eyes. He needed a bailout of government funds, or a strikebreaker. Not more headaches in the form of inmates. "I'm not absorbing the cost of housing and feeding and controlling millions of people who won't work."

Furious bickering broke out between billionaires over who would foot the bill and absorb the cost of the political unrest. They glared at each other, refusing to shell out a penny, lobbing insults and accusations in a vicious Ping-Pong match of blame laying and haggling.

Friend cleared his throat.

"It seems, gentlemen and ladies, that those irascible dandelions have got you by the neck. You'll simply have to give them what they want."

"Rent control?! Debt forgiveness? Abolition of debt prison?" scoffed an heiress. "I'm not paying for that."

"No one said you would," Friend answered soothingly.

The bickerers fell silent. Eyes swung toward the unassuming politician. Ears pricked up.

"So, who's paying?" the head of student financing at a major bank growled, getting straight to the point.

Friend's smile would make the Devil cringe.

"They are."

CHAPTER TEN

. . . . .

Un Pequeño Milagro

At five o'clock on a sharp-edged autumn evening, Zadie and Inez squeezed onto the warm red couch in Pilar Maria's apartment in the city. Behind them, Jesus on his cross rolled his eyes heavenward. Inez' stout mother fingered her rosary and muttered prayers to St. Anthony, patron saint of lost causes and long shots. Pilar bore a leathery blend of determination and pride in her features. A few white strands laced her jet-black hair and she had begun to wonder just how many more miracles she could finagle out of God in her remaining years. Her whole life, she had lived one step from death's door with all the familiar disdain of a neighbor who argues about the placement of garbage cans in the walkway. Pilar Maria Ignacia Hernandez had tricked God and the Devil into giving her extra decades of life. She hoped she'd last long enough to see some justice in this world.

The neighborhood hung in a breathless moment of tension, quivering like the last dry leaves clinging to the branches outside the window. Rumor had it that tonight, John C. Friend and several Congress members would introduce the Dandelion Insurrection's version of the Relief Bill. Every few minutes, the media tantalized the viewer with promises of information, but the day had passed with nothing more than the usual congressional speeches defending the necessity of the mass surveillance program and strong domestic security measures.

Half an hour ago, the news channels began to report that John C. Friend would address Congress at five o'clock. The commercial break ended. Pilar's fingers gripped a rosary bead so hard it cracked. She swore on one breath and recited a Hail Mary on the next. These days, she kept a box of spare beads on the kitchen counter. Every altar and *retablo* mounted on the walls gleamed with a flickering votive candle. Earlier today, she'd made Zadie and Inez buy a dozen candles for the prayer altar at Father Ramon's church.

Por favor, Dios Mio, hear our pleas. For once, do something magnificent - move the bastards' hearts even if you have to resurrect them in their dead chests like Jesus, himself. Un pequeño milagro, she begged. Just enough to get her last remaining beloved daughter Inez out of martyrdom's way. On the wall behind the television, her daughter Guadalupe Dolores' portrait smiled back at her. *Go bend God's ear, hija,* Pilar willed her silently, *tell Him that He took you too early, and I want Inez longer by my side.*

Beside her, Will Sharp leaned against the doorjamb, expressionless, avoiding Pilar's glaring glances. The *vieja* detested him. They were cut out of similar cloths, rugged and cynical, beaten by life, and willing to bargain hard for daily survival. He'd heard Inez state proudly that Pilar Maria would outlive death, taxes, and cockroaches. Will suspected that if it came down to she and him, the old woman would be the last one standing.

The news channel cut to the floor of Congress, the members scattered among the vacant seats. The camera zoomed in as Friend approached the podium.

"We've got him," Zadie declared, scooting to the edge of the couch and jiggling her legs.

"He's going to fold," Inez predicted, her knuckles turning white as she clenched Zadie's fingers.

Five hundred miles south, Charlie and Tansy knocked into one another in nervous agitation as they paced the living room.

Twilight hissed with blusters of wind. The boughs over the house thrashed and moaned, throwing off leaves. Charlie tossed his limbs into an armchair then sprang back to his feet. On the computer screen propped open on the table, Friend shook hands with the Speaker of the House who would be presiding over this congressional session.

Like sentinels, Charlie and Tansy stilled, standing shoulder-to-shoulder, staring at the screen. Charlie watched with lead in his stomach. Nervousness churned his veins into jittery highways of unease. He rubbed the hair down on the back of his neck. It had been too easy. Charlie simply couldn't believe the ruling elites would go down without a hotter fight.

"I don't like it," he commented, steeling not for victory, but for the next blow. The entire weight of brutal history had demonstrated the ruthlessness of the rich and powerful.

On the screen, John C. Friend cleared his throat and began by acknowledging the validity of the people's demands, empathizing with the challenges they faced.

"The people have spoken loud and clear," he said, wincing and rubbing his ear for effect. A smattering of chuckles broke out for the headaches of the past weeks.

"Poverty and debt have led to an untenable situation. These . . . demands . . . that have been recently put forward arise from just grievances - "

"Get to the point," Charlie growled impatiently, as Friend droned on, restating the obvious.

" - and so, along with several Congress members, I am introducing and urging you to pass the Poverty and Debt Relief Act: ending debt prison, providing debt relief, reinstituting the Food Assistance Program that our predecessors so unwisely terminated, issuing instructions for temporary rent control nationwide for the duration of the Interim Government, and finally, implementing a Jobs and Economic Stimulus Program to provide families with much-needed income."

A smattering of polite applause sounded across the seats of Congress. A few scowls wrinkled jowly faces as they called up the bill on their desk screens. Not a whisper of the ordinary citizens' stunned euphoria reached their ears, but in Pilar's apartment, the hoots and whistles of celebration flooded in the open window. The neighbors banged on the iron rail of the fire escape with a cooking spoon. In the street below, two women held phones aloft with the news, screaming and leaping arm-in-arm together when Friend called for the abolition of debt prison and the launch of a government subsidy program designed to aid the affected industries in transitioning to minimum wage employment models. In Pilar's neighborhood, the jubilation erupted into a cacophony of cheers, whistles, blowing car horns, banging pots and pans until she couldn't hear Friend talking even at full volume.

"Keep it down, idiots! It hasn't passed yet!" Pilar shouted out the window, parting the white lace with an impatient hand. She slammed the window closed to block the nonsense of false hopes.

In the interdepartmental IT support offices, Alex Kelley scowled at the screen of her computer, ignoring her work to watch Friend's speech. Her intuition churned in a stomach-aching worry. She curled the narrow bones of her body in a hunch of anxiety over her keyboard, leaned her elbows on her desk, and clenched the spikes of her short hair in her fingers.

"What's the hook?" Alex muttered through gritted teeth.

Friend cleared his throat and took a sip of water. He waved his hand in a good-humored call for silence.

"Now, as you all know, money doesn't grow on trees, and we can't just wave a magic wand and solve all our problems.

Paying for these programs will require collective sacrifice and shared vision, a feeling of solidarity and brotherhood for all of our citizens. We, as Americans, must work together and put our resources on the table to help one another."

Alex jolted and keyed in a search inquiry so fast her fingers blurred. Her eyes leapt from Friend to the text of the Poverty and Debt Relief Act, scrolling rapidly through the sections and clauses.

"Therefore," Friend continued, "the Poverty and Debt Relief Act also contains authorization for the expedient procurement of funds. In the spirit of determination we shall find our nation rising to the challenge of liberating our brothers and sisters from the shackles of poverty. We shall do whatever it takes to address this crisis for the greatest good."

Alex's eyes widened. She swore.

"I knew it."

As Friend concluded his remarks and the Congress members stood in ovation, she looked up and frantically dialed the home phone number of Tansy Beaulisle. This was too big and complex to send as a leaked message from the Mouse. They were going to need help stopping this brewing nightmare. She would have to come out of hiding and offer them assistance. Her heart thundered in her chest. As the phone rang, she ducked out of the office and paced the empty streets in front of the building. Charlie Rider answered. She could hear the sounds of celebration in the background.

"My name is Alex Kelley. We have to talk. There's something you ought to know."

Friend was unleashing the plunder monkeys.

CHAPTER ELEVEN

. . . . .

Plunder Monkeys

The cackle of flying monkeys. Mocking screeches from the dark shadows. Red rimmed eyes and barred teeth hissing. Charlie's mind reeled with images as Alex spoke. The diminutive tech worker had raced over to the house quick as a mouse and twice as nervous. Tansy studied the boyish woman with her close-cropped hair, man's shirt tucked into beige pants, flat tennis shoes, and glasses perched on her head. She claimed to be an ally in the government, and when Tansy challenged her to prove it, she quietly said,

"I'm the one who locked the government bank accounts and stopped the illegitimate president from stealing billions of dollars on his way out the door."

Tansy sat back, stunned and satisfied. Few people knew about the attempted theft or the locking of the bank accounts. It was a tremendous breach of security, twice over - once when the president tried to take the money, twice when an unknown person had blocked him. Tansy only heard about it in strict confidence when someone asked if the attempted theft could be added to the list of criminal charges slapped on the former president's files.

But, according to Alex, the plunder monkeys made the old president's attempted theft look like shoplifting breath mints by comparison.

"Years ago," Alex explained, "when that business tycoon managed to install himself in the Oval Office, a host of greed-sucking fiends rode in on his gilded coattails and attempted to privatize every public asset in sight. Their grubby paws fondled monuments and memorial parks. They salivated over public lands. Mineral rights were tossed up on the auction block. Their corporations snapped up toll bridges and highways for cheap prices."

Tansy harrumphed knowingly, remembering the backbreaking legal load she took on trying to save the people's assets from the thieves.

"It was sheer, unbridled theft," Alex spat out in disgust. "They plundered the nation. A famous novelist - Steven King - called them *the motley crew of plunder monkeys* - and he knew a horror story when he saw it. Over the years, certain public assets, such as the schools and public parks, have been saved or regained. The wholesale giving away of water utilities was halted . . . but this," Alex groaned, "is round two, the return of the plunder monkeys."

The plunder monkeys formed the bricks and mortar of the hidden corporate dictatorship. Politicians could be run out of office, but the ranks of the corporate class continuously circled like vultures, hoping to snatch another bite of the rotting beast of the national economy. Thousands of them scurried around searching for deals. They had grown fat on the gravy train of the old regime. The pinch of withdrawal hit them as the Dandelion Insurrection cut off their bulging profits. Undoubtedly, the plunder monkeys had been lobbying the Interim Government with the nerve-addled insistence of addicts.

To finance its programs, the Poverty and Debt Relief Act authorized the sale of the last remaining public assets to private individuals and companies. Schools, libraries, community centers, parks, water systems, streetlights, parking lots - literally *any* public asset could now be sold for pennies on the dollar of its real value.

"We'll fight it," Charlie promised with determination. The terms of the Relief Act rankled the soul. It was giving away freebies to the wealthy at the expense of the poor. It would further impoverish communities for generations yet to come. It stole the sweat and lifeblood of the people whose tax dollars and volunteer efforts had built and supported those schools and libraries.

The plunder monkeys had to be stopped . . . and fast.

"They're exploiting the lawless window before the elections," Alex pointed out, "attempting to loot everything off before a popularly-elected government cracks down on the free-for-all."

"Friend called this collective sacrifice, but he's dead wrong," Charlie fumed. "The wealthy already hold more than sixty percent of the wealth of the nation. They've been receiving tax breaks for decades. Their corporations and private foundations pay virtually nothing in taxes. This nation has plenty of money to right the wrongs and address the gross inequities that exist. We just have to tax the rich."

"Don't tell me," Alex retorted, waving her hand to the rest of the world. "Tell them. Rip the Interim Government to shreds for this. Scorch them with your words."

"We need more than words," Charlie sighed. "We need a plan."

Alex rubbed her palms together, eyes lighting up as she cleared off the coffee table. This, she could help with. Together, she and Charlie began to plot out a strategy of resistance, bringing out large sheets of blank paper and scribbling notes on the white board that hung on the opposite wall. To Charlie's delighted surprise, Alex Kelley turned out to be a diabolically clever thinker with the cool enthusiasm of a chess master. A lifelong DC resident, she ceaselessly studied the board of power and politics, mapping out the moves of hundreds of pawns and major players. She watched industry, finance, Capitol Hill, the military industrial complex, popular movements, and the seething frustrations of the people - in short, the millions of factors flowing into the winds of change.

More importantly, she was a walking encyclopedia on nonviolent struggle. Alex could recite the hundred and ninety-eight methods of nonviolent action from memory, compare and contrast Kingian and Gandhian nonviolence, and cross analyze the difference between pragmatic and principled philosophies. She cited historical examples dating from 411 BC - when Egyptian workers went on strike at the pyramids - to present, and invariably had a story to reference when a current issue reared up. Alex had resources from around the globe - success stories and failures, crowning victories and major setbacks. She stayed current with new data on civil resistance, as the researchers called it, and followed global struggles more avidly than sports enthusiasts tracked their favorite teams.

"We need a list of the poor communities," she commented, thinking furiously.

"Inez has a list of the cities and neighborhoods that have been in resistance this past month," Charlie offered.

Alex shook her head.

"We can start with that, but we'll need to use a census database . . . the plunder monkeys might go for the jugular of the resistance, or they might pick off the weaker municipalities first, seeking the low-hanging fruits."

She called up the public records on community assets on her computer and began to pin color-coded flags on a map, running an analysis on which would be most enticing to the plunder monkeys.

"We need to know where, when, and why they'll strike so we can block 'em at every turn."

"Can't we just assume they'll be everywhere?" Charlie asked.

"Well, we already know they're not going to go after the wealthy communities that don't need relief funds. We need to send out a clear nationwide message, rejecting the terms of the Act, and demonstrating that we are organized and ready to stop them from stealing from our communities."

Alex's mind raced twice as fast as her hands and eyes. As she put together the database of assets and organizers, she mentally cross-analyzed it with current political views and public sentiment. She leaned back thoughtfully. They were going to have to shore up local organizers. The people desperately needed funds . . . many would be tempted to take the deal. Their lives depended on some kind of change - and they might fall for a short-term relief, rather than the long-term solution. Alex wanted to compile a list of which communities would hold strong, which would waver, and who would fold - and why. She wanted to know the top twenty targets the plunder monkeys would pressure, threaten, and intimidate. Their best defense was a unified, solid rejection of the terms of the Act. The more communities united on this, the better. Once some sold out and got their relief funds, it made the resistance all the more difficult for everyone else.

"I wish there were some way to catalogue where the Dandelion Insurrection organizing is weakest and strongest," she sighed.

"Tucker would know," Charlie commented absently.

"Who?"

"Tucker Jones," he replied, blinking in surprise, as he realized not everyone knew the reclusive, brilliant computer programmer who had helped design the Alternet.

"Get ahold of him, then," Alex commanded. "And put on the coffee pot. It's going to be a long night."

Charlie grinned, already headed toward the kitchen. The lines of his next essay roared in his head. He dove for his notebook and jotted the words down.

Stand strong, he scribbled. *Hold fast to your roots, to the clarity of justice. This is wrong. We know it. They know it. We must unconditionally reject and resist this new assault of injustice.*

By eleven o'clock that night, the map was peppered with pins and notes. Charlie wrote ferociously in the study. Zadie and Inez had called to strategize. Tucker had responded to his query with streams of database information that made Alex's eyes glow. The first coffee pot had been drained and Charlie's body jittered with lack of sleep and excess caffeine. He rubbed his eyes and stood up to stretch, peering around the doorway into the living room. Alex had kicked off her shoes and appeared ready to work until dawn, propelled by raw energy. Her hair flung out in odd directions from absently rubbing her head in a vast collision of thoughts. She stood barefoot by the white board, frowning, her computer balanced on one arm, a pad of sticky notes in her teeth, a pencil behind one ear, and a pen tucked over the other. Charlie guessed she would work until daybreak, stumble through her workday, and continue like this in a fit of fascinated obsession until the solution or strategy emerged.

"What we need - " she muttered over the pad of notes.

"Is some sleep?" Charlie suggested.

"No," she replied, taking the sticky notes out of her mouth. "We need a catalyst, a spark. One ground zero of resistance to catch the imagination of the others. We need a model to take a stand and tell the story of why this is unacceptable in very human, real ways."

"And you need this for strategic reasons?" Charlie asked, yawning.

"For human reasons," Alex clarified, studying her notes for answers, "which are often surprisingly strategic. People don't move into action because of statistics. They move because of their hearts. We're hardwired with empathy neurons, billions of them, and human beings are evolutionarily programmed to help one another. So, simply saying *people are resisting the plunder monkeys* isn't enough. We have to see the faces, know the names, feel like the struggle is just next door or happening to our children and friends. That requires stories from real people in specific places, not generalizations."

"Then you need a school," Charlie pointed out. "A highway just doesn't have the same heartstring tugging charm as a bunch of kids determined not to let the howling thieves take their playground."

"Exactly," Alex agreed, frowning at the database.

"And, it's got to have some resistance background," Charlie added thoughtfully, "because we need to act fast, not spend weeks convincing, training, and preparing."

"Mmm-hmm," Alex murmured, "and it's got to be a little jewel the monkeys can't help but try to snatch."

"Los Jardineros," Charlie exclaimed, remembering with wide-eyed delight. "Just outside Chicago, there's an elementary school that trains the students and families in nonviolent resistance. It's in a poor, mostly minority neighborhood that's definitely on Tucker's list of Dandelion Insurrection hotspots and also Inez' more recent group of campaigners for the Relief Act."

Charlie pointed to the map on Alex's computer.

"They'd be perfect . . . and game for the challenge," he said. "I wrote about them in the early days as an example of organized resistance. Their school was on the chopping block even back then."

Charlie's eyes clouded suddenly. He sighed.

"There's just one problem," he confessed.

"What's that?" Alex asked, her heart sinking.

"Well, I mean, the plunder monkeys couldn't be that stupid, right? They've got to know the history of the school. They wouldn't go after it, would they?"

Alex chuckled wickedly.

"Never underestimate the power of greed, Charlie. It makes sane men crazy, clear-sighted women blind as bats, and normally smart people idiotic."

She placed a bright yellow dandelion of a flag on the map near Chicago. There was a trick to catching monkeys: put a treat inside a hollow coconut and they'd reach into the narrow hole greedily. They'd clench the goodie in their fist - and they wouldn't be able to pull their hand back out. Weighed down by greed, the coconut turned a fast monkey into a sitting duck. In Alex's case, she didn't need dead monkeys, but she did need to show the nation the nasty, screeching, bared-teeth dangerous truth of the plunder monkeys, so no one would be duped into selling out. For that, the trap had to be livestreamed nationwide. She needed a media circus onsite when it happened.

"Charlie," she said with a gleam in her eye, "I think it's time you and Zadie went on a date."

CHAPTER TWELVE

· · · · ·

Little Dandelions

The lights of the elementary school spilled out into the dark night like hopeful eyes illuminated in the faces of children. The sky shivered, reluctant to confess that winter's grip was tightening over the last days of autumn. Spits of snow flurries darted through the headlights. Charlie drummed his fingers on the armrest as Zadie pulled into the parking lot.

Not here. Not us. Not our school.

The words of Idah Robbins echoed in his thoughts. The fifth grade teacher's voice rang with fierce determination and a deep love of her students, school, and community. *A public school is more than a set of buildings,* she had said, *it is a vital part of the community, a pillar of functional democracy.* Charlie had quoted her in his recent essay urging resistance to the plunder monkeys.

"We teach *all* students," Idah had stated. "Every child in this nation is welcome here. We do not discriminate based on aptitude or wealth. No private school can honestly claim the same. If we are ever to have a truly democratic nation, the door of education must be held open equally to all children."

Charlie had called Idah Robbins on a phone number listed in Inez' database of organizers and, after a week of crossed messages, finally caught her just moments after she finished a tense meeting with their local species of plunder monkeys, a private school corporation called Aldler's Champion Schools. The teacher's voice roared with indignation.

"They marched in here flaunting arrogance and authority - and we gave them quite a shock of resistance, let me tell you!"

Idah Robbins recounted the story to Charlie, crackling the phone line with her passionate retelling. Aldler's Champion Schools' Acquisitions and Transitions Team had arrived at Los Jardineros with a small army of lawyers and administrators in tow. Phyllis Devanne, head of the team, was a tall and narrow woman with a craven face marked by a prominent jaw and sunken cheeks. Her powder did not quite mask the papery sallowness of her skin. Her off-blonde hair bore the texture of too many years of dyes, rough and stiff despite the professional styling.

"This school has been seized by eminent domain and was sold to Howard Aldler's Champion Schools Corporation," Devanne announced in her nasal drone, ignoring all words of respectful welcome.

"It was an illegal seizure and we refuse to pass over the school," Idah replied, politely, but firmly. The principal of the school rubbed her forehead as Aldler's people burst out with protests. She gestured them into her office. The room shrank to the tightness of a sardine can stuffed with the drab gray suits of the Acquisitions and Transitions Team. Phyllis Devanne dropped a stack of paperwork on the desk with a thump and eyed the cluttered shelves with a possessive gleam.

"The seizure is quite legal," one of the lawyers stated. "Your municipality applied for and was approved to receive funds from the Poverty and Debt Relief Act. Now, as per Amendment Six, it owes a debt to the Federal Government. This school property was seized as partial satisfaction of the debt."

"The seizure is illegal because we have not consented," Idah snapped back. "You have no signatures from our school board, the only power holders who can authorize this transaction."

"We have a waiver of that formality," Devanne smirked, "and a license from the Illinois Department of Education."

The principal tapped her fingers together.

"Quite frankly," she said, "we don't care what the paperwork says or where the shifting sands of legal documents drift. We intend to keep this school in public ownership as an asset of the community."

"I recommend," Idah added as she eyeballed them over the top of her glasses, "that you return to company headquarters and warn them to back off from the purchase of this school. We are a poor investment. This neighborhood will never consent to private rule."

"Now, Ms. Robbins, I do believe there's been a lot of miscommunication," said a representative of Aldler's Champion Schools in a placating tone. "Aldler's has a lot to offer this community: resources, technology improvements, a proven track record in turning schools around from utter dysfunction to the discipline of a well-oiled machine. We plan to improve the playground and cafeteria, and to upgrade the computers."

"My, my, my," Idah drawled with all the irony of a well-studied history teacher, "haven't you come bearing fancy beads and flintlocks." Her tone altered abruptly into the commanding crack she used on the goofballs in the back row.

"Those who don't know history are doomed to repeat it . . . and it looks like you all have some homework to do. We aren't interested in your oily machine. I happen to know," she added, eyeing him disdainfully, "quite a bit about Aldler's Champion Schools. Your methods are widely known among the National Association of Teachers. We know what happens when you buy up a 'failing school'."

"There have been instances," Devanne began.

"I may teach history to children," Idah snapped, "but I am quite capable of understanding statistics. Eighty-five percent of your schools use private security to maintain discipline and funnel children into the school-to-prison pipeline. Your CEO owns sizable stock options in the security and prison industries, in fact.

"And while you do bring in new technology systems, you fail to upgrade them, choosing to fund your hired guns instead," Idah continued in a disgusted tone. "Your teacher turnover rates are appalling and the average experience level of your instructors is less than one year. Once Aldler's owns a school, a series of fees are implemented for uniforms, books, lunches, extra-curricular activities, unidentified expenses, penalties for misbehaviors, supplies for certain subjects such as art or science.

"And very soon," Idah concluded hotly, "the low-income families simply cannot afford a thousand dollars per year per child for school. Ironically, the very complaints lodged against the public schools end up applying to your schools."

"Something tells us this is not the route to go," the principal concluded, rising and stretching out her hand. "Ms. Robbins, please escort our guests out. Thank you and good day."

From the way Idah told the story over the phone to Charlie, he could just picture Devanne's expression as her team squatted in their seats like sullen toads and refused to leave.

"We're not going anywhere," Devanne had declared.

"You will never take over this school," Idah had retorted hotly.

One of the lawyers leaned over and whispered to Devanne. She nodded and flashed a tight-lipped nasty smile.

"We wish to tour the school."

"No."

She blinked.

"Excuse me?" she protested.

"The teachers and students will escort you to the front door, Ms. Devanne, and then they will return to their classes."

"Students?" she asked, confused.

Idah pointed to the window in the door of the office. The hallway was packed shoulder-to-shoulder with students. The taller heads of the teachers rose above them. Whispers, giggles, and shushing could be heard through the door.

"I believe they intend to open a path for you to exit from here to the main door," Idah explained, "but should you unwisely choose to try to enter the school any further, I think the kindergarteners might, ah, get in the way."

The history teacher suppressed her smile and gave a subtle thumbs-up to her fifth graders. Just last week she had shown them video footage of the Singing Revolution in Estonia surrounding the Soviet Army as it attempted to reoccupy the parliament building and disband the independent Congress of Estonia. Unarmed, peaceful, and fearless, the Estonians had forced the Soviets to retreat. Now her fifth graders were putting history into practice. *Top marks for those students*, she cheered silently.

Checkmated, Devanne and the lawyers rose. Idah opened the door. An eerie, watchful silence fell. The students nudged each other and stepped backwards. A path opened wide enough for the visitors to exit. The children stood silently - though Idah noticed the teachers tapping the more rambunctious on the shoulders just as they opened their mouths. Several hands were intercepted in midair. A small flying object was confiscated.

When the latch on the front door closed with its familiar click-clunk, the hall erupted into cheers.

The principal rubbed off the board next to the office, clearing the usual notices such as number of days of good behavior, birthday announcements, and upcoming holidays. She wrote *Plunder Monkeys* on one side and *Little Dandelions* on the other. The she struck a bold, solid line under the school's side.

"Score one for us!" she laughed.

"If we win, can we have an ice cream party?" a third grader cried out.

"Yes," she replied.

If they won, she'd cash in her savings account and buy ice cream for the whole school.

Over the phone, Idah finished her story with a bellow of laughter. Charlie grinned. Idah warned Charlie that even though they'd thrown the plunder monkeys out once, the struggle would not be easy. Aldler's Champion Schools was prepared to fight dirty. They had threatened to call on the police, the state guard, and private security to seize the school. The whole community was coming together over the weekend for a strategy session and, when Charlie explained his purpose for calling, Idah invited both he and Zadie to come out and join them.

They accepted. The news that Charlie Rider and Zadie Byrd Gray were coming to support the struggle electrified everyone. The young couple seemed legendary to the children. They were larger than life characters who strode across headlines, living revolutionaries who had overthrown the corporate dictatorship. As they sat parked in front of the school, Charlie sighed and hoped they could live up to expectations. Zadie shot him a grin as she shut off the engine. The heat dissipated as cold fingers of air crawled into the car.

"Come on," Zadie urged. "They're waiting."

Charlie opened the door, bracing against the bite of cold as they scurried across the icy parking lot. The building beamed with warmth, dispelling the chill of the night as soon as they crossed the threshold. Idah Robbins turned from her conversation with another teacher and smiled. The compact, intense woman crossed the hall with a firm stride and held out her hand. Kindness softened the edges of her scrutiny. Her lips pressed together knowingly as the sight of Charlie and Zadie confirmed her impressions over the phone. She smoothed her black hair back into its tight bun and adjusted the glasses perched on the tip of her nose. Idah moved with the same matter-of-factness that infused her voice. She was a woman of gracious precision, an exacting but nurturing figure in the life of the school. A pair of students waved from the water fountain down the corridor, jostling to drink first. Idah cleared her throat and planted her hands on the waist of her lily-patterned dress. The toe of her heeled shoes tapped three times. The jostling desisted. Zadie bit back a grin.

"Welcome to Los Jardineros," Idah said warmly, inviting them on a quick tour of the school before the parents, teachers, and students arrived. "This is quite an experience for our community. We've struggled so hard for this school over the years - literally standing in front of the bulldozers at one point - but this is the first major challenge since we decided to be a nonviolent school."

Years ago, after the close shave with demolition, Idah and others felt strongly that the community should not be taken unawares again. The hastily formed Resistance Committee that had saved the school turned its efforts to long-term training and education. Afterschool courses turned into an elective curriculum in community organizing for middle-high school students. Weekend workshops made the knowledge available to older community members. Parent and student volunteers shared creative and inspiring stories of change makers with elementary school children.

"Over the years, this notion of ourselves as a nonviolent school grew," Idah explained, "until two years ago, we decided to throw in our hats and make it official."

She winked at them. The decision was just in time for the nationwide eruption of the Dandelion Insurrection. The school took no official stand, of course, but a great deal of organizing meetings had occurred in empty classrooms after hours.

"The principles and practices of nonviolence shape far more than our resistance," Idah told them, explaining that restorative justice was used for handling conflicts, a social justice curriculum connected history to current events for students, and a hearty critique of the culture of violence challenged and transformed people's views from kindergarteners all the way up to the grandparents in the community.

The walls boasted murals every inch of the way. Dr. King, Cesar Chavez, Mohandas Gandhi made their necessary appearances, but the lesser known examples of collective struggle appeared, too, telling the stories of the Singing Revolution in Latvia, Lithuania, and Estonia; the tree-hugging Chipko Movement of India; the Women of Liberia's Mass Action for Peace that ended the second civil war, and much more. Dr. King's words threaded through the images reminding the students to *be against injustice, not people; choose love instead of hate;* and that *nonviolence is a way of life for courageous people.*

In the midst of explaining a scene showing an Indigenous rubber-tappers' resistance to clear-cutting in Brazil, Idah suddenly frowned and peered over Zadie's shoulder down the corridor.

"Is that man a friend of yours?" she asked in a low, concerned tone.

Charlie glanced behind them, the hair raising up his spine. Zadie craned to see the shadowy figure looking through classroom doors.

"Will?!" Zadie exclaimed. "What are you doing here?"

A flash of intense dislike laced Charlie's blood. His brow darkened as he glared at Will Sharp. Idah's quick gaze leapt from one face to the next, confused by the conflicting reactions.

Will shrugged and approached.

"Just doing my job, Zades."

Charlie bristled at the nickname, but couldn't think of a retort that didn't sound juvenile. Will smirked at him then wiped it off as he introduced himself to Idah. The woman studied him with a closed expression and a noncommittal welcome.

Fighting the urge to throw him out into the snowy night, Charlie gritted his teeth and gestured Will to the side.

"Give us a moment, will you?" he muttered to Zadie and Idah.

Zadie frowned, but Charlie didn't give her a chance to argue, stalking down the corridor toward the school library, nearly stepping on Will's heels to get him moving. The lights at this end of the school were off and Charlie strode into the half-shadows.

"Get out of here, Will," he spat out. "We don't need your help."

"I already told you, I'm here on someone else's orders. What the Roots and I do is not up to you, Charlie," he argued in an amiable, but uncompromising tone.

"It's my life," Charlie retorted, "and I don't want you in it."

Will bit back a flash of irritation. The shadows carved his features and cast a bronze gleam over his chestnut skin.

"Look," he told Charlie in a low, urgent tone, "not to scare you, but there are a lot of powerful, disgruntled people who are scrambling to stop the Dandelion Insurrection from making good on its promises. People who cross these guys have an alarmingly high suicide and fatal accident rate. There's a reason all the real political players in the country have tight security."

"We aren't elites or politicians," Charlie stated. "We're people. Our safety resides in our respect and integrity."

Will lifted a mocking eyebrow.

"And when the elites shoot a lead bullet through that imaginary line? What then, Charlie? They'll praise your integrity to the moon once you're six feet underground. They'll even name streets and parks after you."

"I refuse to live in fear - "

"How about guilt?" Will argued. "If a sniper aims for you, but takes out one of the kids in this school, how are you going to live with your guilt?"

Charlie turned away angrily, but Will darted in front of him and shoved him back with a hand on his chest.

"And if they kill Zadie because of your pigheaded ideals, what then?" Will hissed, eyes hard. "Risk your own life if you want, but don't let the others get hurt."

Charlie glanced down the corridor to where Idah and Zadie were murmuring in quiet voices.

"C'mon Charlie," Will urged softly. "No one likes having to live in the cage of security . . . but it's a case of picking your poison. The Roots are on your side."

"Friend says he's on our side, too," Charlie pointed out in a skeptical mutter.

Will smiled. He could feel the sandy-haired writer's resolve crumbling. One more nudge and he'd fold.

"It's not about us, Charlie," he said quietly, glancing over his shoulder Idah and Zadie. "It's about them. I'd just as soon let the hit men take potshots at your stubborn mug."

A hint of humor lurked in Will's tone. Charlie felt a smile twitch in the corner of his lips at the admission of mutual dislike. He sighed. They stared at each other until something cracked the hard edges of animosity. Charlie nodded grudgingly. He didn't want Will Sharp hanging around, but if Zadie trusted him, then he'd put up with the irritating man for her sake.

"Might as well get used to me, Charlie," Will told him. "I've been here since the beginning, and I'm not going anywhere now."

"I liked you better when you were invisible and silent," Charlie muttered.

"Yeah?" Will retorted under his breath. "I liked you better when you were an obscure small town reporter."

Charlie didn't reply. He turned on his heel and walked back to the two women, explaining to Idah that Will would be joining them in the Los Jardineros effort. He explained nothing more about Will's role, and neither the young man nor Zadie spoke up. Idah nodded briskly then shot Will a look that raked his conscience and reminded him strongly of his mother.

"I was just telling your friends," she informed him curtly, "that this is a nonviolent school."

"So I gathered," Will commented with a sardonic gesture at the walls.

Idah scowled at his tone.

"You think it naive?" she suggested with a glint in her eye.

"Well, this is a kid's school," Will shrugged. "I don't expect you'd be advocating anything else."

Idah chuckled.

"Children are remarkable resisters. Just think of a candy aisle tantrum," she said with a wry grin. "Since they're usually over-matched in physical force, they often resort to acts of noncooperation and protest. The troublemakers in the back row of my classroom are quite good at defying authority and resisting domination. I may not appreciate it in the middle of a history lesson, but those capacities come in handy in a movement."

Will gave her a skeptical look.

"Nonviolence is fine as long as it works," he said, quoting Malcolm X.

"It works," Idah said sternly. "In fact, it has been shown to be twice as effective as violence, succeeds in a third of the amount of time, and with a fraction of the casualties." She rattled off a list of case studies: Zambia, Ghana, and Malawi's resistance to British colonial control; Mali, Portugal, and Greece's rejection of military rule; El Salvador and Chile ousting dictatorial regimes; Argentina stopping a coup.

Will shrugged.

"Every nonviolent movement that has succeeded has been backed up by the threat of violence," he argued. "The Deacons of Defense shored up the Civil Rights Movement, and the - "

"That's a popular misconception," Idah replied sourly. She had heard that argument too many times. "A broader study of the historical record indicates nonviolent movements succeed *in spite of* violent flanks. Not because of them."

Will drew breath to scoff, but a babble of voices broke off their heated exchange. The front doors burst open as the first families arrived. Parents and teachers headed toward the auditorium for the main meeting. One child spotted Charlie and Zadie and let out a cry of delight.

"They're here!" she shouted.

Within minutes, the corridor was packed with excited parents reaching out for handshakes and children jumping up and down. Zadie took it all in stride as Charlie scratched the back of his neck and looked sheepish. In the commotion, Idah drew close to Will.

"This is a nonviolent school," she said softly in a voice that reached only as far as his ears. "The next time you enter, you will come unarmed, is that clear?"

She indicated his concealed weapon with a tilt of her chin.

"I'm their protection. It's my job," Will countered, nodding at Charlie and Zadie.

"No, *we* are their protection while they are here," Idah said firmly. "And yours, and everyone else's. You are in violation of our principles, not to mention our rules."

Will said nothing. Idah cleared her throat in irritation.

"We are defending our school against a takeover using the most powerful tools at our disposal: nonviolence. The presence of your weapon undermines our effectiveness. Do you understand? Leave it behind or stay out of our way."

Will sighed but nodded. He had plenty of unarmed training under his belt to do his work. Idah stepped back then and let him pass as Charlie and Zadie moved toward the auditorium flanked by exuberant parents. He could feel her eyes watching him, though, like a laser drilling into his back.

Just before Zadie entered the auditorium, a mural caught her eye. She paused to examine it more closely.

"Idah," she called, catching the teacher by the arm and pointing excitedly, "what if we pulled a Denmark on Devanne?"

Idah frowned for a moment. Then her face lit up. Her eyes widened. A smile blossomed.

"Oh my," she chuckled, "that's quite an idea!"

"Pull a Denmark?" Charlie asked, confused.

The two women exchanged mischievous glances.

"We let her occupy the school," Zadie said.

"But that's all we let her do," Idah finished with a determined look in her eye.

CHAPTER THIRTEEN

· · · · ·

Pulling a Denmark

On Monday morning, Devanne's team took over the school in forty-five unexciting minutes. The new administration marched in. The principal handed Phyllis Devanne the keys and managed to secure the teachers' jobs for the next six months, arguing that a smooth transition required their knowledge. She marked one score for the plunder monkeys before reluctantly wiping the board clean and leaving the school. The secretary watched everything with a blank slate of a face, quietly locking the school's administrative files against Devanne's staff members as she sat at her desk impassively.

In the principal's office, Phyllis Devanne settled into the oak chair with a shiver of delight, but throughout the school, a crackle of mischievous anticipation jittered from student to student, thinking of Idah Robbins' talk during the weekend community strategy session.

"In 1940," Idah had told the families, "the German army invaded Denmark in less than six hours. The tiny Danish army did not launch a militarized counter offensive. Instead, the Danes allowed the Nazis to occupy their country physically, but they maintained a constant resistance, stalling and obstructing all of the Nazis' plans.

"The Nazis wanted Denmark's food supply, and they wanted Danish shipyards to build warships and tanks. The Danes resisted with work slow-downs, even to the point of unscrewing the screws they had just put in. They took many 'breaks' and there were numerous 'equipment failures'. By the end of the war, not a single warship had been completed! When the Nazis officially disbanded the Danish government, the citizens went into full resistance mode. No one cooperated with the Nazis . . . although they often appeared to on the surface. When the news leaked that the Nazis were going to round up all of the Jews and send them to concentration camps, the non-Jewish Danes, in less than thirty-six hours, hid six thousand Jews in their homes and businesses. The hospitals even checked in Jews under false names to hide them. Then, in a matter of days, the Danes helped all but a few hundred Jews flee to safety across the sea to Sweden."

A girl in the front row gasped. Idah Robbins smiled. The history of courageous action by ordinary people was, indeed, breathtaking. She closed her talk with a snippet of black and white film footage of the incredible two minute stop: a bell rang in a Copenhagen square and hundreds and thousands of Danes froze in place in public protest of the Nazis. The people stood eerily still. The streetcars and horse carts halted at odd angles. For two whole minutes, without a word, the city stopped as if magically frozen in place.

"I propose," she had said to her community, "that we use this strategy on Devanne."

They would let her into the school . . . and then utterly non-cooperate with everything she tried to do.

By midweek, Phyllis Devanne sat in the office, nervously gulping her third cup of coffee. She had overseen the transitions of nearly fifty schools in her long career . . . and Los Jardineros still gave her hot-and-cold flashes each morning. The staff was openly hostile, the teachers coolly rebellious, and the children completely undisciplined. The singular goal of the entire school seemed to be hindering her every move. From filing paperwork to coming in from recess, nothing went simply or smoothly. If she stepped into the gymnasium, hordes of screeching students hurled basketballs toward her, hollering, "Play with us!" When she attempted to ascertain the state of the school inventory - paper, pencils, and so on - the school secretary stumbled over a computer glitch and told her the numbers simply weren't available. Keys didn't work in locks. Records jammed in the systems. The P.A. broke every time she tried to make an announcement.

The hallways brimmed with mischief and trouble. Despite the long and growing list of banned activities - jostling, shouting, Frisbee tossing, ball throwing - the students appeared particularly inventive in circumventing the rules in ways that blocked, stalled, and dragged down the traffic in between classrooms.

One simply couldn't prohibit everything! Devanne fumed silently. After all, those third graders hadn't meant to explode their science project volcano outside her office.

The Little Dandelions of Los Jardineros, Charlie wrote, *are showing the nation that without our consent would-be dictators and tyrants cannot expect the cooperation they require to rule. From the smallest kindergartener to the oldest teacher, this entire school is determined to throw off the objectionable yoke of Aldler's Champion Schools.*

"It will settle down," Devanne's supervisor at Aldler's main office advised her.

But it didn't.

The fire alarm went off nine times in three days and despite her admonition to the teachers to ignore the shrieking alerts and flashing lights, the school staff insisted on filing the students outdoors just in case. After the sixth episode, the fire chief reminded Devanne that he would be obliged to charge

Aldler's Champion Schools for these . . . taxpayers shouldn't pay for her lack of ability to clamp down on pranksters.

Her supervisor was not pleased.

"It's all about discipline, Phyllis," he chided her. "Take a firmer hand and show them who's in charge."

"This struggle is about democracy," Zadie told the reporters, "and the right of a community - not a corporation - to run their public school. The education of our students must involve our communities. Whoever educates the children controls the future. If we want a democratic future, we must plant the seeds in our little dandelions nationwide and ensure that our education is governed of, by, and for the people."

On Friday afternoon, the secretary closed her computer and turned cheerfully to Devanne.

"See you on Monday for the state tests," she called out merrily.

"The what?"

But the door had already slammed behind the secretary.

The next week was agony. The tests were a complete fiasco. The students were worse than unprepared. Their answers - written and multiple choice - were ludicrous. The state examiner's office called Devanne directly, wanting to know the meaning of this insult to the importance of the exams.

"Your students are mocking the tests! These answers - " she spluttered, rifling through stacks of papers, " - a dinosaur is a crocodile that lives in New England? The Earth is a trapezoid? Benjamin Franklin invented the Internet?"

"We'll retake the exams," Devanne said weakly.

"You'd better," the examiner snapped. "Your funding and license depend on these results."

Devanne blanched.

The following week, the students walked out on the exams and refused to come back to school to take them. The police chief sent out his solitary truancy officer, but she didn't turn in a single student.

Devanne took drastic measures: she fired the staff and teachers, and brought in her own people. A six-month state testing reprieve was negotiated with the state examiner's office. Strongly worded letters were sent to parents reminding them that they were legally mandated to send their children to school. If the students were not in class on Monday, or a note had not been provided, they would hear from the truancy officer, the state child welfare office, or both.

Fifty letters of protest were returned to the school as "absence notices" from irate parents. The rest of the students were in their seats by the Pledge of Allegiance on Monday. Every one of them wore a tee shirt that read, *Down With Dictators!* and featured an image of a toppling statue of the trademarked logo bust of Charles Aldler, founder of Aldler's Champion Schools.

Devanne implemented a dress code, requiring parents to purchase uniforms from the company catalogue. The students rebelled. The fourth graders refused to follow the dress code. The fifth graders marched out of class. The teachers Devanne had fired, alerted by text messages from students, met them in front of the schoolyard and accompanied them down the streets in protest. Near City Hall, parents and community members joined the demonstration, picketing outside the building and holding a sit-in inside public offices.

The struggle burst into national attention like a firework in the black sky. The media circus flocked to the walkouts and sit-ins like flies to a feast. The Alternet erupted with stories and photos of children marching in the snow, arguing with authorities, and demanding their school back from Aldler's Champion Schools.

Plunder Monkeys Pillage School, the headlines blared, *Little Dandelions Resist.*

"We think all communities should be as courageous as the Little Dandelions of Los Jardineros," Zadie Byrd Gray told reporters. "The Interim Government passed a rotten deal of an act. The people of this country, especially the children, should not be sacrificed to rich people's greed."

She hit the nail on the head with an accuracy that made the rich and powerful shriek with fury. Charlie hammered away at the Interim Government's refusal to tax the wealthy and the corporations. The couple were lambasted by the corporate press and accused of using innocent children to advance their radical ideologies.

The accusation better describes plunder monkeys like Devanne, the Man From the North wrote, *when the extreme ideology of private wealth strips communities of the democratic control of the schools their tax dollars and lifework have built.*

All across the country, similar struggles were erupting. Students walked out in protest of take-overs or in solidarity with those threatened. Protest blockades of privatized bridges shut down traffic. Toll highway booths were peacefully occupied and the vehicles waived through free of charge. People swarmed the Interim Government representative offices, demanding a renegotiation of the terms of the Poverty and Debt Relief Act. They showed up in city council meetings and pressured officials to reject the Act and to speak out against the unfairness.

Los Jardineros' Resistance Committee set up a Solidarity Hotline to advise other communities. Idah was delighted.

"We've always wanted to expand community resistance education to other places. This is an excellent opportunity."

Charlie wondered if coffee ran in her veins instead of blood. She rose at dawn, answered resistance messages over breakfast, organized with the community until noon, tutored students until late evening, and advised the hotline until midnight. Charlie often spotted her speaking - or arguing - with Will.

"Your friend questions our approach," Idah remarked when Charlie asked. "I'm scratching the itch of his skepticism and settling the issue with knowledge."

Every day, it seemed that more parents were pulling their kids out of school in protest of the administration. Idah pursed her lips.

"They can't just stay home watching television," she told the parents. "Bring them to the Community Center. The teachers and I will keep their minds from atrophying."

When word got out, their critics slammed the teachers for undermining the children's education for political and petty goals.

"We believe that resistance skills that are as essential to these times as computer studies, reading, and mathematics," Idah Robbins responded. "We are also offering classes at the Community Center which cover the subjects the state requires each student to know. When Los Jardineros Elementary School is free of the private company that has taken it over against our consent, we will be happy to return to our regular classrooms. Our students will take the state exams . . . and they will pass with flying colors. The credit for that, however, will remain with the students, and not be used to justify Aldler's Champion Schools' administration."

Idah Robbins announced that the teachers Devanne had fired were opening a full curriculum parallel school in the

Community Center, calling it the "Penny Elementary" as a spin-off of the Penny Universities of the sixties which charged one copper penny for admission. The Solidarity Committee organized a nationwide funding appeal. Charlie and Zadie posted essays and gave online speeches encouraging people to support the teachers' salaries for the duration of the struggle.

Two days later, the old school was deserted.

"Remember," Idah told the community at the six o'clock potluck celebration and strategy meeting, "if Devanne has no students, she has no funding. If her students do not take or pass the state exams, Aldler's will most likely lose their license to operate the school. It is a waiting game now, and we have to stand strong until we win."

Devanne called upon the police to form a truancy squad to round up the children. The chief flatly refused. She demanded that the state shut down the Penny Elementary for operating without a license. The parents filed as a homeschooling collective, and Devanne's request was denied. The Penny Elementary was unusual, but not illegal.

Upon hearing about the situation, the state examiner rescinded the state exam extension she had granted to Devanne. *If that woman couldn't even keep the kids in her school,* the examiner fumed, *the state simply couldn't give Devanne any further support.* The nationwide school resistance to privatization was spreading quickly. If it continued, half the country would wind up in open rebellion. The state examiner had no intention of ending up on the wrong side of history. She pressured the state board to revoke the license they had granted to Aldler's Champion Schools to run Los Jardineros. The company blustered, bribed, bluffed, but in the end, the State Department of Education voted against them. Aldler's filed a lawsuit to appeal and refused to vacate the premises of the school. The local school board declared that, under the law, the company staff and instructors were - and potentially always had been - occupying the school illegally. With that pronouncement, the community decided enough was enough: it was time to take back their school.

Phyllis Devanne was pounding the keys of the computer so loudly she didn't hear them coming. Her stubby fingernails clicked like beetles, followed by a smack of flesh like grasshoppers crushed on the car windshield. Her head throbbed with exultant righteousness as she reported the insubordination of the police department to the Interim Government Oversight Committee. She puckered her lips over a sour lemon smile, satisfied to heap trouble on someone else's doorstep for a change. Her mouse was hovering over the send button, one triumphant moment away from clicking, when she heard voices outside the window.

Frowning, she swiveled in the chair.

Down the road, hordes marched from the Penny Elementary toward the schoolyard. They sprawled across the entire street - children, teenagers, parents, grandparents, teachers, community members with a cop car escort clearing the intersections and - Phyllis squinted to be certain - yes, that was the mayor holding one end of the huge banner. As the crowd poured into the parking lot and a few children broke free of the front ranks to leap for the doors, Devanne's chest constricted in panic.

They couldn't! her mind screeched in shock.

But they did.

In moments, they had swarmed the office and packed the halls, falling into an eerie quiet as Idah Robbins and the former principal informed Devanne that she and her teachers and staff were to leave the premise freely and quickly . . . or the police would escort them out.

In less time than it took for the principal to order gallons of ice cream for the promised celebratory party, Devanne and company barreled out of the school entrance, red in the face and refusing to answer the questions lobbed by the media.

Before their cars had even peeled out of the schoolyard, the soon-to-be iconic photograph of Charlie, Zadie and a pack of cheering children shot across the Alternet like a meteor.

Victory! Little Dandelions of Los Jardineros Win!

CHAPTER FOURTEEN

. . . . .

Participation Matters

If there were a rooftop of the world, Will sighed, perhaps a person could stand on that vantage point and see some sensibility or logic in the madness. He stared at his cellphone with reluctance, finger hovering over the dial button. A rare stillness hung above the town as the gyroscopic churnings of a storm sucked the air backward over the great lake. A few flakes of snow tumbled half-heartedly from the low, overcast clouds. Will scanned the playground from the roof of the school and ground out the stub of the cigarette he had just shared with the janitor.

He liked the kids, and found, to his surprise, they liked him back. He'd read stories to kindergarteners, tossed ball with eight-year-olds, and held the end of the jump rope for the third grade girls.

Should have been a teacher or mentor or something, he thought with a rueful smile. The vast gulf between his career path and the joys of his hidden heart sorrowed him.

Somebody's got to protect the babies, he'd told Charlie months ago as they stood in the maternity ward. He looked at the children racing across the playground, shrieking and shouting exuberantly.

"We are your protection," Idah Robbins had audaciously informed him.

He had scoffed then, but those parents, teachers, kids, and grandparents had defended their school against lawyers, plunder monkeys, and educational boards: the faces of an occupying,

121

unwanted regime. He would roll his eyes, except . . . he still had scars from his beatings from his years at a school run by Aldler's Champion Schools. Oh, it hadn't been official; they had other ways. In his case, the inner ring of the boxing club surrounded him on his walk home from school after being egged on by their instructor. *He'd left more scars than he carried,* Will thought with grim satisfaction, but then again, his record carried the invisible scar that sealed his path through life. His mother had refused to speak out against the school.

"People like us don't win these fights," Angeline had muttered fiercely. "You keep your head down and survive until you can fight smarter and harder, you hear me?"

So, while teachers scowled at him, mocked him, singled him out for humiliation in front of the classes, failed him, sent him to detention for insolent looks, shoved him up against lockers to yell red-faced disciplinary orders over minor infractions, smacked him upside the head, looked the other way when the students tormented him; Will pulled his ferocity into his inner core and stoically beat the other kids at boxing, becoming the school champion no one cheered for. He trounced the chess club and got thrown out. He passed the state exams with top scores while his teachers failed him year after year. He took the insults, beatings, and injustices with a cool darkness that turned whispers of scorn into fearful admiration.

He stared at the children playing in the schoolyard as a realization dawned in his mind: they're better at defending their school than me. He might have beaten a few bullies, but these children and this community had thwarted the same private school corporation that had made his childhood.

He'd been taught that people like him were necessary to protect the infants, grandmothers, defenseless families; that someone had to be armed and dangerous to defend others from harm. But if these weak, defenseless, unarmed grannies and mothers were twice as effective at the job . . . then what was he doing?

He studied the children below. What if, as Idah said, they were protecting him? Or rather, the whole community was protecting each other, using tools that had proved effective, engaging everyone in a form of defense that ran counter to everything he had been taught, but stood squarely on a foundation of truth.

Nonviolent action is twice as effective as violent means, Idah had told him, *because in conflicts, participation matters.*

"In this type of struggle, like in democracy," Idah explained, "everyone has a role to play. The kids can run around in a chaotic swarm, the teenagers can march, the grown-ups can blockade, the grandmothers can sit-in . . . we can all participate somehow. If this were a violent conflict, it'd be the people with strong backs and the ability to shoot straight, not the rest of us."

He nodded, thinking of the military's rugged physical demands.

"And, if participation matters," Idah went on to argue, "then sheer numbers matter. And so, the tactics that involve the most people on the broadest scale of denying the opposition resources are going to work."

Like an ecosystem needing water, or an economic system reliant on capital and commerce, participation matters to all systems, including the political. If the people cooperate with the dictator, the tyrant can give orders and see them carried out. But if the people refuse, the dictator is just a little man in a room having a temper tantrum.

Phyllis Devanne couldn't run a school without kids. When the parents pulled the children out and enrolled them in the Penny Elementary, her power collapsed like a sail without wind.

The strength of a movement also relied on participation. Nonviolent campaigns succeeded or failed by the numbers of people willing to get in the way of injustice, or withdraw support from tyrants, or put their hands on the freedom plow and sow the seeds of change.

"And that's why," Idah mentioned, "whenever a movement turns violent, the likelihood of success drops."

"Because violence lowers the active participation rate?" Will reasoned.

"Yes."

"What if it's the dictator who gets violent?" he pushed back.

"Then, the movement can shift from street demonstrations, which are dangerous if an oppressor opens fire, to boycotts or stay-at-home strikes, which can often maintain pressure while keeping people's bodies out of harm's way," Idah pointed out. "Those who use nonviolent action have over two hundred different methods of struggle, but violent conflict can only throw more violence into the equation. And the movements are generally outgunned."

"So, in violent conflicts, is your potential force actually . . . smaller?" he blinked at the absurdity of the idea.

"Well, you won't see me toting a machine gun over rugged terrain or dodging bullets with my bad back," Idah remarked wryly. "A sit-down strike is more my style, and I know a lot more people like me than I do strapping young people like yourself."

Will shot her a wry glance, trying - and failing - to imagine Idah Robbins on the battlefield.

"That's why I told you to leave your weapons at home," Idah mentioned. "Because if you carry them, others will, too . . . but not all others. Some parents might, the teenage boys, and perhaps some of the high school girls, but none of the smaller children and the grandparents."

Will swore. He shifted uncomfortably and paced the length of Idah's classroom.

"That's how infiltration works," she commented. "You get a few violent actors on the scene, support for the movement fades, and the whole thing falls apart."

He pivoted sharply and caught Idah's eye.

"You're vulnerable," he told her urgently. "A few agent provocateurs and . . . "

"We know," Idah replied calmly. "Why do you think we train, practice, and drill; insist on the importance of maintaining discipline, sign pledges, and organize so that we know each and every person? These are all ways of minimizing our risk."

Will scratched his head sheepishly.

"I always figured you were just obsessed fanatics."

Idah grinned back.

"No, just strategic."

Will shook his head back and forth.

"I gotta go. I got a lot to think about."

Idah nodded, suspecting more about the young man than she let on. After the first meeting with the parents, he had approached her with a question.

"In your talk," he had commented, "you mentioned something called civilian . . . "

"Civilian-based defense, a method by which people can protect their country and each other without weapons."

"How does it work?" Will asked.

Idah regarded the young man, reading sincere interest in his face. He truly yearned to know the answer. This was not about foreign invasions or even ousting Devanne, she realized. Beneath the mask of his social defenses, Idah sensed she had rattled something deep within Will Sharp. He waited for her answer as if a seismic tremor had cracked the foundation of his worldview. His life was on the line, everything he knew, his beliefs, the very principles by which he had guided his existence. Idah's eyebrows rose.

I hope he's ready for the earthquake of my answer, Idah thought starkly. She did not believe in comforting lies or soothing people back to sleep. She dealt in truth: groundbreaking, world upheaving, revolutionary truth. She could ruin - and save - his life with her answer.

"If you are truly interested and willing to study hard, I'll be happy to share with you what I know."

A world opened up to him of courageous resistance under duress and danger. Idah explained civilian-based defense, how citizens, especially government workers, could non-cooperate and refuse to serve invaders, occupiers, or rising dictators, denying them access to the computers, records, offices, and resources needed to control the country. She went on to describe how nonviolent action had been used to expel invasions and thwart coups. He read about people switching street signs to mislead an invading army. He tried to comprehend the sheer scale of the strikes organized effectively by the early labor movement in the United States. He studied the pragmatic visionaries in Lithuania who, after gaining independence from the Soviet Union, became the first nation in the world to include nonviolent struggle in their Constitution as a form of national defense. He learned that nonviolence worked not because it melted the heart of the oppressor, but because people seized their social, political, and economic power, and refused to let business-as-usual continue until their demands were met. Workers went on strike. Citizens blocked roads. People bought local goods instead of the products of their colonial overlords.

"Participation matters, Will," she repeated carefully. "Through every action we take, we build the world, for better or for worse. Think carefully about the role you choose to play."

Will's hair stood up on the back of his neck. A shiver ran down his spine. Idah held his eye a moment longer. Then he spun on his heel and left.

All these weeks later, Will stood on the rooftop of the school wishing he could climb to the top of the world and study the complex patterns below. Where is the continental divide between right and wrong? Where is the meridian of truth and lies? The equator of good and evil?

The world wasn't divided so clearly, he thought. All of his life, he had wanted to protect - himself, the smaller kids, his country - but what if the path he was on wasn't protecting the defenseless? What if it was all a lie?

He sighed. Idah Robbins had suspected infiltration by agents. He doubted she knew how close such dangers lay.

Will stood with his finger over the dial button of his phone.

What role will you play? Idah's voice confronted him. Every action matters.

He tapped the phone. It rang and connected.

"So?" the familiar voice answered. "Is it done?"

"We can't win the schools," Will replied. "There is no way to advance. They're too united, organized, and trained. I scoped all the usual ploys. There's no way to disrupt meetings; the facilitators are too good. If there's a disgruntled faction, I've yet to find it. And you can't get near sabotage or violence with a ten-foot pole around here."

He laughed dryly. Everyone from the kindergarteners to the high school football team would tackle you to ensure discipline.

"There must be weak spots," the Boss insisted. "Where can we break them?"

Will fixed his eyes on a boy down below in the schoolyard, a little scrapper that reminded him of his younger self.

"You can't."

These kids would never be broken. He would make sure of that.

CHAPTER FIFTEEN

· · · · ·

Fish To Fry

Friend swiveled in his oak desk chair, tapped his fingers together thoughtfully, and stared out at the snow. The flakes had lost the delicateness of the early season and now sullenly marched across the gray sky. The holidays closed like a book and the nation's bureaucracy surrendered to the New Year's paper shuffling and reports. Beyond the walls of the Oval Office, the grumble of voices slogged through the day. The slight lightening of the storms of conflict over the holidays had ended last week with the crushing slam of charging factions returning to battle.

The Los Jardineros revolt triggered solidarity from school districts nationwide. People dug in their heels. Stubborn resistance mounted. In one community after another, the people refused to sell their schools, parks, and other assets. Charlie and Zadie traveled in patterns that would make a butterfly dizzy, crisscrossing the country in support of local struggles. They popped up in the Pacific Northwest like mushrooms after a rain, blockading bridges that had been possessed by plunder monkeys. In Boston, they trained a Dandelion Swarm to apply the old tactic of occupying toll plazas, waving cars through the cash-only lanes in protest of the plunder monkeys' seizure of the highways. In Colorado, they joined the Little League strike demanding the return of stolen bases and community baseball diamonds. They camped out in St. Louis' Tent City to block construction of high-rise luxury condos on a lot that had been meant for affordable housing projects. In Atlanta, the Book

Barricades stopped just shy of literally throwing the book at the plunder monkeys that were trying to privatize the public libraries. In Central California, a similar attempt to sell a library inspired an exhausting filibuster reading of *The Grapes of Wrath*, concluding with a hair-raising hundred-person rendition of Tom Joad's famous promise: *I'll be there.* As the old year rolled over into the new, Charlie and Zadie circled back to the District of Columbia to leverage the unrest into getting legislators to tax the rich.

Everywhere you looked, the Dandelion Insurrection reared its golden head. The plunder monkeys stopped salivating over what once looked like low-hanging fruit and started screeching at John C. Friend to do something. Friend made appropriate noises at the appropriate times on his end of the telephone, assured each caller that he understood completely, and then ended the connection.

Friend chuckled. He had them all exactly where he wanted them. The Dandelion Insurrection was forcing the rich into a corner, chipping away at their power and strength, weakening the wealthy in ways that ultimately strengthened Friend's position. He'd crush those pernicious weeds in his own good time while the rich cracked and crumbled into petty internecine squabbles. He would be the winner of it all.

His eyes fell on Charlie's latest essay, laying on his desk. *Let the rich pay for the cake of the Poverty and Debt Relief Act. Why must we sell our souls and the last vestiges of our commonwealth to achieve justice? Don't make this Devil's bargain. Resist until the terms are changed in our favor.*

"Atta boy, Charlie," he commented, "fight 'em tooth and nail."

Let the Dandelion Insurrection run in endless circles chasing plunder monkeys. As the masses fought the elite for schools and parks, he had other fish to fry.

The snow thickened, cast into frantic swirls like schools of fish trying to dart free of ocean nets. Through the flurries, a figure in a long dark coat paced the whitened sidewalks of the National Mall, her shoulders hunched up to her ears. Her arms clenched tight against her sides and her hands shoved deep down into her coat pockets. The wind flipped her dark curls wildly, but, lost in thought, the woman merely tossed them out of her eyes. She stared up at the snow with a clouded gaze.

Zadie fumed as she strode through the snowstorm, trying to churn her anxious thoughts into a flame of warmth. Charlie was still talking to that patronizing moron of a senator. She'd stalked out in disgust, muttering to Charlie that she'd meet him back at Tansy's. She had to get some air before a scream of frustration burst out of her throat like dragon fire. These politicians sat in cozy little congressional offices, making deals with each other while families struggled to keep the heat on, the roof overhead, food on the table, loved ones out of prison, debts and bills held at bay, and the thousand tasks of a movement slogging forward despite the obstruction and delays of chubby little men in suits and well-heeled heartless women.

I should never have agreed to come back to DC with Charlie, she fumed. *Let him and Tansy argue with politicians.* She couldn't stand the futility of hundreds of hours in legislators' offices, trying to cram common sense into greed-clouded minds. Zadie longed for the road, the people, the community struggles to save schools and bridges, the heat of the actions, and the humbling solidarity of real faces, real people, and real lives.

The snow whipped around and stung her eyes, blinding her momentarily. She shivered, thinking of the people all across the country who were reeling from the sheer profusion of attempted plunder monkey grabs. At every turn, poor communities caught another wealthy corporation fondling their utility or snatching at urban parks and greenbelt lots. The Dandelion Insurrection wheeled in a desperate race, striving to hold off the attacks while pressuring the Interim Government to revise the Act and tax the rich.

Obstacles surrounded them on all sides. A certain percentage of the populace, tired of the unrest, had begun to look favorably on the Interim Government's law-and-order rhetoric, increasing the ranks of those who obstinately maintained that the authorities knew best. Another section of the country, seasick from all the boat rocking, hollered at the Dandelion Insurrection to sit down and shut up. Some grumbled that the activists should just be grateful for what they had already gotten. The crowd that disliked change on principle complained that it was high time to get on with business-as-usual. They were echoed by the establishment groupies who snapped at the dandelions to quit causing mayhem and focus on electing good candidates.

Day by day, the special elections in the states rushed closer and the people, exhausted and overburdened, found little time to mount campaigns for the open seats. The remaining politicians jostled for leading positions, spouting nothing but empty promises. Zadie had no patience for them. These politicians came straight out of the same old disastrous collection of corporate pawns and wealthy elites. Inez placed phone call after phone call to organizers and activists trying to bring their vision of dandelion politics into action, but it was like trying to catch the swirling snow: the gusts of plunder monkeys tossed them all into crisis. The days passed and few candidates of the people stepped forward. They were distracted, exhausted, and out-maneuvered. They needed to rest and catch their breath, but couldn't.

Zadie heard the snow hiss off her cheeks, melted into steam by the heat of her temper. An updraft of wind suspended the white curtain overhead. For a moment, the storm stilled. Zadie glanced up to find her long stride had carried her far down the National Mall. Across the lawn, the tall spire of the Washington Memorial darted in and out of the flurries. To her right, the national museums loomed ghostly in the grayness. A few dark, bundled figures hurried across the paths, heads bowed against the wind.

Zadie shivered. A gust flung the snow aside. The curtain fell. In the thickness, the nation's capital looked as bleak and desolate as a North Dakota winter. Stripped of its symbols and myths, it offered only coldness.

Who are we without the lies we tell ourselves? Zadie thought bitterly. Our values of equality and justice were myths. Our pride, false. Our ideals, hollow and unrealized. Every great accomplishment we crowed over turned out to be an illusion built on a foundation of bones. Every victory was soaked in an unspeakable bloodbath. Our pomposity erected monuments to our self-deception, celebrating the dead instead of caring for the living.

The problem with being in the capital, Zadie realized, *was that it allowed politicians to forget the faces of the people.* At the far end of the Mall, veiled in snow, Lincoln's large and iconic gaze towered over the upturned agony of the humans below. Marble columns and business suits clouded the eyes from the grime and misery of the rundown, forgotten, and neglected corners of the nation. Sterile statistics stood in for the wailing grief of mothers who had lost their children. Politicians never had to see the desperation of people denied homes or healthcare. Lobbyists did not evict families with their bare hands; they left the tossing out of pillows and photo albums to others. Zadie longed to haul the Congress members by the scruff of their suits down into the gutters of the nation. Her fists clenched in her coat pockets. She yearned to throw the whole lot of those closed-hearted, stubborn mules into the heart of the misery their policies created.

She had lost patience with the pretty niceties of national delusions. The reality stung like a festering sore. She wanted to roll up her sleeves and scrub out the gangrene. She was willing to tear up patriotism along with the flag and use it as tourniquets to save her fellow citizens. What good was all our posturing and lies? Better to tell the heart-breaking truth, to let us gag at the sight of ourselves, to mourn our brokenness, to drop our jaws in horrified shock at the people we have become.

A cluster of snowflakes slipped down her collar and she flinched. *Go home*, she told herself as she turned her feet in the direction of the subway station. *Draw a hot bath. Make tea. Remember all the people working for change. Remember the saving graces and good hearts.*

She muttered these instructions like a mantra, biting down on her bitterness, desperately trying to cut through her mood before it immobilized her. Despair was a treacherous slope, muddy and slick, pocketed with hidden cliffs. Zadie trudged through the storm, trying to remember spring, cherry blossoms, bright blue skies, and the exact color of dandelions against the green grass.

Her stride nearly carried her onto the steps of the Capitol Building before she blinked and saw where she stood. Her breath froze in her lungs. Shiny tears iced along the rims of her eyes. Her gaze fixed on the spot where the drone had struck, midway between the courthouse steps and the Capitol Building.

The crater of the blast had been repaved. There were no indications of the panic of the explosion. The echoes of screams rang only in Zadie's mind, not in the ears of the few tourists wandering the streets. She'd heard the Interim Government had mounted a plaque on the site, but the sidewalk was plastered with the gray slush of the street.

Zadie choked on a sense that the march, the attack, and her mother's life had been swept away in the river of time; that all of their losses had been for nothing; that the Interim Government's stalling would prove as cruel as the previous regime's greedy control. The snow fell white and ghostly. The trees, fences, park, streetlights turned stark under their thin blankets. Zadie hugged her coat tighter, chilled in her bones, crying and shivering. She yearned for her mother, longing to lay her head on Ellen's shoulder and confess her worries for the movement.

The snow fell silently in a harsh, aching emptiness. Grief hollowed out its beauty. Loss sharpened the sting of the cold. Zadie spun away with a gasp, running for the bustling shelter of the subway, seeking relief from the loneliness of sorrow.

All through January, dandelions and plunder monkeys remained clenched in gridlock. Solid opposition slammed up like ice in a winter-bound river. Pressures mounted. Communities refused to sell out. Poverty and Debt Relief Act funds froze. Groans of frustration wracked all sides as the struggle prolonged, deepened, and yet, refused to budge one way or another.

Something's got to give, Alex Kelley thought with a long sigh as she flipped her wall calendar to February. Under the surface,

135

she sensed frigid black water creeping beneath the solid jam, seeking another option. She kept her ear to the ground, listening for hints, watching Friend's visitor schedule like a hawk, trying to decipher the hidden meanings of seemingly unrelated details. There was something moving under the political gridlock.

What's he after? Alex wondered.

The hum of subtle activity and the hiss of unseen motion haunted her. When the ice jam broke apart, Alex suspected Friend's plans would be revealed. Alex sniffed and searched quietly. The days passed closer to spring. The snow banks shrank. The ice began to pop and crack. The ground thawed. Unseen roots sprouted.

And then, all at once, everything started to move.

CHAPTER SIXTEEN

. . . . .

Oil and Water

Zadie spotted him first. She was sprawled across the plump paisley armchair in Tansy's living room, legs dangling over the side, following the coverage of Friend's latest speech to the Interim Government. Spring warmth teased the cooler edges of the day, flirting and darting away under the shadows of passing clouds. Zadie listened with one ear as he repeated his usual hollow words about the necessity of funding the Poverty and Debt Relief Act through any means necessary.

"Except taxing the rich," she muttered automatically. That logical option never crossed Friend's lips.

She craned her neck to make a face at the screen and shrieked. Charlie bolted upright from a half doze on the couch.

"He's back!" Zadie cried, pointing to the livestream.

"Friend?" he asked groggily.

"No. The Butcher."

He stood behind Friend, another suit among the wall of grays and blacks. He looked older and harder than before. Rumor claimed the sharp-nosed, rough-chiseled man had fled the country after resigning as the head of the military, an invention of a position created by the old president. The Butcher's ties to the military industrial complex twisted through shadows and intrigues. He had launched illegal wars on hyped-up fears of terrorism and brokered weapons deals to every side of violent international conflicts. Charlie shuddered. The Butcher had been the ruling hand and devious mind behind the expansion of mass surveillance and the increase of the domestic security state. The hated Greenbacks that had harassed and terrorized the Dandelion Insurrection were his creation. Charlie was not surprised to see the Butcher back. The people wanted to slash the bloated military budget guzzled by contractors and reapply the funds to social support programs. Trillions of dollars of business assets lay vulnerable.

He threaded his clammy fingers through Zadie's, the metallic taste of fear zinging his throat. Charlie's phone rang. They flinched. He picked it up.

"Oil and water," Alex Kelley stated without a greeting.

"Huh?" Charlie asked.

"That's what he's after."

"The Butcher?"

"No, Friend . . . is the Butcher back? Makes total sense."

"Standing beside Friend in Congress today," Charlie commented, staring at the screen.

"In light of citizen objection," Friend was saying, "to previous funding sources for the popularly demanded Poverty and Debt Relief Act, we have found another option by tapping into the resources of the Federal Government."

He put the phone on speaker volume so Zadie could hear Alex's comments.

"Oil and water," Alex growled. "He won't say it, but that's what he means. I found the paperwork on the lease sales, permits, and licenses allowing companies to extract water, fossil fuels, and minerals from all federal lands, including parks and national monuments. The amendment includes new laws for private security and Interim Government forces to protect the companies' right of extraction."

"That's why the Butcher's back," Zadie concluded grimly. "Security for the thieves."

Zadie snarled the final words, her anger burning hot in her chest. She simultaneously wanted to weep and hurl breakable objects across the room. *Everywhere we turn,* she fumed silently, *they're fighting us. Just once could they leave us alone or do something good?*

They were old enemies, these dinosaurs of power, railing on their deathbeds, refusing to surrender or transform their businesses. They were as old as the enclosures of the commons, the colonization of the New World, and the enslavement and murder of millions. The sun was setting on that era. The people, the earth, democracy, and love were rising with the dawn, but the old guard were fighters, sharp-toothed dominators, rigidly addicted to power and control. They gripped their old ways, white-knuckled, veins of fury pulsing in their brows. In their death throes, they were willing to massacre others for survival. Already, they guzzled the lifeblood of resources, laundering the moneys of genocides through the socially accepted forms of bloated subsidies to dying industries, paid for by budget cuts to social programs and the continued assault on commonwealth. They wanted to steal the resources of the continent, to suck the oil and exude the noxious gases into the global commons of the air. They wanted the water to sell and pollute. They wanted all the little people to get out of their way.

Well, Zadie thought stubbornly, *we won't.*

In fact, they would get directly in the way.

Zadie's blood sung with life's determination. In her rose the strength of the boxing hare out-darting the coyote pack, the baby caribou's burst of speed evading the chasing wolf, and the endurance of the migrating albatross winging silently across the sea. The fertile ground of existence that gave rise to countless species throughout the Earth also formed the throbbing hearts of humanity. Again and again, the people had risen up for life, in tiny towns and massive cities, in remote landscapes and familiar suburbs. They blocked export terminals, oil trains, construction equipment, and drilling rigs. They had disrupted the churning machinery of permits and licenses that ground humanity toward extinction. They shoved the financial equation over, tipping the scales of profitability to slow the addictive reliance on fossil fuels.

And if water was next, they would rise to protect that as well.

Zadie's lungs flooded with breath. The budding branches of the trees unfurled tiny leaves. The dandelions shot up in the short, spring grass. She would rise to this challenge. They all would. The blood in her veins, the beat in her heart, the beauty of life demanded it.

Alex was correct: John C. Friend never once mentioned the exact nature of what federal resources were being put on the auction block, and Congress passed the amendment in a boringly normal vote. Friend congratulated them on their commitment to the people.

"Alex," Zadie said finally, "can you get the records of the permits and extraction plans?"

Alex promised to jump on it.

"Good," Zadie replied. "Charlie's got to blow the whistle on this before people start cheering the new amendment. Rural people can't be sacrificed for urban populaces' relief funding. Otherwise, you know the usual spin they'll put on this."

Charlie nodded soberly. Politicians pit poor urban people against rural populaces by convincing inner city residents that only rich white people lived out there in the wilderness - or narrow-minded bigots. They spoke of *putting resources to work for everyone*, and neglected to mention the Indigenous communities, small farmers and ranchers, little mountain towns and historic villages that would be threatened by mining, extraction, and water draws. *Those environmentalists want to save the grizzlies*, the smiling politicians said, *but we want to save your children.*

Never mind the children of the rural regions, rendered invisible by the mighty powers of corporate media and the overwhelming masses of the cities. Charlie knew the rhetoric; his Acadian family in Northern Maine lived in a remote valley often threatened by upstream mining, over-foresting, lax restrictions on water standards, and the machinations of politicians hundreds and thousands of miles away.

With climate change hurling devastating storms, droughts, and abnormal frosts across the continent, Charlie also grimly knew that the rural people understood with stark clarity the fragility of the ecosystems. They lost their homes to forest fires. Their grain crops floundered. Their farms went bankrupt.

Every living forest offered humanity a thin green line of hope . . . and yet, the stands were dwindling. Coastal fisherman watched ancestral fisheries collapse. Indigenous communities saw the loss of ancient medicinal plants. Ranchers ran out of water. Every part of the populace held a piece of the puzzle. Tackling climate change would require the cooperation of everyone.

"We have to stand with one another," Charlie murmured. "Our lives depend on it."

That night, Zadie and Charlie lay curled together, wide awake, the adrenaline of the day still coursing through their bloodstream.

"There's a water extraction site in southern Arizona that has asked us to come," Zadie murmured. "Alex thinks it's the first

141

target, according to the permits. The oil company wants to extract the water to use in their proposed mining site nearby."

"When do they want us to come?" he asked.

"As soon as possible," Zadie answered. "There's already an established resistance camp. This isn't the first time they've had the aquifer threatened and they've been readying for another attempt at extraction."

Charlie sighed.

"I've got to meet with Friend and try to get him to set limits on use of force . . . or kick the Butcher out of the country again."

"I could go out now, and you could catch a later flight," Zadie suggested.

He stirred uneasily at the idea.

"We have to be careful, Zadie," he said anxiously. "With the Butcher back, it could get brutal and dangerous again - fast."

For a while, they argued back and forth about where they could do the most good. Zadie insisted that they should be in the desert if the Butcher moved in on the camp. Charlie countered that getting arrested - or worse - was pointless when they could leverage their clout in Friend's office. Zadie shot back that she wasn't going to sit around like a castrated duck in a penguin suit while people got hurt. Charlie retorted that all martyrs suffered from egotistical savior-complexes, but nobody in the camp would want her blood on their hands. Zadie growled in exasperation and told him he was missing the point.

"Let's not fight, Zadie," Charlie interrupted, not wanting to waste his breath arguing when the Butcher circled like a vulture over their lives. "You go out. I'll catch a flight after the meeting with Friend and be there before you miss me. If anything happens while I'm here, I can - I don't know - stage a die-in at the Oval Office until he intervenes, okay?"

Zadie looked taken aback. She bit her lip.

"I don't want to go alone," she murmured quietly.

"Will could go with you," Charlie reminded her with an unhappy sigh.

He rolled over and started working out the logistics to distract himself from the sinking sensation in his gut, fretting over small details, asking her to call when they landed, to please explain it all to the organizers, remind Will to disarm - the camp didn't allow weapons - and he'd be out on the soonest possible flight -

Zadie hushed him with her fingertips.

"I love you, Charlie," she told him.

He grinned sheepishly.

"That's what I meant to say."

"I know," she replied with a smile.

"Don't get dehydrated - " he broke off as she started to laugh and confessed, "I love you, Zadie."

They lay together silently, remembering the Dandelion Insurrectionists who had been killed and injured by the Butcher's Greenbacks. The return of the Butcher revived the terror that had haunted them as reports circulated of friends and organizers attacked outside the grocery store, shot at through the windows of their homes, nearly driven off the roads by cars with blackened windows. Charlie tried to still the dark worry of his racing thoughts, but Zadie could feel his heart pounding against her spine.

"I'm scared, too," Zadie confessed in a whisper.

She rolled over, entwining her body with his, kissing him as if she feared he'd vanish in the next breath of a second. Tree limbs groaned heavily. The house creaked with the night wind. Shadows writhed on the walls. Charlie buried his face in Zadie's hair, inhaling the sweet scent of her rose and honey soap.

Neither spoke. They lay together in the moaning night, holding their fragility and courage like a pair of blue robin's eggs in a twisted nest of twigs. Later, they would talk strategies and plans. This night begged for honest and whispered confessions. Charlie and Zadie pressed their foreheads together and breathed the same breath. No promises or assurances rode their slow exhales, just presence and love. They'd lived in uncertainty until it rested on them, and they within it, with all the familiarity of a rusting tin roof on an old shed. They no longer whistled in the dark or lit false candles of hope. They stayed close and let the roof of the unknown rattle in the dark night winds. In silence, they lay entwined, each lost in thoughts of oil drilling, water bottling, mercenaries, and dangers, counting each breath together as a blessing.

CHAPTER SEVENTEEN

. . . . .

Desert Resistance

The shaggy-haired volunteer from the desert resistance camp met them at the airport, holding a sign with a dandelion drawn with a thick, black marker. His thicket of a beard fanned out in a cloud of white and a leather tie pulled his thinning hair into a ponytail. He wore cut-off shorts and his sleeveless shirt revealed the blistering rite of passage with which the desert welcomed newcomers. He chattered their ears into exhaustion as they collected bags at the carousel and threaded through the crowd. The heat beyond the sliding doors nearly knocked Zadie over. The relentless blue sky cackled at her. As the rattling old car shuddered out of the feverishly baking city, Zadie could sense the desert watching her, waiting.

She sighed. These sparse, hard lands held reckonings. One's soul was laid bare, bleached honest as old bones. For months, the racket of resistance had masked the subterranean moaning of her heart. The desert eyed her knowingly: everything hidden and ignored would be exposed, ripped raw by knives of light and the scouring dusty heat. The desert toyed with human frailty, a behemoth kicking over the forests of the heart like so many blades of grass.

Zadie bit her bottom lip nervously, longing for the buffer of Charlie as the desert cracked her knuckles with wicked anticipation, thirsty for the blood and bone truths Zadie kept hidden inside. The desert wanted them all: her harpy-screeching fury at her mother's murder; her wailing grief, primal as an infant's first gasp of life; her terror-clenched tendons along her spine from the nightmares she could not stop. And, much as she feared the flaying of her outer calm, Zadie ached to surrender those pains that scorched, cut, crushed, and clenched her.

The faltering air conditioner in the car gave a breathless gasp at sixty miles per hour and died. Zadie rolled down the window and leaned the curves of her face into the hot breath of the wind. Her body sweated tears that streaked down the backs of her knees and wept across her ribs. The volunteer driver ran out of chatter and subsided into silence. When he began to weave and sway with sudden jolts of awakening out of half-dozes, Will ordered him to pull over and took the wheel. The man stretched out on the backseat and was asleep in minutes.

They drove onward.

The length of sky and earth made Zadie feel vast and tiny at once. The desert surged with contradictions. A great river of invisible wind swept in constant motion over the ancient stillness of miles of slow-eroding rocks and sand. The silence sang symphonically. The earth flared bright and flat at midday. The cathedral of horizon-less sky stretched unending. Wordlessly, she let it all flow out: sorrow, loss, searing intensity of love, guilt, fury, fear . . . every nuance of blazing emotion poured out unconstrained by propriety or the inadequacy of words.

She rubbed the bottom rims of her eyes as tears welled like a spring hidden in hard rock. The salt dried on her skin in seconds, the desert's mocking baptism. She felt Will's glance, but he said nothing. In the grace of silence, she swallowed. A tremble forced her lips together. All at once, her mother appeared like a madonna riding the hood of the car, laughing, hair thrown back in the hot wind, limbs bent like tree branches as she perched above the front grill, her black curls whipping joyously.

A bite of laughter caught in Zadie's throat then drowned in sorrow. The vision of Ellen wavered in the downpour of tears then she vanished like a mirage. Zadie gasped, her hand leaping up with a faltering stride. The hissing desert rushed into the empty space, slamming its emptiness up like a slap across the face.

Ellen was gone.

Zadie folded her burning arms over her soaked ribs, clenching the shudder that ran up her body.

Will cleared his throat with a sigh.

"Tired?" Zadie asked, cutting off whatever condolences brewed in him. She wanted none of it.

He shook his head.

"Just thinking," he answered.

"About?" Zadie pried, desperate to distract him from her rawness.

"My mother," he answered, honestly enough, though in truth, Angeline had circled through his mess of tangled thoughts about his mission. Secret conflicts and growing doubts plagued him. Will mentioned Angeline as the safe ground in a treacherous quagmire of thoughts he couldn't confess to Zadie. He had orders from above to blend in with the resisters. At this stage in the game, his ears were more valuable than his fighting skills. He had left his weapons at home. Stay close to the target, he had been told, even if you have to disarm. The days of protecting the Dandelion Insurrectionists from assassinations were over; the Roots' mission had shifted.

Will disliked walking defenseless into this frontline struggle. With the kids, he'd been somewhat confident that open fire was unlikely, but all bets were off with the Butcher running the opposition's show. He had his orders, though; his task was to watch, listen, and wait. No heroics or frontline actions were required. He'd stay far away from rubber or live bullets and let the fools take the risks.

On the tail of the concern over risks had come the thought of Angeline. She never worried about the dangers he faced daily - she only worried over his capacity to confront them. She'd encouraged his childhood boxing matches and street scuffles. She wanted her son prepared for the rough realities of life.

"Strange," Zadie murmured, shading her eyes against the sun as she stared out the window, "I was just thinking about mine."

"Yeah. They haunt us like that."

"Tell me about her," Zadie urged.

Will lifted his eyebrows and leaned back in the seat, one hand gripped tight on the wheel, exhaling in a long breath.

"Angeline? She was beautiful - no, really, everyone thinks their mother is beautiful, but Angeline . . . she could literally stop traffic. I saw her do it. She had these high cheekbones, dark skin that was smooth as polished stones from a river, and when she cut her eyes, the world froze."

She could freeze, too, Will remembered. Angeline turned her statuesque poise into a slammed shut door on the world. Only when her secrets piled up high enough to come tumbling out of her eyes did her inner thoughts reveal the depth beneath the implacable surface. All his inquiries about his father received the same automatic reply:

"May he rot in hell."

Which, Will noted, did not indicate who he was or if he still lived.

Angeline stood unmoored in the vast ocean of humanity, unattached to family, location, or history. She never talked about where she had come from, and when Will pressed, she answered in a curt tone.

"Honey, I traded my past and future to the Devil for you . . . and I got the good end of the bargain."

"Does that mean I came from the Devil?" he had asked, frowning.

Angeline laughed so hard she had to stop and catch her breath. She kissed the top of his head, thoughtful.

"Some mothers say the stork brought their children. I suppose, the Devil brought you, but you sure didn't belong with him, nor did you come from him originally. I was just rescuing you, that's all."

Will thought often about that exchange over the years, and took perverse delight in the story, to the point where he wrapped the Devil's bargain around his street legend as it grew. Later, in training, when they asked for his father's name on forms, he told them he had no father, but they could write down "The Devil" if they needed to deliver his ashes to someone's door.

When Angeline died, he wished he'd asked one more time about his father. But, fatal car crashes don't come with deathbed confessions, and she'd left no letter nor hint in her will.

There must be more to the Devil story, though. He knew because of an oddity that had surfaced in the aftermath of the crash. The driver that had run her off the road had filed suit to blame her. In the agony of the court proceedings, the man cruelly claimed that Angeline had been driving recklessly and was obviously off her meds. According to a witness at the crash site, she'd been raving about the accomplices of the Devil.

"She was hallucinating," the driver's lawyer claimed.

The judge agreed and paperwork estates set out to haggle over the details while nineteen-year-old Will sat inscrutable, hearing the eyewitness' chilling recitation of his mother's dying words: *the devil's friend, the devil's friend, somebody tell him about the devil's friend.*

"Never could figure her out," Will muttered to himself.

"What do you mean?" Zadie asked.

He shifted in his seat, surprised.

"She could have done anything, lived anywhere," he commented bitterly, "but she worked a low-wage job as a typist in a shabby bookkeeper's office and lived in a two-room apartment in a rundown poor neighborhood in New York City. Why didn't she get out? Take me with her . . . live in some nice, safer place where the kids don't learn to dodge bullets on the way to school."

Will glared at the endless stretch of road.

"It was like she was always hiding."

"Like you?"

Zadie's question leapt out and stung him. Her hand jumped up to her mouth, belatedly trying to stop it.

"I'm sorry," she added hastily. "I just meant - "

"I know what you meant," Will said with a forced coolness. "I'm a shadows guy. I deal in darkness and night risks, the unseen and half-hidden. My job is to track the things that go bump in the night."

Zadie shook her head. She meant Will was always hiding himself in the shadows, as reluctant as Angeline to bring the full force of who he was into the bright scrutiny of eyes and light.

"I just meant," she said quietly, leaning her head on her hand propped on the open window, so the wind half-swallowed her words, "that you're both hiding your beauty from the world."

Whether he heard or not, he made no reaction. Zadie waited, sighed, then closed her eyes and let the stream of hot desert air pour over her as solidly as water, but achingly dry. She could smell the plants pushing forth new leaves and fresh greenery emerging from their thin sliver of a damp spring. Occasionally, the scent of pine tumbled down from the hills and mixed with all the other aromas of mud and sap and sprouting plants. A sudden thought brought tears to her eyes and the wind of the moving car flung them away.

"She never saw the desert," Zadie murmured. "Ellen always wanted to come to the desert and paint. She never got to."

She stared out the window at the startling lime green of the mesquite. The bold sands of ochre and fawn slid past the long miles to the horizon line.

"She would have loved it."

Zadie's lips trembled and when Will glanced over he could see the thick sheen of tears in her profile. He reached out and squeezed her shoulder.

"I'm sorry, Zadie. It wasn't supposed to happen - "

Will broke off abruptly. His whole body flashed hot and cold. Sweat beads broke out on his forehead. He swallowed. He glanced at Zadie, but she was lost in her thoughts, oblivious to his strange behavior.

"Yeah," she said in a small voice. "It shouldn't have happened, not to her, not like that. She should have gotten to grow old with my father and fill up whole galleries with paintings."

"Yeah," Will agreed, relieved that Zadie hadn't understood his inadvertent slip.

It wasn't supposed to have happened. The drones weren't supposed to have fired. They were meant to scare the people away, not to kill them. And if the military hadn't panicked and raided that drone complex; if that Greenback hadn't been shot and fallen on the command desk; if Will had been in charge of the operation, not those incompetent idiots, Zadie's mother and all the others would still be alive today.

CHAPTER EIGHTEEN

· · · · ·

Kinap

She watched them, silent, the way a stone's shadow timelessly tracks the sun's arc across the sky. Unnoticed, not moving, Kinap followed the newcomers as they parked the dusty car and stretched out into the blinding sunlight. She sat in the shadow of a box truck on one of the low, flat stones that spotted the parking area. Her arms rested on her knees, tan and pulsing with the heat. Dark brown hair hung long down her back. She held a refillable water canteen in one hand and every so often, she would lift it, peer into the cool darkness of the spout then sip. Studying the arrivals, a hum of thought reverberated in her bones.

She was far from her home in the Dawnland, the beautiful river and forested islands of the Penobscot Nation on the East Coast. The dryness parched her skin and sent longing shivers through her for the cool waters of her home. When she returned, Kinap promised her burnt and flaking skin hours of slow soaking. But first, she had to answer the insistent buzz of intuition that hummed louder than the cicadas at sunset.

Kinap came to the resistance that rose up under the harsh blue of the desert sky because the tangled webs of oil and water extraction stretched across the entire continent. Communities distanced by thousands of miles shared ensnarled threats that caught them all like flies in the sticky death hunts of corporate spiders. This tribal nation's lands bordered US federal lands; the watershed ran through them both. Extraction wells sunk on one side of a line on a map stole the water out from under the feet of the tribe. Kinap had been called to come in her capacity as a trainer, an Indigenous rights lawyer, and as someone intimately familiar with the opposition. The oil company that threatened this region owned a subsidiary bottled water company that had sunk wells throughout the tiny towns in Kinap's part of Maine, sucking up the seemingly limitless bounty of wetlands, rivers, and lakes until the water tables shriveled and collapsed beneath the earth, leaving the trees gasping and the historic wells of the region dry. The bottled water was guzzled in the cities. The plastic containers wound up in landfills. Tank loads were shipped to water districts with contaminated local sources. Instead of cleaning up the tap water, corporations bribed public utility officials to buy imported water, raking in the profits as the potable water was sold at high rates to desperate people trapped by politics and poverty. Meanwhile, oil and chemical companies gleefully bought stock in water extraction companies, and let their pipelines, factories, fracking wells, mines, and tankers spill into hundreds of watersheds nationwide, driving up the value of the dwindling drinkable resources.

Kinap's heart ached with sadness at the violation of the sacred. She lost speech in a mute and primal howl of raw emotion at such wanton, destructive greed. The water of the Earth was being intentionally despoiled by the ideological descendants of the colonizers who came, tore the native peoples of this continent to pieces, raped and pillaged, and rose to power.

Kinap rose with a crack of knees and stepped out of the shade. She strode across the lot to greet the pair. She was a tall woman, standing with a straight spine and a proud lift of her chin, close to forty-five with a ruggedness of character that indicated she had weathered more than sun and wind in her life. She had borne children, raised them on her own, and held her granddaughter long before the first white strands laced her hair. She was younger than some, older than most, and carried a couple lifetimes' worth of hard knocks and tough lessons under her belt. Yet, the spirits gave as much as they demanded. She'd been given the strength and knowledge to meet the challenges laid upon her.

"Welcome," she called out. "You are Zadie Byrd Gray and your friend is . . .?"

"Will Sharp," the dark-skinned man answered, stretching out a hand.

Kinap read the callouses on his fingers in the brief handshake and noted what they indicated. She frowned, surprised, and glanced at the man's belt.

So . . . she hummed to herself, seeing he was unarmed.

"My name is Kinap. I am one of the water protectors, a guest in these lands, as are you." She shook hands with Zadie and scanned them with a searching, yet discrete, look. "I'll show you the camp and get you oriented."

She led them down the trail toward the peaks of the tents. The main section of the camp lay in the foothills, situated on tribal lands where the Federal Government had no authority to evict them. A spur ran down to the actual well site. At first, a row of tents had stood along the slight ridge, but these tents ran greater risk of being raided by law enforcement. Twice, they had packed up the spur ahead of rumored raids, choosing not to sustain arrests for camping violations, but rather for blockading the construction workers on the road below. They shifted tactics continuously, valuing adaptability and fluidity. They had re-occupied the spur and well site with water protectors rolled up in sleeping blankets under the stars, ready to disperse or stand their ground without risking equipment and supplies. Currently, a long, painted banner was staked like a fragile barrier from the main camp along the hundreds of feet to the well site. It depicted art and prayers in several languages, providing a visible symbol of resistance even when only a few people spanned the distance. The banner billowed in the wind like a sail of hope. The citizen media team used it in photos and videos as they lifted the struggle out of the lonely desert and sent it into the hearts and minds of people thousands of miles away. Millions of people's lives were connected to this oil company's water grab through their oil heaters and gas stations, the pipelines and refineries that supplied them, the banks that financed them, and the investments and stock portfolios that profited from extraction. Every flick of a light switch, hiss of a gas stove, and turn of a hot water faucet meant contaminated rivers, polluted land, and deadly greenhouse gases. The media team's job was to illuminate those connections, reveal the real cost of convenience, and move people into action in solidarity with the camp. In the long run, the efforts to divest, revoke permits, and increase water protections were essential for stopping extraction.

The main camp extended over a small, flat central gathering place, up and across the rise and fall of hills. They held the higher ground - both morally and physically - and looked down the slope to the well site, and, beyond that, to the dirt road cut into the dust. A bridge over a large culvert spanned the muddy arroyo. The spur crossed the snaking waterway higher up, where the slopes ran steep and the trickle of the stream still sung for a moment before the wide throat of the thirsty flatlands swallowed it. The desert spread raw and wide with endless horizons. The rumble of voices in the camp stirred the yawning silence. One's mortality loomed large in this land.

Kinap led them down the paths between the tents. Trainings happened at eight in the morning, two in the afternoon, and seven o'clock in the evening. Everyone was required to attend three classes whether they needed them or not. Midday camp meetings were mandatory, as were service duties.

"Feels like being back in the military," Will muttered.

Kinap's ears were as sharp as her eyes, and she heard the remark.

"We're facing military and paramilitary forces on the ground. Discipline and commitment are not optional. This is not a vacation spot. You'll find out soon enough the substantial difference between us and the Marines, but the military does not hold a monopoly on structure and training."

As she led them into the center of the resistance camp, Will grew quietly impressed. He didn't think civilians had the organizational capacity this camp exuded.

"Kudos to the leaders for this set-up," Will complimented Kinap.

"That would be about two hundred of us."

"Get out." Will turned, stunned. "Self-organization didn't dig those latrines."

"Indeed it did," Kinap answered with an amused expression.

"Self-organization gets a bad rap because it is so often done under very challenging circumstances with scarce resources and under-skilled people," Zadie put in. "This camp, however, appears to have brought together people with skill and ability."

She nodded her appreciation to Kinap.

"Civil engineers and plumbers built those latrines," Kinap laughed. "They're the most over-designed holes you could imagine. Our kitchen could pass inspection. Our media team has been working together for four years. Our strategic advisory council is local, highly trained, and experienced. *This*," Kinap gestured to the calm efficiency of the camp, "is ideal. It is a model of cooperation built on over a decade of relationships."

She grimaced, remembering earlier struggles. They had learned the hard way about open call, mass invitations - especially in Indigenous communities. The freak show circus that poured into the resistance camps had crippled several campaigns. Tremendous resources had been swallowed up by the necessity of dealing with unprepared people, ego-trip maniacs, freeloaders coming for the food and camping spots, photo-op resistance hoppers, people with Native fetishes, the mentally unstable, the violence-prone, infiltrators and disruptors, Great White Savior complexes, and so much more. When it came down to an intense frontline struggle, they needed trained people with good hearts and balanced minds. They needed strong allies, not more problems to deal with.

"Nonviolence is broadly inclusive," Kinap remarked thoughtfully, "and that's a good thing. Anyone can and should hold a protest sign on a street corner or move their money out of a corrupt bank. But when it comes to situations of direct conflict, where armed agents of repression are present and tension runs high, it is unwise to rely on the unskilled and unprepared."

They were dealing with situations where guns might hold live ammunition; where attack dogs ripped flesh; where police attempted to provoke protesters into violence; where the likelihood of being tear-gassed and beaten was high.

"Even the military knows better than to pluck random people off the street and plunk them down in combat," Kinap pointed out.

"They'd wet their pants and do extremely stupid things," Will confirmed.

"Same in our situation," Kinap reflected. "The dangers we face are similar, even if our methods of handling them differ greatly."

"Peaceful warriors," Will muttered under his breath in a disparaging tone.

She turned on him abruptly. Her brown hair whipped over her shoulder. Will skidded to a halt. Her eyes studied him, thoughtful, seeing more in him than he saw in himself.

"Do you know what *kinap* means?" she asked him in a low, soft tone. "In our language, *kinap* is one of our many words for warrior. But, unlike your culture, we have not enslaved our values of courage, commitment, loyalty, and skillfulness to violence. Our warriors know how to use just enough force to prevent harm from happening . . . and no more. They know how to oppose injustice without lowering their dignity by causing harm to others. *Kinap* is one who stands up to protect, to offer the ultimate sacrifice of his or her life if necessary, but not through killing the other person."

All languages have gaping holes where the cultural imagination fails. English speakers had not found a word for *kinap* in four hundred and fifty years of colonial occupation. The conquering oppressors slapped their images of warrior on top of a people and landscape they feared. With the loss of those crucial and subtle distinctions, an opportunity for healing vanished. They unleashed the devastation of their ailing culture across continents and continued to fall in the gaping holes left in the scarred landscape of their imaginations.

Kinap studied Will Sharp's features with her unrelenting scrutiny. She saw his African and Caribbean ancestors in his skin, hair, and certain curves to his face. She saw European ancestors, too, speaking through his lips and almost Roman nose. They swirled inside his complexion, cream to the thick

159

coffee of one side of his family. Kinap also carried complex stories in her blood and bones. She had some Scottish ancestors among her many Indigenous grandmothers and grandfathers. They forced her to remember that the line between oppressor and oppressed can split down the middle of a person. She held them both, as did Will, and Zadie, too, with her Roma looks and the ruggedness of a woman who has been slammed up against the historic remnants of the witch hunts. Few children of this continent escaped the blessing and the curse of such complexity. All were the descendants of the collected horrors and strengths of history. Billions of stories rested within each fingertip, waiting to be told through living hands. Each person had to choose what history they would embody, which strands of cultural genetics would be activated or sent into dormancy, which ways of life would be preserved, revived, or cast aside.

He could be *kinap,* she thought sternly, if he chose. For all his scoffing, his eyes traced the camp with curiosity. She sensed the young man hung like a bird on the edge of a precipice, uncertain if by leaping, he would fall or fly. And Kinap, who had been soaring for years, felt a sudden lurch of her heart, an unexpected ache of both annoyance and affection. Will Sharp glinted of danger and possibility. Ordinarily, she would speak to the elders quietly about such characters. Infiltrators frequented Native-led resistance and her intuition jangled at the signs. But, Kinap saw other signs, too, messages from her helpers who urged her, strangely, to live her name.

Kinap, warrior, woman of skill and courage; one who could approach the dangers and transform them. If he was an infiltrator, the frontline of resistance lay in his heart. He walked mere footsteps behind Zadie, far too close to the center of the Dandelion Insurrection's core. Kinap eyed him with silent determination. She would grasp whatever danger he represented and change Will Sharp into something that could do them no harm.

The Butcher was waiting. Charlie tensed in the doorway of Friend's office. A rush of adrenaline drowned out the politician's words of welcome. All week, they'd been pestering Friend's secretary with messages, demanding a meeting. For days, they'd gotten delays and cancellations until finally, Charlie threatened to buy a plane ticket for Arizona and go join the resistance. If Friend wouldn't talk, he wasn't going to sit around twiddling his thumbs, worrying about Zadie. Friend's secretary had called back within the hour, but failed to mention that the Butcher would be at the meeting.

The cold man did not rise. He sat in the dark leather chair with one lean leg crossed over the other. His studied ease was belied by the intensity of his gaze. The man's eyes glinted with flecks of amber in a deceptively warm brown. Holding his gaze was like staring down a tiger crouched to pounce. Underneath the surface of the Butcher's olive skin, Charlie suspected the muscular quiver of the impulse to throttle him. A rebellious bolt of confidence unlocked his limbs. He bit back the urge to smile.

A thorn in your side, am I? Charlie crowed, proud of the Dandelion Insurrection's derailment of this man's ambitions. The silence between them hissed with mutual animosity. He gathered his composure and tried to find something appropriate to say.

Tansy didn't waste her breath on niceties.

"Wish we were meeting under more pleasant circumstances," she told the Butcher, "such as your trial at the Hague for crimes against humanity."

Her narrowed eyes gleamed with anticipation of that day.

"Always wanted to ask," she growled, "do you prefer to be called Mr. Calden or can I refer to you as the Butcher like everyone else in the country does?"

Charlie stifled a laugh and a groan.

"Now, now, Ms. Beaulisle," Friend chided, "there's no need to be rude."

"When the truth is ugly, politeness is just another way of lying," Tansy answered.

"Ms. Gray isn't joining us?" the Butcher asked, ignoring Tansy's remarks.

"She's in Arizona," Charlie responded shortly, certain that the Butcher's spies tracked Zadie's whereabouts.

"How . . . unfortunate."

A chill shot down Charlie's spine at the ominous threat lurking behind the words. He clamped down on the reflexive urge to bolt, to call Zadie and scream at her to get out of there, get everyone out of there! With Alex's aid, they had found out that the Butcher wasn't back in any official government position. He'd moved into private security, leveraging his military and governmental connections to seize the contracts associated with the new permits allowed under the amendment to the Poverty and Debt Relief Act. His appearance at the congressional session was intended as a reassurance to the corporate flank: the Butcher was on hand to ensure the plunder monkeys got their payload.

Charlie sat down opposite the older man.

"It's good you're here," he said, "because Friend's going to have to make it clear, in no uncertain terms, that your past tactics have no business in the country."

He pinned Friend's eyes as the man shot him a bemused look over his sagging jowls.

"Charlie," Friend cajoled, "be reasonable."

A bark of scornful laughter broke out of Charlie and Tansy at the same time.

"Murders, beatings, intimidation, house bombs, unfounded arrests, surveillance, drone attacks, indefinite detentions, and smear campaigns are all reasonable?" Tansy ticked off the list of the Butcher's tools. "Sorry, but no. It's your methods - and you - that are going to have to go, along with government suppression of protests, unreasonable use of force, shooting live ammunition into crowds . . . particularly since you're working in the private sector now. Better check with your lawyers. You can't just kill with impunity like in the good ole days."

"Especially since the Dandelion Insurrection fully expects the Interim Government to support a resolution on the prohibited use of force against unarmed protesters," Charlie added, sliding a document across the table to Friend.

He and Tansy had been up all night drafting the bill. It was high time for the administration to reassure the citizens that their civil liberties, human rights, and democratic freedoms would be honored and upheld by the government. The people had lived long enough under the dark shadow of brutal repression, mass surveillance, and the strangulation of political dissent. Tansy wordlessly passed a second copy of the draft to the Butcher, her face scrunching with the struggle to stay straight.

"Well, we can have a committee take a look at it - " Friend began.

"We want it introduced tomorrow and passed no later than the end of the week - " Charlie cut in.

"Impossible!"

"That's the same speed as you've been passing the other bills," he replied pointedly.

Friend began to splutter excuses, but Tansy interrupted impatiently.

"Any day now, *his* security forces are going to collide with a group of resisters who object to a water extraction *you* authorized. You've pitted corporate greed against your citizens, and we think it's *reasonable*, " she stressed the word, "for our government to set clear standards around dissent, protest, and state or private repression."

Friend and Charlie drew breath to lock heads in argument, but the Butcher spoke out.

"I'm sure that can be accomplished," he said in a soft, but uncompromising tone, "so long as . . . "

He made them wait, staring thoughtfully up at the ceiling as if considering his words. He looked down and smiled like a shark.

" . . . so long as the Dandelion Insurrection agrees to stand down at the extraction sites."

A stunned silence greeted the proposal.

"No," Charlie finally stated in flat refusal.

"What's the point?" Tansy snapped. "We don't need political rights and freedoms set up on a pedestal to look at. They're tools to use!"

The Butcher lifted his eyebrows.

"We'll use whatever is necessary to ensure our clients can use *their* rights," he said coolly.

"The right to profit?" Tansy snarled. "Or the right to destroy the Earth?"

"If you allow him to attack the resisters," Charlie warned Friend, "we'll have no choice but to rise up against the Interim Government and denounce your administration for being corporate puppets, no better than the last regime."

Friend cleared his throat and shot the Butcher a nervous look.

"Charlie," he intoned ingratiatingly, "we want to find an agreeable solution to this conundrum. I don't want to see people get hurt - "

"Then make it illegal for them to be shot."

"It is already, you know that."

"Then enforce your own damn laws!" Tansy exploded. She rose up like a lion of justice, roaring, excoriating the previous regime, tearing the Butcher apart for his crimes, demanding that Friend take a stand for justice, not murder and greed. At the end, she sat back down, flushed from neckline to temples, fanning her face with her hand and glaring at them.

Friend exchanged a weighty look with the Butcher. An unseen signal passed between them. Friend appealed to Charlie.

"There is another option," he said carefully. "We could revoke some - not all, you understand - but some of the extraction permits and levy a select tax on certain assets and inheritances."

Charlie blinked. Tax the rich?

" . . . in exchange for the Dandelion Insurrection backing off from the rest of the extraction sites."

He sighed. There was always a catch. Politicians never passed a bill in an act of genuine goodness. A rider, an amendment, a clause - something always sank the noble into the despicable, selling out the rights of one group for the privileges of another, doling out slivers of justice to some while tromping down on others. Charlie felt sick, dirtied by the suggestion that he would betray rural communities to grasp the tantalizing fruit of taxing the rich. No amount of federal funding could ever replace that desert aquifer or the watersheds. And it shouldn't have to.

Charlie stared at Friend as the older man urged him to think carefully, the hopes and dreams of the people lay in his hands, life was full of compromises, and doing the right thing required sacrifice. Tansy snorted and lashed out with a retort. Charlie didn't hear it. The swell of his thoughts crashed over him. The Butcher's gold-flecked eyes bore into him. Charlie swallowed and moistened his lips to speak.

"I can't. I can't make deals like this for the Dandelion Insurrection, for the people. I'm not in charge. But I can tell you that I doubt the resisters would stand down no matter what you offer to the rest of us."

It was their land, their water, and their lifeblood. Charlie explained this until his throat croaked in protest, but the concept baffled the two powerful men. There were people in the world - lots of them - that understood the meaning of sacred. In the dry lands of the desert, water was not a commodity to be bought or sold, or bartered for relief funds. It was as precious as one's children, as beloved as a soul mate, as intimately treasured as the breath in one's chest.

And, as fossil fuel emissions threatened the Earth, millions of human beings were learning to care for the atmosphere as the true source of the life in their lungs, blood, and heart. They would no sooner tear out their organs than allow the breath of the Earth to continue to be poisoned.

Charlie couldn't stop them from resisting. He could only try to help them succeed.

CHAPTER NINETEEN

. . . . .

Water Is Life

The sun slanted toward the horizon like a woman lowering into a hot bath. Zadie and Will sat in their tents, gasping from the intensity of the afternoon and awaiting the fall of darkness. The time of fidgeting with phones and weak cell signals passed. They slumped, hot and exhausted, staring at the black rivers of shadows stretching from the rocks. Even tiny pebbles laid down the ink of shade in bold signature lines across the bleached sand. The tents of the resisters crouched like ancient creatures gathered to growl stories of long-forgotten times.

Rest, Kinap had warned. The desert wears you away like a harsh wind on sandstone, flake by flake, stripping you to the bones. Zadie scratched her itching skin, rubbing dust and dryness off as the desert smirked beyond the thin nylon of her tent. Her phone call to Charlie left her anxious, her heart thumping from shouting over the faltering connection that died just when he crackled something about having to stay in DC longer than expected if Friend -

If Friend what? she thought, resenting the people and forces that kept them apart. She lay back on the sleeping bag and winced as a loose rock ground into her shoulder blade. She closed her eyes against the white glare of the sun as it mellowed into gold.

A few feet to the left, Will stared out the open tent flap at the organized efficiency of the camp. One of Idah Robbins' stories teased the edges of his memory, something about how Lithuania had put nonviolent resistance into its constitution as

167

a form of national defense. In a way, this camp was defending the tribal nation's water resources using the same ideas. Will found it ironic that police, soldiers, the National Guard, and private security could all be mobilized to protect the profits of corporations, but the people couldn't call upon them to protect the water or the land. The authorities would mask the truth under claims of maintaining law and order, but Will had been a soldier, and he cynically knew that beneath the rhetoric of patriotism, most wars were waged for the profits of the rich.

Kinap's lecture on warriors had triggered an onslaught of parallels between his military service and the determined proficiency of this resistance. He had the uneasy sense of history hurtling in circles as Natives tribes defended the sacred land of their nations against unwanted invaders. Will wondered - not for the first time - about his position in this looming battle. Soon, tomorrow at the latest, he would need to hike up into the hills to call the Boss on the cell coverage he hid from everyone. Only military, top-rank private security, or corporate bigwigs had this level of reception so far from cell towers. Camp techies were still scrambling to put a decent system together to link to the Alternet. Will chewed on his mental report. He would have to warn the Boss about the high levels of organization.

Peaceful actions took place daily on the main road to the well access points. Hour by hour, the resistance stalled, delayed, and turned back drilling trucks. They organized actions in the closest town, coordinated demonstrations at the state capital, supported solidarity events nationwide, advised similar struggles, and sent envoys of water protectors to the oil company's regional headquarters.

Over the decades, extraction resistance campaigns had matured, first through the efforts to slow fossil fuel development, and more recently to halt water extraction. The once scattered, loosely connected, multi-nodal network had grown into a behemoth of strategic coordination sharing resources of trainers, best practices, slogans, medical teams, funding sources, and legal aid. It offered support to hundreds of groups in thousands of towns and communities. Across the country, data-crunching organizers figured out how best to hit industry where it counted, leveraging industry weaknesses with the skill of surgeons.

Oil and water don't mix, and when the forces of greed came to extract them both, the swarm rose, intelligent and coordinated - the exact social phenomenon the elites feared most. Without a central command, the people had figured out how to hound corporations at every end of the operation.

As the plunder monkeys took up the hastily abandoned plans of the previous regime's Operation American Extraction, the people merely dug in their heels. They'd been on the front lines for decades, increasing in numbers with unwavering commitment. These were their homes: the tribal lands, backyards of rural homeowners, farmlands and woodlots, grazing pastures of ranchers; all were beloved by those who dwelled there.

Water is life, the native elders said.

Not in our names, their allies told the corporations.

Across the country, people in every nook and cranny, hill and holler, valley and plain, mountain and forest hunkered down and prepared to resist.

To Will, who had never seen a human being sing to a river or bow to a tree or greet the deer as his brother - or even seen a wild deer - the camp was unsettling. *Which was the mass delusion?* he thought. *That the earth is our mother? Or that the earth is a dead object to possess?*

He had always thought of business people as the rational, practical ones, not the Native tribes, environmentalists, bunny-lovers, tree-huggers, or these resisters at the camp. But it was hard to argue with the logic that *water is life* when the desert sucked moisture straight out of his skin, leaving him with a parched throat, cracked lips, and lightheaded.

To refill their water containers, he had to go to the well, where Kinap would always invite him to thank the aquifer for the gift of life in his veins. She watched him with her dark-eyed stare as he took a sip.

"Feel it?" she asked him as the cold water slid down his throat.

A drop spilled onto his lip, absorbing directly through the membrane of skin into his thirst.

"Thousands of years, this entire watershed, hundreds of feet of protecting mineral rock have conspired to become the water that has now travelled up this well and into your body so that you can protect this land," she told him.

Kinap searched him with her knowing eyes.

"You are the land, protecting itself. You are the water, defending your right to refuse to be enslaved to extraction and exploitation. You are the air, the earth, the animals, the plants, all of life protecting yourself."

Will squinted and wrinkled his nose.

"Oh really?" he replied skeptically, thinking of his secret assignments.

"The earth called you here," Kinap insisted, though she also looked dubious of his worthiness. "It does not want to give up this water to the oil company."

"How do you know?" he challenged her.

"Because," she answered simply, "we are here."

Will resisted the urge to roll his eyes. He hefted the full container out from under the spigot and replaced it with the empty one. There was no arguing with Kinap. The broad planes of her face were often tilted as if she listened to voices no one else could hear. Sometimes, Will had the eerie feeling that Kinap saw the world with her liquid eyes blurring the past and present. She had one foot planted solidly on the earth and the other foot in the realms beyond this one.

She's a madwoman, he thought as he trudged back to the camp with the heavy containers of water. Still, she had perspectives that kept him up late at night. Stretched out under the clarity of the black sky outside his tent, looking up at the canopy of the stars, he felt that sip of water in his cells. Lying on his back against the cooling ground, he thought of the aquifer far beneath him, and the oil further down, and how one was essential for life and the other poisonous to humanity and the planet.

The desert has called you here, Kinap had told him at the well.

"She got the call," Will had flippantly remarked, pointing toward Zadie. "I just followed her."

Kinap shook her head and refused to change her opinion.

Drink, she said, *you are the water protecting itself.*

No, I'm not, he had wanted to say, but the cool sweet water silenced him.

Now, you are, it whispered inside him.

Will fought the urge to weep, suddenly flooded with an indescribable ache.

Kinap told him that her people saw the river as their kin, as much a part of their family as their own flesh and blood relatives.

"You would not allow your child, mother, or sister to be harmed, would you?" Kinap asked him, waiting until he shook

171

his head. "In this way, we cannot abandon our river. She is one of us."

The people here felt the same way about the water that he had felt about the children at the school. They were sacred. Humanity had an unarguable duty to protect water and children, both.

You tricked me, he said silently to Kinap across the night. Like all sorceresses at wells of immortality and life, she had let him drink without revealing the exact nature of the bargain.

The water was in him. Life surged in his veins. He could not ignore the truth as it throbbed inside him. The desert had offered up its most precious treasure, hidden underground, given freely to those who walked into the camp to protect this land, the water, and the earth. Kinap was right. The people here, in opposition to the extraction companies, were proof that life wanted to live and would call the people into action.

He could feel that truth singing in the very aliveness of his cells.

Dusk cradled the camp in gentle, gold palms. After the long day of trainings, the resisters unwound around the central fire by the kitchen tents. All week, they had watched the ranks of security forces increase. Everyone suspected the company was about to launch a strong offensive to take and hold the main road. Enough of the construction vehicles had gotten through that all it would take was a few more days of drilling for the main well to be complete. There were other ways to hinder the company - the transport pipeline across the desert still needed massive work - but stopping or stalling this phase of drilling was crucial.

Someone strummed a guitar then lapsed into conversation as strategies were bandied back and forth. The clink of dishes being washed and stacked eased onto the soft air. A starry-eyed girl who had dropped out of college to join the resistance yammered away to Zadie, marvelously idealistic and impassioned. Zadie felt a million years old and worked to hide her smile as the girl complained about her parents' indignation over her departure from school.

"They can't help it," Zadie told her. "They love you, want you safe, and want what's best for you."

"But your mom knew how important this is!" the girl cried.

Zadie struggled for words. By the time the Dandelion Insurrection erupted, she'd already put her parents through the horror of running away as a teenager. Bill and Ellen were radicals in their own right. They had been movement organizers for decades. In a way, Zadie had come home to the familiar world of working for justice. Bill even joked about it being in her blood - the roots of resistance ran back in his family to the Quaker abolitionists.

She began to tell the girl this, but stopped and craned over her shoulder with a frown. A low rumble growled over the open desert. A murmur of confusion rose up around the campfire. Figures popped out of tents and stood poised toward the west like anxious prairie dogs. Hands rose to shade eyes against the sunset. One by one, people turned to squint into the distance. Black specs on the horizon drew closer.

"Drones," Will muttered in Zadie's ear, coming to stand close.

The word punched Zadie in the stomach. Ice ran through her veins, splintering into shards of pain and panic.

"Stay calm!" a voice bellowed.

The group swiveled toward Kinap.

"We have prepared for this. We drafted plans for this contingency. We have drilled. What comes first?"

Zadie's teeth were clenched so hard against her fear she couldn't breathe, but everyone else took a collective breath.

"That's right. Cut through panic," Kinap encouraged them. "Keep your head clear and squarely on your shoulders."

Will snorted softly in incredulous disgust. On the other hand, there wasn't much they could do - predator drones could fire from miles away. Scattering from the camp might save some of them, but the tents and gear would be lost. As his mind ran down the grimly short list of options, Will stepped around the side of the kitchen tent and texted the Roots. They all knew where he was, and one of them - if not all - would know the Butcher's plans for the approaching drones. The Boss hired them to stay on top of these things.

Drones? Armed or not? he typed.

Surveillance, came the reply.

Will nodded and returned to Zadie's side.

"They're unarmed surveillance drones," he announced.

"How do you know that?" someone asked him.

"Special ops training in the US military," Will said quickly, letting them assume drone identification had been part of the curriculum.

"They're here to watch us, not to shoot us," another woman declared.

Will sighed over civilian naiveté.

"They're here to terrorize you," he explained, "to intimidate and harass you. They are counting on your ignorance of drones to use the sound and presence to instill fear, grate on your nerves, agitate you, shorten tempers, and cause friction in the camp."

To his surprise, Kinap laughed.

"They will not succeed, then. Will they?" she challenged the group. Then she spoke directly to Will. "Our emphasis on prayerful, peaceful activism may look curious on the outside, but on the inside, the moral fiber of this community contains an arsenal of spiritual practice and mental discipline that makes *those*," she pointed to the approaching drones, "look like pathetic child's toys. All of us who have gathered here have the skills to maintain mental clarity and stay grounded. We are prepared to deal with this.

"For weeks," Kinap raised her voice to reach the whole group, "our frontlines have been on the bridge and roads. Today, the struggle lies here."

She placed her hand on her heart.

Will gave them credit for preparation and planning. He turned to Zadie to comment on it and stopped.

She stood tensed tight, the lines of her muscles taut against her sweating skin. Her fists curled into white-knuckled balls. Her eyes squeezed shut and her shoulders were hunched up to her ears.

"Zadie?" he queried gently.

She did not respond.

"Zadie!" he barked sharply, raising his voice over the sound of the drones.

Her eyes flew open, wild and panicked.

"Shit," he swore and grabbed her arms as she flailed.

At his touch, she moaned and sank onto her heels, throwing her hands over her ears. He crouched down and tried to pry her hands off so she could hear him.

"Leave me alone!" she snarled.

"No. Zadie, listen - "

"Get off! You weren't there - you didn't see - "

"Zadie, you're panicking - "

She began to cry. Shudders wracked her body. Will cursed again. No amount of meditation was going to cut through the trauma-induced panic of someone who had just barely survived a massacre months ago.

Zadie lashed out, her nails raking his arm. She got up to run, but he was faster and grabbed her around the waist, pinning her against his side as she kicked to get free.

"Where will you run?" he shouted, trying to get through to her. "There's nowhere."

"That's what I said! *There's nowhere to run,*" she choked out in broken moans. "And they all died because of me."

"These aren't armed. No one's going to die."

"But they did. It's all my fault."

He shook her.

"There was nothing else you could do. There were millions of people packed in the streets - "

All at once, the fight drained out of Zadie and left her shuddering. Her legs turned to jelly as the adrenaline fled. Her body sagged, heavy as stone, and Will crouched down, lowering her into the dust without letting go. Her fingers clenched his forearm in a painful vise of fear. He could feel iron bands of tension running up her back.

Will had a startling flashback of holding a brother-in-arms in the midst of an episode of PTSD. He'd let go and his friend had launched himself through a window to his death. He held onto Zadie as if he could redeem that moment by persevering now.

"You didn't kill Ellen," he said, his voice in her ear, closer than the rising thunder of the drones. "It's not your fault."

Will kept talking as she cried, repeating himself over and over, knowing she clung to the sound of his voice.

"I keep seeing the - the bodies - " she choked out.

"I know," he murmured.

And he did know. Grimly. Far too well, he knew the kinds of horrors that shot across the mind and returned in dreams, that gripped you in the grocery store and made you clench a box of cereal into powder as the past exploded in front of the ingredient label.

Damn you, he cursed the drones and his long history. The sounds brought back memories for him, too, but he'd spent too much time crippled like Zadie was now, curled into a sobbing ball on his apartment floor, watching ghost children from his neighborhood get shot; watching gun fights and knifings in the gangs; watching his fellow soldiers die. The old anger rose in him, vicious and ferocious, the unnamed rage at the whole world, the insanity and cruelty, the drones overhead. He loosened his grip on Zadie, suddenly afraid of his hands.

"Don't go."

He froze, neither comforting nor fleeing, stuck as equally as she in the horrors of the past. And as the drones circled, they huddled in the dust. Overhead, a drone raked its prying gaze across them. Neither noticed . . . but the moment would come back to haunt them.

CHAPTER TWENTY

· · · · ·

For Life, Liberty . . . and Love?

For life, liberty . . . and love?

The question mark at the end of the headline knifed Charlie's heart as he stared at the front page of the website. The twisting of the movement's slogan stabbed him cruelly. It was a corporate journal, one that suppressed climate change news and glossed over the costs of the wars. Plastered across the screen were photos of Zadie and Will curled together.

It was typical tabloid copy - all sensation, no real story. It was a trick, a distraction from the fact that Friend had allowed drone use against the camp. Charlie used every rationalization at hand and invented several on the spot, but there was that photo, unmistakably Zadie nestled in Will's intimate embrace.

Dammit Zadie, he swore silently as a triple wave of anger, jealousy, and sorrow slammed him. He slouched back in the chair, resisting the urge to kick the computer off the desk. He gripped his hair in his fist and squeezed his eyes shut, but when he tentatively opened them, the photo was still on the screen.

"You could have told me," he muttered furiously. Everyone else must have known . . . they'd been tiptoeing around him all day, averting their eyes as they mumbled and asked if he'd seen.

"Seen what?" he had replied, blindly, innocently.

Finally, Tansy steered him by the elbow into the study and blurted it out.

"Charlie, don't go exploding like a case of fireworks - ain't nothing more than cheap jackals selling tabloids - "

"What is?"

" - 'course it's being picked up by the major news, the big stations, and large journals, but they'd print scandal about their own mothers if someone paid 'em enough. Sure as gravity goes down, there's an explanation for this. I mean, these days, they can alter photos to make John C. Friend look like Marilyn Monroe, so don't go losing your head like Marie Antoinette over this - "

"Tansy," Charlie sighed, indicating that she should spit it out.

"Zadie's having an affair."

Charlie actually laughed.

"That's nonsense," he replied dismissively. "Those same tabloids said that I was a terrorist and that climate change was a hoax. It's not true."

"They have photos," Tansy said quietly.

Charlie stared at her, then spun and woke up the computer. Will nuzzling Zadie's neck on the homepage of the National Post. The two sitting cradled on the ground on the Insider Times' site. The pair spooning in the Capitol Hill Journal. Tansy rose and left him in privacy as he gawked in disbelief, bringing up one website after another. He slouched in the chair, speechless. Then, furious, he leapt to his feet and barreled toward the front door, seeking space to clear his wildly reeling head.

"Charlie, don't - "

He yanked the door open against Tansy's warning and an explosion of cameras and questions assaulted him. He stumbled back and slammed the door shut, swiveling and pounding the wall with the side of his clenched fist.

"Maybe it's a look-alike," Tansy suggested.

"It's her," Charlie admitted bleakly.

The hanging wall phone in the kitchen began to ring jarringly. Tansy answered.

"It's for you, Charlie."

"I don't want to talk to anyone - "

"It's Zadie."

He darted for the phone, skidding around the doorjamb to snatch the earpiece out of Tansy's hand. The older woman sighed. Youth. Always racing. She personally would have used any excuse to delay while she strategized a sane approach to the conversation waiting on the other end of the line.

"Dammit, Zadie, how could you?" Charlie snapped into the receiver.

Tansy winced. Definitely not a good opening.

"It's all over the media," Charlie retorted. "No, I won't just calm down and listen. I'm ready to hop on a plane and come pound him into bits."

There went his nonviolence commitment, Tansy thought, shaking her head.

"Oh? What was it like then?"

Tansy could hear parts of Zadie's muffled reply . . . something about a drone.

"You want to know how I feel?" Charlie asked, incredulous. "I'll tell you - hang on."

He spun to glare at Tansy as she tapped insistently on his shoulder.

"Cut that out," he snapped.

"Not until you stop acting like you've got balls for brains," Tansy replied, gesturing to the reporters outside. "The government is recording every word, which will undoubtedly be shared with all your fans in the corporate ranks. It was probably their drone that took those aerial photos."

Charlie's face contorted. His jaw clenched. He shifted left and right, unconsciously seeking an escape from a boxed-in situation.

"Yeah, I'm still here," he told Zadie as a shine of frustrated tears reddened his eyes. "Look, we can't talk about this over the phone."

He paused, listening.

"Well, find a stable Alternet connection and call me back online."

Tansy heard Zadie say something that sounded suspiciously like *I love you, Charlie.* The young man shut his eyes and rubbed his hand over them.

"Just call me back later, okay?"

He hung up.

Charlie leaned his forehead against the wall. Tansy's words melted into a blur of sound as the room spun and his thoughts reeled in a queasy lurch. He hadn't been this jealous of anyone since high school when Zadie boldly seduced the captain of the soccer team. Charlie swallowed down the ostrich-egg size lump choking his throat, feeling just as gangly and unsure as his adolescent self. Everything about Will Sharp galled him - his secretive ways, militant attitudes, aloof superiority, his scoffing and sneering.

The atmosphere in the house turned sour with his bottled-up envy and acrid from the sting of his anger. Tansy did her best. She believed in meddling the way Catholics have faith in a string of beads and muttered prayers. A nose stuck out from one's face for a reason, after all. She waited all day with Charlie in the hopes that Zadie would get a connection. She talked him out of plane tickets and hired investigators, agreed that Will Sharp had a special place in hell waiting for him, and tried a dozen times to break through the thick smog of the boy's fury and misery.

Finally, Tansy Bealisle conceded to defeat. She needed reinforcement. Popping out to pick up Chinese take-out, or so she told Charlie, she called the one person who'd ever talked sense into the nation's most famous revolutionary. He was a man no one recognized, but whose work had touched every citizen's life. Tansy had a knack for sitting on secrets like a hen brooding on eggs. She returned with take-out and nagged Charlie to eat like a Jewish mother. He moped and stared off with dark looks as noodles hung off his chopsticks. When she cracked his fortune cookie open and read the paper slip aloud it said: *Help is on the way.*

Damn straight it is, Tansy thought smugly.

The following morning, returning to the house in her jogging shorts, she hollered up the stairs.

"Get down here, Chuck," she told him bracingly. "I got a surprise for you."

"I don't need more surprises - "

"You'll like this one, I promise," she vowed.

He stood leaning against the back of the couch as calm and quiet as the first time Charlie had met him. He seemed lost in thought, one hand absently running through his head of spiky black hair, the other curled in a fist under his chin. His wiry frame was small and self-contained. The toe of his left sneaker twitched as it crossed over the right.

"Tucker."

Relief slipped out of Charlie with the name. Tucker glanced up, broke into a knowing smile, and pushed away from the couch.

"Tansy said I ought to come out," he told the youth simply. Then he pulled him into a hug.

The terrible, solitary weight Charlie had been carrying eased slightly. Unshed tears shuddered in his spine. Tucker caught Tansy's expression over Charlie's shoulder and gave a barely perceptible nod. She had called Tucker Jones in Kansas the day before and talked his ear off, hung up, and redialed to chew the other one off his head.

"That boy needs help, Tucker. For all he's done, he's just a kid. These tabloids are tearing him to shreds with lies. He's been under enough pressure to turn coal into diamonds. He's going to crack and the last thing we need is to have to cry over split eggs."

"Spilt milk," Tucker corrected mildly.

"Same difference. Get out here and give him a shoulder to lean on, would you?"

Tucker doubted his narrow shoulder could properly handle the load, but the size of his heart would have to pick up the slack. He left his assistant in charge of the local print shop he ran, packed up his computer, closed up the house, and prepared to stay with Charlie as long as needed. The rumbling tornado of rumors twisted in the sky, dark with danger. The landscape of change howled with gossip. If Charlie needed a calm eye in the middle of the storm, Tucker could offer that to his friend.

He held Charlie at arm's length and gave him a searching look. Tansy left the pair, explaining that she had a workload the size of Texas and twice as stubborn piling up at her office.

Tucker Jones' wry glance loosened the dam of Charlie's silence. Frustration, hurt, anger, worry, and jealousy poured out of him. He lit into Will, spit out furious insults about Zadie, and concluded with the infuriated nausea he felt at the sight of the photos.

"I've loved her since eighth grade," Charlie protested, pacing the kitchen, knocking into chairs, and pounding the countertops. "How could she do this?"

Tucker cleared his throat.

"I'll make you some coffee."

"I don't want any."

"Sit down and have some coffee, Charlie," Tucker ordered shortly.

The sandy-haired youth glanced up in surprise at the commanding tone in his friend's voice.

"I don't need advice from a bachelor," Charlie muttered sourly.

"Why not? I've probably broken up with far more lovers than you've even dreamed of dating," Tucker replied with a knowing laugh as Charlie stared at him.

"I'm not breaking up with Zadie."

"Sounded like it from what Tansy told me," Tucker said frankly.

"She's the one that - "

"Do you know for certain?"

"No, but the photos - "

"What did she say?"

"She said she freaked out over the drones and Will *comforted her*," Charlie snarled the words.

"So, instead of being grateful that someone - anyone - was there to help the woman you love through a shockingly painful and terrifying experience, you're jealous, angry, and joining the rest of the world in doubting her integrity."

Charlie opened his mouth to argue, but Tucker waved him into silence.

"You might have *listened* to her, Charlie."

"You're on her side?"

"What if it's true?" Tucker shot back fiercely. "What if Zadie's telling you the real story? What if she really did see replays of that drone attack - which is still giving you nightmares, Tansy says - and what if you were her, afterward, seeing how the media is spinning those photos to drive you two apart?"

Charlie slouched in the kitchen chair, resistant, but considering Tucker's points.

"I'd be furious . . . and frightened. It's the old *Zadie the Slut* line they've used since middle-high school."

"And you fell for it hook, line, and sinker, just like everybody else."

Charlie winced. He had taken on kids twice his size for talking dirt about Zadie. Freshman year, he had challenged the valedictorian of the senior class for whistling and catcalling at her. He'd gotten suspended over locker room scuffles when he'd known what the boys were saying *was* true about her. He'd watched lawyers try to slant juries against her by slandering her character. He had even seen the media spin this line before.

"I fell for it," he admitted, avoiding Tucker's knowing gaze. He swore. "What should I do, Tucker?"

"Call her back and apologize. Set up a time to talk online. Listen to her. Then tear those media vultures apart like only the Man From the North can."

A storm raged in Zadie's tent, raw emotions pinging off the relentlessly cheery nylon as she stewed, cross-legged and furious with Charlie, waiting for the camp techies to get the Alternet stable. They swore to her that some weird interference - probably military - was blocking their connection. Sharp crackles of her thoughts burst out like jagged lightning as a deluge of hurt feelings rumbled under her breastbone.

She had called Charlie expecting understanding and support. After all, he knew the slander-lust of the media. He'd been torn to shreds and seen her ripped to pieces. Zadie blinked back tears. She couldn't believe he'd fallen for those outrageous headlines. Didn't he trust her at all? No.

No one did. She could hear murmured conversations drop off as people neared her tent, undoubtedly gossiping. Zadie hadn't joined the main circle since the first shock of these tabloids hit. She wasn't hungry and couldn't stand the way people avoided her eye. Minds raced with suspicions, and Zadie was too stung by Charlie's betrayal of faith to go set people straight. She fumed and brooded and waited.

The desert waited, too.

Beyond the fragile cloth of the tent, the desert crouched, ancient and cackling, in the wind's grit. Hour by hour, she scoured down Zadie's defenses until her vulnerability shone translucent. As dusk fell, the desert folded the wings of her heat and light across her back, shed the snakeskin of the day, and coiled slick as night in the whispering hills. There, pooling in the black-blue shadows, she waited with tense patience. The desert nudged the woman from the eastern river who had traveled so far to protect the water in the dry land's womb.

Bring her to me, hissed the desert in a sigh of wind.

Kinap glanced up from the bustle of the kitchen tents. Beyond the firelight, she sensed the crouching spirit. She set her plate aside and let her feet lead her to Zadie's tent.

"Why are you hiding?" she queried softly.

"I'm not hiding!" Zadie exclaimed, indignantly covering the sting of truth.

Kinap let loose a peal of disbelieving laughter. Zadie was glad the growing darkness hid her blush.

"You haven't done anything. Just wrap your heart up in the dignity of Great Love and walk down to dinner," Kinap told her.

Great Love. Zadie stirred uneasily and cleared her throat. She knew that lightning crack of fiercely intense love. She had been called by it, strengthened by it, propelled into action and launched across the landscape of change by it. Now, she feared it. She had handled it like a novice, overconfident in its protective powers . . . and her mother had died.

Kinap noticed her hedging.

The desert licked her teeth.

Bring her to me, she hissed through the hills. *Let me crack her love open again.*

Kinap froze, listening. Her dark eyes flicked to Zadie, who was slumped on her sleeping bag, miserable and lonely, shivering in fear of the ferocious love she had once unleashed.

So, you parted worlds, worked a miracle, experienced loss, and clammed up tighter than a mollusk in fear and pain, she thought. *We'll have to do something about that.*

Kinap's name meant *warrior,* and she stood strong through lifetime after lifetime, returning in different bodies, different births, but always with the same unshakeable conviction. She was as human as any other, with faults and flaws, but she was also an archetype embodied, an ancient and undaunted spirit, here to serve the people - all of them, human, forest, river, animal - in their greatest times of need.

Kinap was not alone, either. She had met eyes with old souls in bodies from all backgrounds. She recognized the spiritual warriors returning under many names: satyagrahis, bodhisattvas, love warriors, spiritual activists. Across the continent and around the globe, she counted them by the hundreds of thousands, all immersed in struggles, speaking hundreds of tongues and one common language of love.

Zadie Byrd Gray was one of them.

Kinap had known this since the day she watched the livestream of the drone attack in Washington, DC. As the ominous machines circled over the crowd swelling around the courthouse steps, Kinap had seen Zadie crack open the body of reality and allow Love to come walking through millions of human hearts. The girl was stumbling through life at one tenth of the strength she ought to have pulsing out of her fingertips right now.

"Up."

Kinap's tone forbade argument or negotiation, but Zadie remained curled into a tight ball on the blanket.

"Go away," Zadie muttered.

Kinap pressed her lips together. *Going to be difficult, eh?* She darted forward, grabbed the edge of the blanket, and hauled upward, sending Zadie sprawling.

"Up!"

Kinap leapt, seized Zadie's arm, and pulled her to her feet before her rattled mind could protest. She silenced the young woman's stuttered objections and hauled Zadie along by the elbow until the stars shone brighter than firelight. The Milky Way sprawled in a breathless gasp overhead. The stunted junipers twisted into human-shaped witnesses huddled in the dark. In a hiss of motion, the desert coiled around them, an invisible serpent of cool breezes and hot breaths of air.

"You once split reality and let Great Love walk into us," Kinap's voice rang out, challenging and encouraging at the same time. "You once embodied the values of midwife to the coming world."

"Kinap, I - "

189

"You once," Kinap cut her off with a tone of thunder no louder than a murmur, "made your mother proud."

"How dare you!"

"And now you're hiding, fearful, curled into your own misery," Kinap stated. She had to break through the fog that choked the young woman.

"What do you want me to do?" Zadie burst out, frustrated.

She glared at the older woman, but could not find her eyes in the darkness. Kinap's proud stance stood large against the expanse of night, slightly uphill, framed by midnight blues. Beyond her, the desert laughed, one part mocking challenge, another part a woman's knowing laugh filled with the strength of birthing mothers and enduring grandmothers, ancient saline oceans and tides of planetary pulls, vast silences of empty spaces and the hum of darkness caressing light. Kinap breathed in primordial time and exhaled infinity in her words.

"Split reality and bring back Love."

"I can't. I never knew how I did it - "

"Try."

"Fine, I will - "

"Now."

"Now?" Zadie repeated, stunned. "Are you crazy? Why now?"

"The water is moving," Kinap stated inscrutably, crossing her arms. "The oil is spilling. Fires sparking. Now. There's more to this than you know."

This is madness, Zadie thought. She shifted on the rough dirt of the hillside, looking around at the silence of the night.

"I can't," she whispered.

"It takes a single spark to set the world on fire," Kinap hinted. "The desert will help you."

Zadie sensed her then, the creature that stripped bones bare and bleached the rocks. As if parting a veil, the desert whittled the night into nothing, revealing the force gathering behind the curtains of the star-strewn sky. Just beyond the edge of ordinary sight, Love churned as vast as plate tectonics and as powerful as earthquakes. It pressed against the edges of reality, seeking to crack the barriers of awareness that blocked it. Zadie recognized this Great Love - the kind that sears the soul and hauls us back from human folly, the Love reverberating in revolutions of the heart, the Love that scorches cruelty away as it rises, the Love that breaks our hearts and turns out its contents to those in need.

Life wants to live, but more than that, it wants to love. Simple survival is not enough. Mere procreation leaves mothers turning their faces to the wall and fathers hanging from the rafters. Fallen in the wasteland, thirst alone may leave us collapsed, abandoning our bodies to the vultures. But love? For the hope of saving our children, seeing our beloved, or protecting our communities, we stagger to our feet and stumble forward on the burning sand. To save her granddaughter, an elderly woman can find the strength to lift a crushing vehicle. For his father, a son plunges into the flames of a burning house. We shoulder the unbearable, accomplish the impossible, and endure the unthinkable by the intensity of our love.

These stories of love emerge on every continent, in every town. Multiplied by millions, they create a song of life louder than the small-hearted survivalists, and richer than the death mongers and their addictions. More enduring than despair, more grounded than hope, this song reverberates in the genetic strands of humanity, woven into the biological structure of human life. Deep in history, our foremothers loved their children. Far in the future, our descendants love their families.

In this present moment, which hangs like a bead of dew on the grass stem of time, where the life of the planet lies clouded by question marks and the body of humanity sprawls in a wasteland of our own making, the love song of our ancestors and descendants is calling to us to rise. The hymn of life hums in the throats of our brothers and sisters. The chords of evolution roar and bark, howl and hiss, warble and moan from the tongues of fellow animals. The wind strikes the harp strings of the forests and marshes, prairies and mountains. The great tympani of the coasts booms and crashes across the cymbals of sands and the drum barrels of rocks.

All that is needed is to listen. The love song of the world enters our souls through the language of life. Our touchstone of strength forms the shape of our beloveds. Courage surges into our limbs. We rise. One foot steps in the direction of change. This is the Love that thrusts the world through eternity and carries us forward into the infinity of tomorrow. It sings overhead, scouring the barriers of reality, looking for an opening.

"Let it in," Kinap said softly.

"I'm afraid," Zadie confessed. She had split the veil and brought Love through before . . . who would die this time?

"Many will be saved," Kinap murmured, uncannily responding to her unspoken thoughts. "There can be no life without this Love. It is water to the desert of our world."

And it was true. Without Love, humanity dies of thirst, grasps at riches, destroys the earth through insatiable greed. Without Love, we are walking dust, dead matter stumbling from the dawn of birth to the dusk of death. Without Love, our Earth is stripped of beingness, left barren and lifeless, a pile of rocks and resources, objects to possess and control. Without

Love, humanity sleepwalks as automatons, controlled, manipulated, and shoved through a nightmarish existence.

"But with Love . . . " Zadie murmured, reaching her hand up into the night to touch the force that pulsed so tangibly, so close.

With Love, the pivot of change emerges, the lever stretches long enough to move the world, the arc of the universe bends toward justice, the spirit of humanity soars, and the flood of life revives.

"Let it in," Kinap urged.

"I'll lose it," Zadie wept.

"Let it in again."

Tears streaked down her face. Her fingers curled against her palm. She squeezed her fist. Her heart answered with a throb of hope. She looked up. A coyote howled. The song of the pack echoed in the night. The desert rose, ran her talons down the borders of reality, and shredded the veil that blinds the human heart.

"Now!" Kinap cried.

Zadie uncurled her fingers, her heart, her mind, her spirit, her body, breath, and being. She opened everything she embodied.

The door of possibilities swung open.

Love seized the day and entered.

CHAPTER TWENTY-ONE

. . . . .

The Front Line

The dust. The sun. The rock under her foot. The trickle of a sweat bead falling down the slow curve of her cheek. The sharp edges of details hammered like flat blades across Zadie's mind, stinging and dull at once. A stream of air moved on her skin. The reverberations of the night before sang in her blood. Love streamed like sunshine through her heart.

"Get up," Kinap had said, rousing her at dawn. "Today, you go down to the front line."

Beside her, Kinap and the women prayed. Behind her, she could feel the heat and presence of the men. Before her, the elders sang in words older than the centuries of greed that came to steal land, people, water, and lives.

Beyond the bridge, a drilling rig idled. Further back, black and steel armored cars with mounted rifles glinted, along with overbuilt police vehicles, menacing vans lined up to cart off protesters, lines of shielded and helmeted cops, and - most worrying - the anonymous uniformed agents of private security forces.

A motion to the right caught her eye as a media livestreamer repositioned. She stared ahead as the camera lingered in her direction. She heard her name and another update on the tense and waiting scene. She had given a round of statements, explaining their position as protectors of the aquifer. She repeated the demand that the permit be revoked: water was not a commodity and the plunderers needed to leave; the Poverty and Debt Relief Act could not be funded this way.

195

Beyond the media team, medics grimly waited for the inevitable collision. Above them on the ridgeline, the second, third, and fourth sets of action cohorts were ready to replace the first.

Zadie's gaze launched skyward, suddenly viewing the scene in a hawk's eye circle overhead. The sun roared over the rise of the hill and the metal shells of the armored cars glinted like insects in the road. The resisters formed a frail, thin line of defense against the solid determination of metal-laden plunder monkeys. For a moment, her heart plummeted. Then the wing beats of knowledge and hope caught the invisible current of trust. Threads of signals from the livestreamers to Dandelion Insurrectionists far and wide created a gossamer spider's web of connection. Zadie knew her presence helped to focus the lens of nationwide concern to this bridge, this watershed, this tribe, these people, turning the desert resistance into a symbolic struggle for them all. More than a bridge and a well were at stake. This day had to pull the mask off the lies and forked tongues of the Interim Government. Today, once and for all, they would see whether the hand of the Interim Government would rise to aid the people, or fall like a fist dashing their hopes.

Now is the time, Charlie had written, throwing the gauntlet down at Friend's feet, *revoke the permits and send the Butcher packing.*

Zadie's heart ached, thinking of him. Knowing he would be watching the livestream, she turned and made the old symbolic gestures of the Dandelion Insurrection. A smile meant *be kind.* A lift of fingers as if reaching to touch stood for *be connected.* And the meeting of eyes reminded everyone to *be unafraid.* In the days of the old regime, the insurrectionists had used the silent symbols as a form of subtle solidarity. Now, Zadie sent a message to Charlie's heart: *I love you. I wish you were here.*

The song. The drumbeat. The somber weight of the scorching sun rising in an arc. The morning prayer circle had spoken of the sadness and the shame that this crossroads had been reached again, that the armored cars were circling like military wagons of old, that the gentle body of the people would once more be exposed to the brutalities of violent greed.

Remember to pray, Kinap had told the circle, *and to keep your hearts strong. Remember why we are here today.*

Each strike of the drumming thundered in Zadie along with her heartbeat. A whirl of dust lifted. A cross breeze suspended the fine particles. Slowly, they fell. For an instant, Zadie saw her mother standing ahead of her on the road, the drilling rig visible through her delicate outline in the dust. Ellen turned over her shoulder and caught her daughter's eye.

Then the wind lifted and she vanished.

Zadie blinked back dusty tears and a parched smile cracked her lips. She tasted salt and blood, the milk of life. Someone passed a water bottle. She sipped and offered it to the next person. Three tribal members from these desert lands had locked down to anchor points sunk into the road where it climbed over the large culvert. In the rainy season, a flood creek surged through the deeply carved arroyo. Today, the lingering spring run-off still dampened the bottom, though the banks stood dry. The drilling rig and its support trucks could not climb the arroyo's steep and crumbling slopes, nor would the driver risk sinking the heavy equipment into the unplumbed depths of the mud in the center. It had to pass over the culvert bridge, but it could not, unless the driver was willing to run people over.

The resisters knew him - Frank was his name - nice guy, had a wife and two kids and lived in the next town over. He took a job with the drilling company because he needed the work. Up until now, he'd been sinking routine residential wells in uncontested areas. Then the company assigned him to this nightmare.

Frank stared at the resisters. They smiled back as they always did. He'd been blessed by them, prayed for, smudged with sage, treated with respect, and offered water, food, and conversation every single day he drove out here. For weeks, he'd been sitting stalled at this bridge, eating up company payroll without any progress. Joe or Walter sometimes swapped out with him, but they hated the gig as much as he did.

"They jes' stand there and tell me they love me, for chrissakes," Joe complained. "They get it, you know? Everybody's got to work; we're not in charge of company decisions. Hell, they even ask how my kids are doing."

"I'm not running them over," Walter grumbled. "My job isn't worth manslaughter or murder charges. Boss can just swallow this deal. No skin off my back to just sit there idling."

Frank felt the same way. But today . . . he sighed. The cops were supposed to clear the bridge and he didn't feel good about this at all.

Move, he willed them silently. *Don't get hurt, just move.*

But they didn't. They couldn't. Safety lay in numbers and they stood as protection for the three chained down to the road.

The opening sallies of conversation began. Frank listened with half an ear. The old guy there could talk until sunset without letting up. He had done so on several occasions, winning another day for the resistance. The old woman next to him, if she got started, would call out to the cops and company workers, reminding them that water was life and they were good people caught in a bad situation. By the time she got done, Frank half-wanted to just get out of the truck and stand with them.

At an unseen signal, the heavily armored security forces - a mixture of corporate and state police - began to advance. The commanding officer ordered the resisters to disperse or be arrested. The media livestreamers crept closer. The prayer chants grew louder. A tear gas canister was launched. A resister darted forward, grabbed it, and hurled it out to the west, far away from everyone. A second, third, fourth canister came hurtling in. Each time, a resister darted forward. Medic crewmembers helped the canister clearers who inhaled the fumes or received an eyeful.

"We are not leaving today," an elder warned. "We hold the bridge in defense of the water . . . and we are prepared."

She pointed to the hillside above them. A thousand people watched the standoff. In the front rows were the next waves of protectors, ready to take the place of those arrested or injured.

"Even if you arrest us," the elder told the police, "more will come."

The security forces could do a lot of damage, Frank thought, *but the old lady was probably right.* They could block the bridge enough to stop him . . . especially since he refused to run over any dead or unconscious bodies. That wasn't in his job description.

The commanding officer again ordered them to disperse. No one budged. On the bridge, the prayers sang out. When the resistance refused to scatter like frightened rabbits, the officer in charge renewed the assault. A line of officers moved in and began arresting people, throwing them to the ground or hauling them roughly from the line. The second flank of resisters moved down the hill, readying at the medics' station as the ranks of injured grew. Across the nation, people watched as wave after wave of protectors faced the onslaught on the bridge. Kinap told Zadie to stand back by the three locked down to the bridge and to delay her arrest as she continued feeding comments to the livestreamers. The police vans filled with the arrested. The heat intensified. The singing and drumming fell off as elders were hogtied with plastic cuffs, along with their younger companions. A man, father of two small children, saw his grandmother taken away and her drum flung out among the rocks and dust. He muttered under his breath, strode down the hill, and snatched up the drum. Stationing himself near the medics, he loosened a bellow of song that echoed off the hills.

Heads turned. Hearts lifted. The struggle continued, resolute.

As the vans grew packed and began departing for the jail, the lead officer eyed the figures on the hill and calculated that he could not arrest them all . . . not until the vans returned from the ninety-minute round-trip to the jail. He snapped an order to step up the use of force. His officers balked. The head of the private security force hired by the oil company proffered a document for the lead commander to sign. He blinked at the legal jargon, listened to the private security man assure him it was legitimate, common across the country, in fact, and then signed the responsibility for the operation over to the newly sub-contracted temporary officers specializing in these kinds of operations.

When a private security agent with an assault rifle and a nasty smile told Frank to move his truck out of the way, the drilling rig operator nodded shortly without meeting the man's eye. Sweat soaked his company shirt despite the full blast of the air conditioner. He shifted gears and checked the side mirrors. The armored vehicles crawled like insects, amassing for . . .

something. One large vehicle revved its engine - a private security truck, Frank noted - behind him on the road, leaving Frank enough space to maneuver out of the way. He began to back up, his alarm shrilling, overhead light feebly flashing under the glare of the sun.

Frank's eyes flicked to the bridge. He blinked. In front of him, standing boldly unafraid was Zadie Byrd Gray. He recognized her from the news, black hair tossing in the hot wind, long limbs defiantly taking a firm stance on the bridge. She caught Frank's eyes and held them. The rest of the chaotic struggle fell away.

She smiled at him: *be kind.*

Frank's heart lurched as he remembered the gesture from the old days.

She lifted her fingers up in the air: *be connected.*

His hand twitched on the steering wheel, rising to meet hers.

She held his eyes steady: *be unafraid.*

He swallowed down the lump of fear and nerves and indecision.

It takes a single spark to set the world on fire, Kinap had said.

Then let that spark be Love, Zadie answered silently.

With a breathless laugh, she ignited the torch of compassion lying dormant in Frank's heart. With a shock like cold rain cracking open in a desert sky, she poured the cataract of Love through the fierce fragile vessel of her being, turning the full force onto bewildered Frank Novaro. He had no words to describe what was happening; something split the toughened shells of his rugged heart and poured a burning love into his veins.

Behind Zadie, he could see three people locked down to the road. In back of him, the black truck revved its engine like a bull pawing the ground before the charge. The vehicle was aimed straight at the bridge. A security officer hollered for Frank to back up and move to the side.

He swore. Even if Zadie dodged, the trio couldn't get out of the way. He thought for a moment. Zadie continued to stare at him with gentle eyes. His veins burned with a sense of injustice - everything about this job was wrong. He set his jaw and pulled the wheel to the left. Before anyone could object, Frank angled the truck off the road, shifted into first and nudged the wheels forward. Then he slammed the brake on and put the gears into park, blocking the bridge with his rig.

Nobody was going to ram that bridge.

He killed the engine and yanked the keys out, sliding across to the passenger side as the security forces hollered and lurched forward.

"Hey!" he shouted at Zadie, hopping out and walking toward the bridge. "Take these and don't let them get 'em!"

He hurled the keys, silver flashing, through the air. Zadie's astonished hands reached out like a prayer. She caught them, looked up at Frank then bolted like lightning up the hill toward the safety of the camp. Frank turned back to the security officers and prepared to be arrested. He didn't care if it cost him his job.

Nobody was running over people. Not here.

As the wrath of the security team landed, Frank heard a sound rising over the shouting, over the rumbling engines, over the bridge: the people were cheering, wildly, peppered with tears and shocked laughing joy. And though he couldn't hear them, the whole nation watching the livestream echoed the astonished celebration ripping through the resisters.

Frank Novaro lost his job . . . but he won the respect of the nation.

CHAPTER TWENTY-TWO

· · · · ·

Let's Be Frank

Like a spark to a blaze, thousands - millions - of people saw Frank Novaro's refusal to let murder happen and felt the fire of love ignite in their hearts.

Let's be Frank about this, they said, driving to sites of extraction, parking lengthwise across the roads, and hiding the keys. Towing companies received frantic phone calls from megacorporations. Fleets of haulers arrived, began to turn around, and then came to a halt across the road.

"Haul your own damn cars," the tow truck drivers growled. "The towing union is on strike."

There is no towing union, the plunder monkeys screeched.

There is now, came the answer.

Pandemonium erupted nationwide. People walked to work with euphoric grins and arranged car pools with a sense of jubilation. Local police were sent license numbers and told to cite people for blocking public roads. Fines were levied. Judges threw them out and dismissed the charges.

Let's be Frank about this, the people chanted. Teenagers pooled their money to buy old junkers and wheeze their last breaths into a protest song of road blockades.

Let's be Frank about this, said one community after another until hundreds of roadblocks barred the paths of new extraction points. The citizenry simply refused to allow plunder monkey profits to come at the expense of their air, water, and land.

Find another way to finance the Relief Act, they demanded. *Try taxing the rich. They have all the money.*

In DC, Charlie boxed and cornered Friend with the grim satisfaction of a scrapper who knows he's got a bully on the run.

"Call off the Butcher and tax the rich," he told Friend, knowing the people could continue these actions for months so long as the tow truck drivers and judges backed them up.

Friend had a harder and harder time concealing his dislike of Charlie Rider. The boy was a young wolf on the rise - and an old dog like him had to guard carefully against hotshot usurpers. This youth had to be weakened - and fast.

After the drone images of Will and Zadie had been released, Charlie's essay on the subject had streaked across the Alternet and scorched the corporate media with blistering hot truth. People salivated over the essay as the media tried to roast Charlie alive. Instead, he kicked over the fire and tore free, charging the real culprits with his words.

The use of those drones subjected the woman I love - a woman who could have been your love, your daughter, your best friend - to an intentional act of corporate terrorism. The fear they intended to strike into the peaceful protectors of our Earth failed, but it hit the mark of a vulnerable target - a woman who had just months earlier survived a drone attack we all condemned, a massacre that took the life of her mother and friends, violently and brutally before our eyes.

Charlie lifted the mighty pen not just in defense of Zadie, but also to slice through the sticky webs of deception spun by the corporate media. The tabloids' gossipy headlines didn't worry him - the corporate media's wickedly gleeful versions of the story did. It reeked of a coordinated smear campaign, designed as a distraction. Charlie attacked the puppet strings of the media's control of public opinion and pointed out the elephant in the room.

Friend allowed the use of corporate drones just as he nodded to the violence of corporate thugs assaulting protesting citizens. And the media willingly distracted us from this alarming fact. Instead, slapping salt on a painful wound, the media took photos out of context and invented this affair out of thin air. At best, the media displayed poor journalistic integrity, receiving photos from a biased source and failing to investigate the story behind the images. At worst - and we have learned from hard experience to expect the worst - the corporate media has once again demonstrated itself to be the pawns of the corporate-government state.

The essay struck boldly in the long-standing literary battle between the Man From the North and the corporate media gladiators. Every pent-up frustration became fuel for the fire of his writing. He was a tiny bee pestering the behemoths, harrying and tormenting them while the people cheered him on.

The utter lack of journalistic integrity in this country undermines functional democracy and empowers tyranny regardless of issue or agenda. Sensationalism has replaced critical thinking, propaganda stifles truth, biased slants are so steep that citizens plummet into confusion and division, smashed on the jagged rocks of falsehoods and deceptions.

Fact had devolved into a matter of opinion. During the hidden corporate dictatorship, censorship determined news. Facts were announced by corporations. Studies reinforced profits. Dissent led to jail. Truth tellers slogged against the uphill climb of mass deception. Charlie had thought the end of the old repressive regime would liberate the pens of the media, but he was wrong. Their budgets still derived from the same advertisers. Their owners still tested the winds of political change and believed corporations would rule once the blip of the Dandelion Insurrection died. Their bets were hedged on the same old power players that had always run the show. Charlie couldn't blame them . . . but he could call them out and parry them into a corner where they couldn't destroy the movement so easily.

As he crossed literary swords with corporate media giants, a band of scrappy and determined writers, journalists, livestreamers, radio show hosts, and filmmakers came to his aid, heaving the weight of their skills and platforms into the fray. Charlie's impossible duel with giants swelled into a battle over propaganda and truth.

All stories had slants. Everyone had an agenda. But a report guided by the effort to resolve a conflict or promote deeper understanding sounded very different than an inflammatory article designed to divide and conquer, conceal and distort.

Sleek glossy lies are still lies, Charlie wrote as the citizen journalists turned the raw edge of scrutiny on the corporate media, exposing the shameless propagandists like grubs writhing under a bright light. *Shut them down by shutting them off. Tune into the stories gathered by ordinary citizens whose programming is determined not by corporate sponsorship, but by conscience and heart.*

Charlie's essays called upon people to black out the corporate media and boycott their major sponsors. The behemoth of the companies roared, declaring Charlie Rider and the citizen journalists to be *fake news.* They lobbed lawsuits at Charlie like hard pitches aimed to smash him in the face. Tansy Beaulisle rolled up her sleeves and went to bat, cracking those cases into the outfield, letting foul plays get called out by the umpires, and slamming down an out-of-the-park home run of an injunction against further baseless slander lawsuits.

The citizen media fought fast and furious. The corporate giants staggered, pricked by thousands of tiny gnats. Charlie's call for a blackout and boycott began to take hold. Advertisers panicked as ratings and viewership plummeted. Worrying reports of intimidation and harassment of citizen media teams sent a shockwave of fear through the movement. Charlie lifted his pen and sent a warning to corporate media.

Your hired goons will not stop us, he declared furiously. *They are fuel to the fire of our resistance. The more you attack, the hotter we blaze, the brighter the light of our truth shines.*

Media was a weapon in the grip of the power hungry. One day soon, it had to become a tool in the hands of a citizenry striving for truth and mutual understanding. Functional democracy required facts and information. It could never be achieved while the fawning lapdogs of corporate media pranced to their advertisers' tunes. The efforts of people across the nation to build local, community-based democracy would be next to worthless if the general populace could still be deceived by the same corporations who had held them in the grip of mass propaganda.

Either you stand for journalistic integrity, he warned the corporate media, *or you are mere pawns of someone else's agenda.*

His essays rested on the foundation of love and the architecture of truth, refocusing the national conversation onto the real story of betrayal: the misinformation and propaganda churned out relentlessly by the corporate controlled media. Charlie allowed himself an ironic grin . . . it was a good thing he had quit being a reporter to be an insurrectionist. His own bias for respect, honesty, and above all love, roared in every line of his writing.

How does he do it? Will snorted in a mix of admiration and annoyance, reading one of Charlie's essays. Despite his initial dislike of the man, he'd grown a grudging respect for his writings. Will shaded the text on his phone and squinted against the sun's glare as he sat on a rock just beyond his tent, baking in the heat. The camp stirred quietly today. An occasional helicopter passed overhead, but no company trucks had been spotted from the lookout point further off. Rumor had it that the oil company was plotting a new assault, but for now, all was quiet.

Behind him, in her tent, he could hear Zadie talking to Charlie over the newly stabilized Alternet connection. Will scanned the desert's long flat horizon line, shaking his head at Charlie's audacity. By the time he read the last paragraph, he was ready to sling mud back at the mudslingers, and utterly convinced that the only hope for humanity was to love a little deeper, hold fast to truth a little longer, and stand up with blazing courage for one another.

Charlie Rider was a foolish idealist, Will thought begrudgingly, *but he was one fine writer.* He dared to write about the world we all want to live in, the world we long for in our quiet moments of impossible hope.

Careful Will, he cautioned himself. *If you don't watch out, you'll start believing in that world and ole Chuck will have caught you in his devious trap.*

That was the dangerous part of his assignment. Will had been embedded in the Dandelion Insurrection for over a year. And, while they couldn't kill you with nonviolence, they could seduce you with kindness, connection, and courage. He had to sternly discipline his thoughts to avoid getting sucked into believing them. After all, the real world crouched out there, harsh and unforgiving. Brutality and cruelty abounded. Only a firm hand at the top could crack down on the sheer evil, that's what the Boss said, and that's why Will worked for him. He was a realist. These bright little dandelions would try to use group therapy on genocidal maniacs and all wind up dead. The country had to be run by someone who knew the ropes, not these impractical citizens professing democracy. It was a nice idea, but . . . Will shrugged. He wished the world could be as they envisioned it, but it wasn't, and he was betting on the least of the evils he knew lurked in the belly of the political beast. Better to have a benevolent dictator than a genocidal tyrant.

Will shifted uneasily on the rock. His usual arguments sounded hollow and flat to his own mind. He had caught Kinap studying him with a thoughtful expression. He had never been allowed down to the front lines, not even when Zadie was asked to go. Will avoided Kinap's piercing gaze, acutely aware that he had grown to value her esteem. Suddenly, desperately, he did not want to be found lacking. Whatever qualities were required - courage, conviction, discipline - he knew he held them. He could face the challenges on the front line as well as any other person in the camp. A hot blush climbed his neck as he realized he wanted the madwoman's respect - and Zadie's and the resistance's. As Kinap studied him, Will yearned for the chance to prove his worth among them. He had the discipline of a stoic, had endured pain and hardship, and could grip his mind in a vise of iron control when needed.

Remember why you're here, he commanded, shocked by the direction of his thoughts. *You have an assignment.*

He scowled. Contact with the Roots had been spotty, but the last conversation with the Boss troubled him.

"Excellent," the Boss had crowed approvingly about the tabloids. "Those photos were gold. Give me more."

"How?" Will had stupidly asked.

"Seduce her," the Boss spat out. "I'll take care of the publicity."

He warned the Boss that it wouldn't work. Zadie's heart was firmly planted in Charlie.

"We don't need her to love you to make the world think something's going on," the Boss pointed out.

When Will argued that Charlie could make the tactic backfire, the Boss had laughed.

"Let me handle our man Charlie. You do your job, Will. You've done this before, remember?"

He did. Many of the Roots had used seduction as a tactic to insinuate themselves into movements. It wouldn't work on Zadie. Will shifted restlessly, perturbed by the idea, and bothered by the way it rankled him. He was losing his nerve.

Zadie's laugh rang out, bright and clear. Will narrowed his eyes. He wouldn't. He couldn't. No matter if it cost him his job, he refused to cooperate with the Boss' plan. Some things, like schools and kids, were sacred. He couldn't betray Zadie's trust. Not like this.

CHAPTER TWENTY-THREE

· · · · ·

The Mouse and The Cybermonk

Alex Kelley sat in meditation, absorbed in thought, studying the chessboard of the nation. She laid out a web of understanding, piece by piece, watching the interlocking systems, tracking the patterns, threads, and connections. The wall of Tansy's living room had become a solid sheet of sticky notes, scribbles on napkins, and sketches of strategy.

She could sense their opponents amassing for a renewed assault. They were mad as wet cats about the resistance to the plunder monkeys. The elections drew closer by the day, and the people acted as if they were skipping through the daisy fields of democracy while the armies of the wealthy prepared for slaughter on the battlefield. Thousands of years of human history spun like a crushing wheel of time. Poor people struggled for dignity and justice; rich people fought for more, more, more. The ghosts of nobles and serfs, kings and peasants, princesses and peons, masters and slaves lined up in the living bodies of the present. The coming elections were a showdown of epic dimensions and Alex worried that the people were about to lose, yet again.

Know your enemy and know yourself, wrote Sun Tzu in *The Art of War.* So, Alex meditated on John C. Friend and the elites . . . because there was something in the equation she was missing. Something she was not seeing. Something that affected the patterns that moved them all.

Alex sighed and let the tangled web of her thoughts suspend. She couldn't see it. Not yet. The sounds of Tansy's house began to rush through the wall of her concentration. She heard the tapping of Charlie's keyboard upstairs and the murmur of Tucker Jones' calm explanation of the loopholes in most election verification software. Inez' voice - slightly distorted by the Alternet connection - exploded with sharp ferocity over the latest dithering of the Elections Commission.

"Can't you come up with something real?" Inez implored. "Those elections are coming up fast and we're going to be destroyed if there's no proper verification system in place."

Slick suits pounded the campaign trail with slogans of change packaged up with million-dollar marketing firm glossiness. Dozens of state and local elections loomed, fraught with controversy and accusations. Two Elections Commission members had resigned in protest, a third died in suspicious circumstances, and a fourth made a frantic escape to Canada where he warned that elections tampering was rampant, but refused to offer details on who was tinkering with the system.

"It's not us," Inez stated with a bitter laugh, "we're too busy trying to survive the plunder monkeys."

People viewed the elections as an answer to their prayers. *Elect real people, get real change,* ran the popular slogan of the scrappy local candidates who stood on the frontlines of plunder monkey resistance and had pushed for the Relief Act. The remaining members of the Interim Government's Election Commission had suddenly - and unsurprisingly - developed cold feet over paper ballots and were now thrusting a suspiciously unverifiable electronic voting machine into production.

"There are verifiable systems," Tucker commented, "especially with the paper ballot back-up. I've had an online program ready and waiting for years, but it has to be implemented, and the Elections Commission won't do it."

"They've all been bought off," Inez griped sourly.

Tucker sighed. The Elections Commission refused to consider his program, though he had tried to bring it to their attention many times.

"If the corporate candidates are thinking of stealing the vote," Tucker pointed out, "they won't let the Elections Commission put in a real system."

"*Por Dios*, of course they're going to try to steal the election," Inez commented in disgust. "We're not going to elect them into office!"

Tucker conceded her point and promised to see if he could find their trail of digital crumbs either tampering with the system or trying to bribe, badger, and bully the Elections Commission members. She signed off with a stream of affection for the wiry programmer - Tucker Jones had always been a welcome calm in the storm of flaming personalities and impassioned activists that made up the constant madness of the movement.

In the living room, Alex chewed the edge of her fingernail and scowled, thinking about the possibilities of corporate counter-revolutions. If they pulled another coup, she doubted it would be as slow and subtle as the first one. They were too addicted to massive profits backed up by the power of the state. She wished she could just shut down the government with a switch - like the old president had tried with the Internet - and deny the corporations and their minions access to the whole system.

She sighed. *How did the Alternet rise up to replace the Internet?* When the old president had tried to plunge the nation into darkness, he had triggered a viral surge of adaptation that thrust the secure Alternet into prominence. She had pestered Cybermonk - the online alias of her fellow programmer whom she suspected had masterminded the switch - but thus far, a cheeky winking emoticon had been the only response.

"Wish I knew," she sighed, stretching her folded legs out.

"Knew what?" Tucker asked, carrying an iron teapot and a pair of cups into the living room, figuring she needed stamina for whatever she was working on.

"I was wondering how Cybermonk crashed the Internet," Alex answered, rubbing the tension out of her scalp. Her fingers froze as she heard him stiffen. She swore at her inadvertent slip. She never mentioned aliases aloud. She carefully concealed everything that had to do with the team that built the Alternet, even going so far as to cover up the bulk of her technical skills at work. No one knew that boyish Alex Kelley from the Interdepartmental IT Support Office had the skills or interest to have programmed the watchdog sentinel that garbled Alternet messages if intercepted. She had left numerous false trails in her work, feigning frustration over problems that she could solve in her sleep.

Tucker Jones carefully set the teapot down on the low table, cautiously considering his next words, not wanting to get caught. Alex was brilliant - far smarter than she let on, actually - and ferocious in her strategic thought process, Machiavellian at times.

"Do you know this Cybermonk?" he asked, finally. "Why do you think that's who is behind the switch?"

He's a spy, Alex thought in panic.

Tucker looked at the tense figure curled against the sofa, looking for all the world like a frightened -

"Mouse?" he asked in quiet amazement.

A jolt of shock electrocuted her. Wide eyes leapt up in fear. Tucker dropped a teacup. It bounced on the carpet.

"You're the Mouse," he said in awe. The watchdog programmer, one of his anonymous colleagues in the network that built the Alternet, a staunch advocate of releasing it, and, Tucker realized, the hinge agent that had gotten it through the government firewalls to infiltrate those systems. He had designed the mechanism that allowed the Alternet to replace the Internet, but it was the Mouse's work that made the system hold up under the enormous strain. He started to laugh in delighted, shocked surprise, dropping to crouch on his heels . . . and saw her terrified eyes.

"Mouse," he said, "I'm Cybermonk."

Her face fell down like a collapsing bridge.

"Prove it," she demanded in a hoarse tone, her caution refusing to believe.

Tucker raised a wry eyebrow and rose to standing.

"Ask Cybermonk what his favorite food is," he said, pointing to her computer.

Then he walked into the kitchen to fetch his laptop, holding it balanced on his forearm as he returned. Alex tugged hers across the table and typed in the question to her online collaborator. Tucker pecked out a long sentence with one finger.

"Watermelon on a hot day or butternut squash soup as it snows," Tucker said as the same words appeared on the screen.

An eruption of shrieks and laughter shot out of the pair as they jumped up and down like a set of kindergarten punk rockers, hugging in wild disbelief. Tucker swiveled to face the strategy wall. This made a lot more sense to him now. It was exactly the style of thought he'd seen in the Mouse's programming year after year. He was amazed that she had survived under the old regime.

"How did you manage to keep your job all these years?"

"By letting the guys in my department pretend to be the smarties," she confessed. "Any time security suspected anything, they'd get hauled in on the carpet, but when asked about me, they all said I didn't have the skills to pull off the security breach in question."

A laugh slid out of Tucker, soft and awed. When Charlie came down later, their conversation had fallen into an indecipherable code of technical jargon and their heads were bent together like a pair of school kids plotting mischief.

"It could work," Tucker said, frowning, "but it's risky."

"What is?" Charlie asked.

They jerked around with guilty surprise.

"Nothing," Alex said hastily.

"I'm going to make dinner," Charlie told them, since they obviously weren't going to tell him their scheme. Over the clang of pots and running water, he caught fragments of their ideas: switches . . . trigger events . . . it's been done before . . . if we could put in place civilian-based defense strategies . . . but how to spread . . . might work. By the time he hollered that the pasta was done, they came in brimming with so much excitement that Alex barely ate a noodle and Tucker wolfed down two plates without noticing.

"You two are impossible," Charlie complained with an eye roll, retreating upstairs as their thick-as-thieves energy made him miss Zadie like a long lost twin.

"How did you end up in government service?" Tucker asked Alex as he began washing the dishes.

Alex smiled enigmatically.

"I grew up in a conservative military family in the Beltway," she shared cautiously. "Every member of my immediate and extended family for multiple generations has been in some kind of military or public service. I made the mistake of believing the professed values of this country and wound up with a blind spot to hypocrisy that stretched from sea to shining sea, as they say."

Tucker rinsed the spoons and pried.

"So . . . you went into government tech support?"

"Well, first I applied to the CIA."

A clatter of silverware hit the metal basin of the sink.

"Don't worry," Alex assured him hastily, "they rejected me. My psych evaluation showed too high results in ethics and integrity. I matched their profiles on whistleblowers."

Tucker chuckled.

"Can't have that in the CIA."

"No," Alex sighed. "The interviewer was quite blunt. He told me my career would likely end with a bullet in the back and I should consider seeking employment elsewhere."

"So, you wound up supporting a movement that was undoubtedly infiltrated and sabotaged by them?"

"Oh, I wouldn't assume the CIA's against you," she argued.

Tucker raised his eyebrows.

"I'm not saying they're for you," Alex added. "Just that it's an unfounded assumption either way. If the CIA wanted domestic regime change, you'd be a handy way to get it done."

Tucker sighed and waved a soapy hand at her.

"Don't ruin my simplistic innocence. I'm just a cybermonk praying for world peace." He shuddered at the thought of the CIA supporting the Dandelion Insurrection.

Alex shrugged. They'd done it before in other countries . . . and just like drones, mass surveillance, and indefinite detention, what goes around the world comes around, and ends up roosting on American soil.

She smiled cheerfully.

"Well, we'll find out soon enough."

"Dare I ask why?" Tucker groaned.

"It's simple," the Mouse answered, hefting the stack of plates into the cupboard. "While they may support regime change, it'll be a cold day in Satan's playground before they support redistribution of wealth, ending extraction, and real democracy. They'll come out and fight you soon enough."

Tucker shook his head and reached for the coffee, gesturing for her to pull up a kitchen chair. He leaned against the counter with his arms crossed over his chest and a thoughtful look in his eyes.

"Thank you," he said.

"For what?"

"Programming, knowledge, everything," he answered, trying to wordlessly convey that he understood the risks she had faced, programming the Alternet while working under the previous regime.

Alex sensed his gaze peering through the window of her eyes into the churnings of the mind, through the neural networks, down deeper into the heart, feeling the pulse and tapping her hidden secrets. Finally, frighteningly, his piercing look scanned her soul, weighing sincerity and flaws, calculating trustworthiness and human fragility.

"Running a background check via retina scan?" she joked, breaking eye contact and tension.

"Nothing that mechanical," Tucker grinned, "but far more sophisticated."

He stalled for a moment, pouring coffee into their cups.

"I've met a fair share of human beings over my forty-two years of life," Tucker said. "Scoundrels, saints, sinners, brilliant nobodies, and terribly flawed geniuses. And, while the young man who claims to run our security team will no doubt do a background check on you through computers, I am content with what I see."

"What's that?" Alex asked daringly.

Tucker studied her with a twist of humor on his lips.

"Why are you hiding behind the moniker of Mouse when your heart is as bold as a tiger and your soul as bright as any dandelion I've ever met?"

Alex felt tears push the backs of her eyes.

"No matter," he said quietly. "Undoubtedly, the Mouse knows why she is hiding."

Alex grinned shakily. That was simple: you had to be smart and careful to bring the fat cats down.

CHAPTER TWENTY-FOUR

. . . . .

Texas Free Rangers

That night, the pipeline exploded. Dramatically. Visibly. An act of protest sabotage blew up the partially constructed water pipeline that stretched across the desert, sixty miles from the resistance camp. The blast surprised the resisters like hail on a warm spring day. The news whipped so fast through the Alternet at the camp that they might as well have been at the scene. As it was, they nearly crashed their server as people tried to stream the last scenes of the fiery destruction. The camp techies texted out a stern warning: share screens or you'll all get nothing. Their second text was a mandatory role call, proving through data log that the protesters were registered at the camp, not at the scene of the explosion.

Previously, flanks of the resisters had slowed the pipeline's progress, but they had pulled back from that front to concentrate on the well site. The initial explosion had caught the dry grass on fire and set off a dramatic blaze around the twisted metal. A dozen masked riders on horses added a touch of absurdity to the images streaming out to viewers nationwide.

"How could they?" Zadie cried in frustration. "And who are they?"

Will scrutinized his live feed, not answering. Between war whoops and the horses shying at the noise and fire, jostling camera feeds and masked saboteurs, he saw enough to set his gut clenching in anger. He didn't blink when the live feed announced that a group called the Texas Free Rangers had claimed responsibility for the destruction. It was a lie. He knew

221

beyond a shred of doubt that those were his twelve Roots riding in circles around the pipeline.

"We do this for all people," a masked rider announced, "for life, liberty, and love! To stop the corporate terrorists and to protect the earth. Be warned: the Dandelion Insurrection has a hardcore edge. We are it."

"They can't," Zadie spluttered, infuriated and dismayed at the same time. "We would never - who on earth are they?"

She turned to Will with a deep appeal in her eyes. He was relieved the night's darkness hid the subtleties of truth in his face.

"We'll find out," he said in a careful non-answer. "Don't worry, Zadie. We'll get to the bottom of this."

Will had burning questions of his own: if the Roots had been ordered to blow up the pipeline, why hadn't he been told?

At two o'clock in the morning, Tansy woke Tucker to tell him the news.

"The Texas Free Rangers?" he repeated. "You're sure that's what they said?"

Tansy confirmed and Tucker lunged for his phone, dialing a number from memory.

Argus Reasonover was half drunk and dodging fists when his cell phone rang. He ducked under his adversary's swing and shot out the bar door into the darkness.

"Tucker! How the hell are you - goddammit all to Satan's fiery oven! No, not you Tuck, I jes got - hold on."

Without hanging up, Gus ran pell-mell down the deserted street, sending a stray alley cat yowling up a drainpipe as the neighbor's dog snarled madly at the end of a short rope. He shouldered his way into the only all-night establishment in that end of town and dove into the plush office of Madam Roxanne with a wink.

"Not again, Gus," she groaned.

"Aw hell, jes' lock the front door a moment, darling. They'll be sweet as calves by morning. They always cool down in the face of cold sobriety and splitting hangovers," he pointed out, kissing her roundly as she rose.

He hooked his hat on the back corner of the chair and slouched into the embroidered upholstery of the seat with a sigh of relief.

"Tuck? Y'all still there?"

"What's going on out there, Gus?" Tucker asked in concern.

"Nothing I can't handle. Some of the Free Rangers got a little testy this ev'ning 'cuz I was winning the pants off them at poker. Then I won their guns and they got mad. A Texan would walk butt-naked down Main Street at high noon so long as he's got his holster on and his gun in hand," Gus sighed, "but take the gun away and he gets a tad insecure."

"So, you weren't blowing up pipelines tonight?" Tucker asked in confusion and hopeful relief.

"Pipelines? What'n the hell are you talking about?"

"Check the news, Gus," Tucker urged and heard the television click on.

Argus Reasonover deemed himself an "undercover agent non-provocateur". Among the widespread fans of the Dandelion Insurrection were several notable groups who wholly supported the aims of the movement, but weren't keen on nonviolence. Among these, the Texas Free Rangers loomed larger than life: humorous, notorious, thoroughly disreputable, and ultimately loveable. Tucker considered them to be both great allies and worrisome liabilities. Years ago, they had shown up at his Kansas print shop to distribute the banned essays of the Man From the North. Tucker had called his old Texan friend Gus to find out the skinny on the Texas Free Rangers.

"Tucker, they're about as likely to commit to nonviolence as the United States Marine Corps," Gus had informed him. "Their idea of peaceful protest is riding their horses down to Austin and firing blanks into the air to piss off the liberals."

"That's hardly peaceful," Tucker noted dryly.

"Well, nobody got hurt," Gus explained.

"I'm surprised the police didn't arrest them all."

"Can't. We're an open carry state. They did get ticketed for letting their horses eat the state capital grass."

Tucker groaned.

"They tell the police they're coming and that they're bringing blanks," Gus added. "For chrissake, the Governor's related to half of them. They're the descendants of old cowboy families that got edged out of business when the bigwigs monopolized the cattle industry, closed off the range, and used big government to ram their railroad down everybody's backyard so they could profit and the little guys could starve."

"So, they're the Jesse James's of today?"

Gus laughed.

"They'd like to think so, but they ain't into robbery, murder, or revenge. They've got higher - and harder - goals."

"Such as what? The second amendment?"

"Tucker, this is Texas. Our guns are safer than our drinking water. The Texas Free Rangers are after the end of crony capitalism and the restoration of the free range as a commons."

Tucker choked.

"And they'll do whatever it takes to achieve that?" Tucker guessed.

"Well, they've been around nearly ten years and nobody's died yet," Gus reasoned. "Though they did cut the barbed wire and run cattle through an oil tycoon's hundred thousand acre backyard."

Tucker frowned, remembering.

"They did a lot more than snip wire, if I remember correctly."

"Sure, they pulled out ten miles of fencing before they were stopped. Just like the ole Levellers and Diggers in England."

"Unlike their predecessors, however," Tucker argued, "that land didn't belong to their ancestors."

"We-yall, that's a matter of some contention. There's some part-natives in the group and they're working on building up a Cowboy-Indian Alliance."

"How's that going?" Tucker asked in a dubious tone.

"Oh, 'bout as well as you'd expect," Gus snorted. "Every time they gain some common ground, some insensitive loud mouth pisses on it."

"Gus," Tucker sighed, "I just don't think we can work with them."

"Aw, come on, Tuck, they can commit on an action-by-action basis, leaving guns at home at the Dandelion Insurrection's say-so. Just so long as they don't have to hammer them into ploughshares and become vegetarians. I'm sure they can go nonviolent for the duration of a protest or a blockade or whatever. Why, just a couple weeks back, they went into a standoff with the Bureau of Land Management openly unarmed."

"They did?"

"Someone tole 'em they were a bunch of lily-livered chicken peckers compared to the Civil Rights Movement. So, they did it on a dare. Ended up gaining some grazing rights, too, as a matter of fact."

"Who was the someone?"

Tucker could hear Gus squirming on the other end of the line.

"I ain't an official member of the Texas Free Rangers, but I sure's hell support the general ideas. We get to drinking and arguing about once a week, and I generally talk 'em out of their more stupid ideas - like taking the Governor hostage. I tole 'em, it don't matter if you're the Governor's goddamn conjoined twin . . . you're gonna get shot or jailed for that harebrained idea."

"Gus . . . "

"Right, sorry. I got sidetracked. Here's what I think y'all ought to do: tell the Free Rangers to avow tactical nonviolence for any Dandelion Insurrection actions they're gonna participate in or organize."

"No sabotage," Tucker mentioned.

"No property damage and no waving guns or firing blanks, no fist fights or violence or threats to nobody," Gus recited.

"But would they agree?" Tucker asked.

"Laying down the terms of a fight isn't nothing new," Gus pointed out with a shrug. "Usually, it's along the lines of 'Joe's back lot, fists, no guns, just you and me at sundown', but if someone put it to 'em in the right way, they'd see the logic of the Dandelion Insurrection's terms."

"But who'd proposition them?" Tucker wondered. "I suppose the Man From the North could write to them."

"Naw, they wouldn't listen to him. Better leave it to me. I can shoot a tin can off a fence at a hundred yards and knock 'em out with a single blow."

"Gus," Tucker sighed, preparing a lecture.

"They all owe me for money, drinks, or saving their lives. I'll hold 'em to the terms. God knows I've talked 'em out of plenty of foolishness before."

And so Gus Reasonover became an undercover agent non-provocateur for the Dandelion Insurrection, holding the Texas Free Rangers to their promises whenever they organized with the movement. Thus far, Gus had succeeded. And, as the replay of the explosion shot across the television screen, he sighed and stuck his boots up on Madame Roxanne's desk.

"Wasn't us, Tucker. I swear."

"They were riding horses, Gus."

"*Bad* horses, and riding like a bunch of weak-kneed shrinking violets who ain't never been on an old nag outside of summer camp. The Texas Free Rangers would shoot anybody who rode that bad."

"They publicly declared that it was them who blew up the pipeline."

"Yeah? I declare it was a bunch of yellow-livered imposters without the gumption to make a reputation for themselves."

"Gus, you're all on video recording firing off guns - "

"- wasting good ammo and risking lead coming down on their heads - "

" - and whooping like spaghetti westerns - "

" - which we consider insulting to the dignity of our profession. We got our own authentic style, you know."

"Can you prove that?" Tucker sighed wearily.

"Tucker, the Texas Free Rangers are the most videotaped, media-covered group of crazies in Texas. There's plenty of documentation. You just send Tansy Beaulisle down here and we'll fight 'em in court and expose who these saboteurs really are."

"You're going to have to convince Tansy before you ever get to the judge and jury," Tucker warned him as Tansy started breathing down his neck demanding to speak to that smart-mouthed, smooth-talking, scandalous son-of-a-drunk-donkey Gus Reasonover.

"Is that Southpaw standing there? Put her on."

A pause. Then an explosion of colorful, only partially decipherable mix of greetings, condemnations, curses, and accusations slammed across the connection. Gus winced and rubbed his ear.

"Ain't us, Tansy."

"You're gonna hafta provide more'n your sweet talk and long standing reputation for trouble to get outta this one, Argus," Tansy Beaulisle drawled.

"Now look, you she-devil, why'n the hell would the Free Rangers ride around in circles like a pack of jackasses just waiting to get caught, huh? We're crazy, not stupid."

Tansy's snort challenged the claim, but she let him go on.

"Furthermore, why weren't those idiots caught? They're on horseback, riding sacks of bone and hide that move about as fast as the glue they're slated to become. The company's got drones, for chrissake. Why weren't they tracked and caught?"

Tansy lifted her eyebrows thoughtfully. He had a point.

"Third of all, there's blue lights coming out from the pipe just 'afore the big bang. That's Dynatight - it's got some long-winded chemical name, but basically, it's a powerful, restricted explosive. Not only would the Texas Free Rangers have a hard time getting ahold of that kind of a controlled substance, it's also a helluva lot cheaper to just make explosives out of stuff you can get at the hardware store."

Gus leaned forward and started taking off his boots as Roxanne nuzzled his neck.

"So, there's your case, Ms. Beaulisle. Hook, line, and sinker. We didn't do it and we probably know who did."

"We do?" Tansy blinked.

"Sure. Even the company would use something cheap to blow up a pipeline. Nope, Dynatight smacks of just one thing: bloated, overfunded government. So, get your sleuths working on it and call me back in the morning. I've got some pressing business to attend to."

With that, Gus Reasonover hung up, tossed his phone in his hat, and turned to the urgent matter of Roxanne.

CHAPTER TWENTY-FIVE

. . . . .

Roots and Offshoots

In a private ranch house situated on twenty thousand acres of cattle grazing land abutting a range of desert mountains, a ring of glasses toasted the explosion with hearty laughs and eager recounting of the escapade.

"Well done, boys," the Boss commented in quiet satisfaction. "And let's remember to toast our friends in high places who agreed to blow up their own pipeline."

"They'll have that section replaced in two days," one man remarked.

"Yes," the Boss said, stroking his chin. "We'll have to point that out in hopes of dissuading the 'insurrectionists' from further sabotage."

"They won't be dissuaded," someone promised, laughing darkly.

One by one, each member of the Roots reported his efforts to infiltrate, undermine, and sabotage the regional endeavors of the Dandelion Insurrection. One reported that Inez Hernandez was still giving him the evil eye, but the priest she worked with seemed to trust him. Another agent had become a key networker at Idah Robbins' Solidarity Hotline. A pair showed up to work security outside Tansy's house, ignoring the lawyer's black looks and muttered imprecations. One of the Roots was working as a volunteer editor at a respected movement journal. Several more were neatly inserting themselves into the leadership of volatile extraction resistance campaigns in Michigan, North Dakota, and Texas; preparing the ground for the next acts of sabotage. The others remained unattached and undercover. While some of the core Dandelion Insurrectionists knew about the existence of the Roots, no one knew exactly who all thirteen were - and no one suspected that their mission was anything other than standing guard over key leaders.

Spirits ran high after the thrill of the explosion. The masks and trappings of the Texas Free Rangers' style provided cover for those situated nearest to core Dandelion Insurrectionists. By morning, they'd all be back in their respective positions, flown there by the Boss' private jets. Their employer listened quietly to their reports, weighing each tidbit of information carefully.

"That's all of us," said the twelfth speaker, "except Will Sharp, of course."

"Yes, regrettably, he couldn't join us. He's positioned where we need him most, however," the Boss drawled, looking around at the Roots.

Over the past months, the Roots had driven down deep and branched out in the darkness, sending out laterals, encouraging others to join them, arming people and training them to fight. They knew their targets: the outliers, the disgruntled and frustrated, the lonely and afraid.

Long before they had joined the Roots, each of the twelve agents had used these same tactics for other missions. Usually, they focused on an individual or a pair, buying them drinks, making friends, plying out their grievances with movement leaders, and finding their vulnerabilities. Then, casually, starting with a joke or flippant remark, they'd open the door of Molotov cocktails, pipe bombs, street fights, and property destruction. Much later, if the target proved worthy, harassment, kidnapping, and assassinations entered the conversation. They'd entrapped, recruited, and nudged people into dangerous, crazy actions that served a purpose few could discern.

Some of the Roots had previously worked for the government, identifying potentially violent characters, ostensibly to arrest them before they caused legitimate harm, but more often to intentionally entrap resisters, weakening the movement's legitimacy in the public eye. Questions lingered after each assignment: would that kid have actually built a pipe bomb if the undercover agent hadn't shown him how to do it? Had the idea of sabotage even crossed their minds?

The Roots who came from corporate backgrounds shrugged. Their missions involved fomenting violence in movements to make public sympathy swing in favor of the company. If the appropriate targets didn't exist, their job was to create them . . . or insert an agent provocateur to do the dirty work.

During the ascent of the Dandelion Insurrection, the Roots' assignment had been to clear away the obstacles in front of the growing movement and to protect key leaders from untimely demises. That mission had been accomplished. The heavy-handed political puppets of the corporate dictatorship had fallen, clearing the stage for new blood.

But it wouldn't be those bright dandelions that took power.

Those idealists had to be kept away from the halls of political office . . . in fact, their brilliant little run needed to come to an end. The Roots had a new mission: to turn the Dandelion Insurrection against itself, split it over tactics, divide and crumble it as acts of sabotage and violence hardened people's hearts against their precious little insurrectionists.

It was wicked. It was ingenious. It was working.

At eight o'clock in the morning, Friend hauled Charlie Rider in on the carpet of his office as the nation woke to the news of the explosion. He steamed with the red-eyed irascibility of an overworked man lacking sleep. The newspapers on Friend's desk screamed headlines about the sabotage and he demanded an explanation from the man he considered the ringleader.

"Wasn't us," Charlie answered.

He'd been up all night, talking to Zadie, Will, and the resistance camp organizers; writing press statements condemning the action, defending the movement, and repeating over and over that the Dandelion Insurrection did not resort to sabotage.

"That's been our line from day one, and we've always adhered to it," he told Friend firmly.

"We'll have to investigate, you understand," Friend informed him sternly. "We can leave no stone unturned."

"We'll be doing our own internal work, too," he retorted coldly. "We don't support sabotage any more than you do."

A quick flash of an ironic smile flickered on Friend's face before vanishing.

"Then you have no objections if I inform the nation at today's press conference that - "

"The Dandelion Insurrection denies the claim that this action was done with our knowledge and support, that we have never endorsed sabotage, and that - "

"The Interim Government will have your full cooperation?" Friend queried pointedly.

Charlie sighed again.

"I'm one person, not the whole movement," he repeated for the thousandth time. "You know my views on this action. My personal press statement condemning it has already gone out. Neither you nor I can make claims about what the Dandelion Insurrection will or will not do in regards to cooperating with the Interim Government. It just doesn't work like that."

Friend looked skeptical, but he merely nodded and said he'd use language carefully, as he always did.

Only when the tired young man turned to leave did John C. Friend allow himself a chuckle. *Never fight with an old dog, boy,* he growled at Charlie Rider, *we know every trick in the book.*

Arrests. Interrogations. Releases. Houses and headquarters raided. Swift and coordinated as a hunting wolf pack, the Interim Government unleashed an investigative task force that hounded Dandelion Insurrection organizers nationwide. The witch-hunt for saboteurs sent shockwaves through the movement. The scale of arrests echoed the repression of the old regime. Organizers often sat behind bars for over a week awaiting questioning. Investigators prowled through the workspaces of the movement, seizing documents and computers, disrupting meetings, and sniffing through cars and apartments for evidence related to the pipeline explosion.

"This is impossible," Inez complained. "They're arresting, detaining, and questioning so many of us, we can't get anything done."

The raids and interrogations continued. So did the sabotage. Fossil fuel extraction equipment was damaged in North Dakota. Another pipeline exploded in Michigan. A refinery in Houston blared into red alert when tampered wires frayed. A series of gas station explosions sent plumes of fire and noxious smoke into the air. A fracking tower toppled. The Butcher ramped up his forces' aggressive intimidation of extraction resistance organizers and raked in a fortune through expanding security contracts - prompting Alex to suspect he was fomenting the sabotage himself.

Every report of sabotage swayed yet another Congress member to oppose Charlie and Tansy's proposed legislation restricting the use of force. *These protesters are dangerous,* they claimed, *and are crossing the line into eco-terrorism.* When the sabotage of a gas well set off a forest fire, Charlie and Tansy's bill was buried under the avalanche of politicians calling for an end to sabotage in an effort to, ironically, protect the environment. The legislators swallowed the words - and bribes - of industry and passed a bill giving private security permission to harass and intimidate protesters as they protected important infrastructure from sabotage.

Tension mounted in the movement. Fear of the Butcher's private security thugs sent shivers through the people. Citizens worried that the Interim Government was sliding back down the slippery slope toward the brutal repression of the last regime, giving a nod of silent complicity to the paid mercenaries of the Butcher.

Some strands of the populace supported the pipeline attacks. With climate change barreling toward them fast and furious, the fate of humanity and the planet was on the line. Something had to be done, they said, and the destruction served the greater good. The fossil fuel companies were getting what they deserved for lying to the public for decades and calling climate change a hoax.

But the saboteurs didn't stop at fossil fuels. They smashed windows of corporate storefronts. They broke into the offices of local officials and ransacked the rooms. They attacked seemingly random targets. A sense of danger rose in all corners of the country as people tensed for the next assault.

To everyone's surprise, Friend appeared on the news and announced that the raids and investigations demonstrated to him that the Dandelion Insurrection had nothing but good intentions for the country and their fellow citizens.

"However," Friend stated with a sigh of regret, "there appear to be some bad apples in the movement, and we will get to the bottom of these sabotages. The safety and security of everyone depends on it."

Rumors abounded about who was organizing the attacks. The Texas Free Rangers scraped clear on the skin of their teeth-gnashing outrage at the affront of the imposters - that and the solidity of their alibi, since their credit card information, eyewitness testimony, and security cameras all confirmed that their whereabouts were getting rip-roaringly drunk at the Lucky Star that night.

Charlie and Zadie denounced each action, but the saboteurs left calling cards of dandelions - flowers in shattered glass, spray paint on government buildings, a slash of yellow on blown-up equipment. Friend blew as hot and cold as a New England spring, blustering with outrage over the attacks then unexpectedly folding to small concessions to the saboteurs' demands.

"It doesn't make any sense," Alex murmured after Friend stepped in to protect a school that had been on the privatization auction block. The PTA had been holding down a successful resistance for months when someone set the headquarters of the highest bidder on fire as a warning to back off. It was a sensational news story of flaming buildings and the pathos of Friend's speech.

"We cannot commend the act of destruction - and we must uphold justice, law and order - but these incidents highlight the understandable outrage of this community," Friend said with tears brimming in his eyes.

Alex glared at the video stream. Her eyebrows frowned in fierce concentration and for days she stalked the house, lost in stony silence.

"What does he want?" she muttered to herself. "Why this hot and cold? It's almost as if he wants the attacks - " she broke off, stunned.

She swallowed hard and blinked as the room spun under her. John C. Friend was undoubtedly the most diabolical, brilliant, terrifying strategist in the twenty-first century. He was so good, no one would ever cite him in the history books, no one would even spot his manipulations. The movement would simply reel, off-balanced and confused, into pits and traps of their own making, leaving him the last man standing.

At least, that's what he thought. But he hadn't calculated on the Mouse.

"Charlie," she said, pulling up a wooden chair and straddling it backwards, "what's the only thing keeping Friend from just doing whatever he wants?"

"Well, us, I suppose," Charlie replied, looking up from his writing with a frown.

"And what would happen if he directly attacked the Dandelion Insurrection?" she asked.

"The whole country would rise up against him, just like we did against the last regime."

"Exactly. So, he's got to stand - or appear to stand - with us."

"Even as he fights us," Charlie complained.

"Think about this for a minute," Alex urged. "How can he weaken and destroy the Dandelion Insurrection without appearing to be fighting us?"

Charlie frowned at the ceiling. A minute ticked slowly by. He blinked.

"Exactly as he's doing ... by *helping* us," he snarled the word with irony, "rout out saboteurs while his horrible investigations and interrogations are actually just hamstringing our ability to organize."

"And . . . " Alex prompted.

"And what?" Charlie frowned back.

She sighed.

"And why is he conceding to the saboteurs?"

"I don't know," Charlie grumbled, "but it's giving everyone the impression that those tactics are working - which then allows him to crack down on us harder - "

His voice broke off into a stunned silence.

Alex nodded.

"We're digging our own grave," Charlie choked.

"Precisely. Meanwhile, the arguments around tactics are splitting us down the middle of the movement."

" - turning people against us faster than new recruits join the self-proclaimed *hardcore edge* of the Dandelion Insurrection."

"Keeping us fighting each other - "

"Instead of him."

"Actually, he comes off smelling like a rose, a good guy, *a friend to the people*," she slurred the last phrase with disgust.

They stared at each other for a long, horrified moment.

"Is this it?" Charlie asked, swallowing hard. "Is this checkmate?"

Alex Kelly grinned.

"Not by a long shot, Charlie Rider. The real game has just begun."

Will sighed and shifted position as he surveyed the crowd packed into the high school auditorium. The scent of the rural Kentucky valley's flowering apple orchards slid in the open doors. Zadie tested the microphone, looking strained and tired against the dark velour curtains and weak stage lights. They'd been traveling continuously for several weeks, speaking out against sabotage and solidifying nonviolence commitments throughout the Dandelion Insurrection. At night, Zadie spoke to large groups. During the day, she met with core organizers. Will handled logistics and security. The police had detained them for questioning twice, but no arrest warrants had been issued. Will missed the silence of the desert camp - which was quieter now that the tribal leaders had won a court injunction against the water-extracting oil company. The locals mounted sentries and let most of the resisters go home. Kinap had sent them greetings from her home in the east, and an offer of welcome should they need a rest.

Will rubbed his hand across his face and thought wistfully of the silent desert as contentious arguments broke out. Many people believed the pipeline explosion had won the court injunction - though the organizers had stated many times that the judge nearly ruled against them because of it. Now, hotheads in large cities and small towns spoke up for further acts of sabotage, arguing that the violence of the corporations justified the destruction of property. Zadie countered by pointing out that, short of exploding half the nation, the sabotage was less likely to cripple the corporations than it was to embolden Friend and the Interim Government to crackdown on the movement. A few nights ago, a pair of night watchmen had been injured in an explosion, and prior to that, a firefighter had died putting out an act of arson. The tide of public sentiment pushed angrily at the movement, blaming them for injuries and the loss of innocent life.

As Will listened, a hornet's nest of conflicting views buzzed in his mind. He knew full well who was coordinating the sabotage. The Boss had confirmed his suspicions that the Roots were involved, but the Roots had thrown up a wall of silence on the subject.

"It's better if you don't know," the Boss had told him.

Will resented working blind. He felt isolated and excluded from the group's plans. A sense of betrayal plagued him as he traveled with Zadie from one community to the next.

Will scowled. The real trouble for Zadie wasn't the Roots - they tended to work silently and secretively - but rather the people he called the Offshoots, citizens who were emboldened by what was happening and opportunistically joined the fray, anonymous and untraceable. He disliked these self-trained amateurs who answered to no authority, yet claimed to be acting under the auspices of the Dandelion Insurrection. They challenged Zadie as she implored people to stay true to the original principles of the movement.

"Our notorious nonviolence has served as our saving grace. We've seen it take the wind out of the sails of the government and corporate forces that used violence against us. Our firm stance held the torch of truth high, and the stark contrast of our choices versus their brutality won us friends and supporters," she argued, night after night, to local groups and organizations who largely nodded - except for the heckler in the midsection, or the guy in the back row, or the set that came up after the talk to hurl insults at her and argue that a diversity of tactics was needed now.

Pandora's box had opened, and the frustrated and unconvinced came screaming out, insisting that nonviolence wasn't working fast enough, and arguing that it was time to terrorize the opposition into concessions. Will wasn't surprised. People had grievances - some just, some not - and violence was as common as sliced cheese to the average American. It was considered a natural reaction to being pushed around and abused by the corporate state. He certainly didn't deny that people had a right to fight back, to protect themselves, to train in self-defense. He'd do it.

But was it an effective tool for justice? Will had serious doubts. The US military would always outgun them. The corporate elite would always find that replacing windows and exploded pipelines was cheaper than environmental or economic justice.

A dispute broke out in the audience as an older woman accused an intense young man of being an agent provocateur. Will hid his ironic smile. The kid could be an agent, but he probably wasn't. The ranks of the Offshoots were filled with people whose bottled up fear and frustration had been pressured to the bursting point. In his experience, the agents were far more skillful than that youth.

Will watched the young man disrupt the community meeting, loud, belligerent, and opinionated. Will had also used the tactics of this malcontent, but he preferred to work more subtly, sowing discontent and weakening the movement without being seen. He would never stand up in a full crowd of people, shouting, claiming to speak for the movement while drowning out the quieter voices in the room.

Will doubted that the majority of the crowd supported the acts of sabotage. He could read their faces like open books: stubborn old women consistently ignored and furious about it; people struggling with health challenges wanting actions they could participate in; the nervous and worried mothers, looking back and forth between the factions, saying little, but pulling back from the movement as it teetered on the edge of violence. The timid, shy, scared, and nervous could be trampled over in a public meeting like this, but that didn't mean they agreed with the loudest stated position. Will could see their heads turning to

Zadie to hear her reply to those defending the recent acts of sabotage. Their expressions were hopeful, not accusatory. The young man challenging Zadie might win or lose this confrontation ... but he didn't have the whole movement behind him.

Sit down, Will thought disdainfully, *wait until you've done the groundwork before attempting a public coup. Amateur.*

"The movement does not belong to Charlie Rider," the young man complained, referencing the most recent essay of the Man From the North in which he denounced sabotage. "And, the Dandelion Insurrection is bigger than you, Zadie Byrd Gray. If this is a leaderful movement, then we each have an equal say in tactics."

Will loosed a sympathetic chuckle at the accusation that the movement didn't belong to Charlie Rider. But was the movement bigger than Zadie Byrd Gray? *No bigger or smaller,* he thought. Hidden in that slender, wild-haired woman was a powerhouse. He'd known her, trailed her, hid her, and watched her every move for over a year. Will thought, possibly, she was one of the most remarkable people he'd ever met. What is a movement, after all, but the embodiment of aspirations turned into organized action by thousands and millions of people? If the Dandelion Insurrection strove for a world of respect, democracy, nonviolence, sustainability, liberty, life, and love ... then Zadie contained those traits in a nutshell.

Will's thoughts turned dark. What kind of movement did he embody? Secrecy, hidden powers, lies, surveillance, armed defense, manipulation, subterfuge.

A quiet part of him countered his scathing assessment. He also represented loyalty, commitment, service, hard work, perseverance, vigilance. The line of good and evil wanders through every person. One man's loyalty is another man's betrayal. Every coin has two sides to its eternal tossing.

You're called the Roots, Charlie had scathingly challenged him one day during their time at the school resistance, *but whose roots? What will you grow into?*

Not dandelions, Will acknowledged silently. And for the first time, he regretted that painful truth.

The deep night ached with loneliness as Zadie lay sleepless, flat on her back, hands laced behind her head, staring at yet another blank slate of a ceiling in someone else's home. She lowered her eyelashes halfway then jerked them open again. No use. The dreaded hour of insomniacs had caught her. She held her body motionless; to move would brush the coolness of the thin cotton sheets against her limbs and reveal the empty space where she longed for Charlie.

Tomorrow, she swore, *we're cancelling the rest of the talks and heading back.* Either that or he should abandon the attempt to argue sense into politicians and come join her. The strain of the nightly debates over tactics left an iron band of a headache tightened on her brow. She wanted to lay her head on his chest and listen to the certainty of his heartbeat telling her the movement would be fine, the new day would dawn, and life would rally once again.

On nights like this, she wrestled with confusion and doubt, replaying the day's heated debates and cursing the points she'd forgotten to make. Every breath mattered. The life of the Dandelion Insurrection hung in contention. How many acts of sabotage would the corporate pawns endure before the full blade of repression swung at anyone who dared to dissent? This tiny window of political freedom, hard won with tragic sacrifice, could slam shut at any moment, plunging them back into dangerous silence.

Everything trembled, tenuous.

Her heart ached to see others going along with the assertion that the time had come to put all options on the table. The gleam of bloodlust entered eyes. Frustration built into the craving to retaliate with violence. Acts of sabotage had risen; shipping truck tires were slashed, warehouses vandalized, a bomb was planted outside a bank. The secretiveness lent the saboteurs a mystique, but the criticism of the actions fell squarely on the Dandelion Insurrection. Former supporters voiced outrage at the tactics. Arguers would retort that sabotage and property damage *were* nonviolent - no one got hurt, at least not intentionally - and besides, the greater violence of pipelines or corporate greed justified the use of such tactics. Zadie urged everyone to weigh tactics on *strategic* value, not their relative position in the gray zones of the spectrum of violence.

"We have to look carefully at the short and long term effects of each action we choose," she said, thinking about the backlash that occurred after every act of sabotage.

Over and over, she countered the claim that every nonviolent movement was backed up by violence. Zadie endlessly explained that the research showed that violent flanks did not increase the success rate of nonviolent movements, and a handful of examples did not outweigh track records built from hundreds of struggles. Squabbles over history would break out, derailing the talks into the past instead of looking squarely at the noticeable cooling effect in popular response to the Dandelion Insurrection. As the supporters of sabotage gained traction, Idah and Inez reported increasing difficulty in gathering participants for actions. Families feared the frequent arrests and interrogations of the Interim Government's Investigative Task Force.

Zadie sighed, trying to unknot the tension in her shoulders. They'd been on edge for the past week after a series of death threats had been sent to her inbox. At tonight's talk, Will had stiffened abruptly, his eyes tracking a figure lurking on the edge of the crowd. He insisted on extra caution as they left and the heightened security measures had left the metallic taste of fear lingering in her veins. Adrenaline singed the frayed edges of her nerves. She rolled onto her side.

A low rumble of a voice murmured in the hall.

Her breath clenched in her chest.

The voice spoke again, replying.

It's just Will, Zadie sighed silently in relief, *talking on the phone.*

She didn't intend to eavesdrop, but in the midst of the silence even a dropping pin would thunder.

"Just hold your position. Don't do anything. I'm coming over."

She heard a few mumbled words: *station, blow, orders,* but Will was moving out of hearing range. Curiosity propelled her out of bed. She pulled on her jeans, threw a dark sweater over her tee shirt, and shoved her bare feet into her boots. Holding her breath, she twisted the doorknob with an upward pressure to silence the thunking of the latch. She swung it open just enough to slip through. Peering over the railing of the landing, she saw Will sliding out the front door. She descended the staircase with only a few hair-raising creaks and groans, and crept out of the house, flattening against the dark shadow of the wall.

Will slunk up the street toward the north end of town. There, the street ended at the sloping embankment that concealed the transformer station. Zadie's heart raced in her chest. That transformer served a large swath of Kentucky's power grid. She darted after Will, grateful that her hiking boots had no heels and that the rubber soles muffled the sound of her steps. She rounded the corner of the last house, plunging into an alley of darkness, and scaled the slope between the swaying black pines. Sharp scents rose from crushed needles as she scrambled up to the top.

The grid of humming wires buzzed in the darkness, lit by a single streetlight and undoubtedly monitored via surveillance camera. She crept through the understory of the trees, falling to her belly as voices sounded to her left.

"Don't blow it," Will said, low and urgent.

"It's a perfect target," another voice argued.

"Half the region's grid will go black," a third added.

"It's all rigged," said the fourth.

Zadie squinted at the hooded figures, frowning. Two of them looked familiar.

"There are things you don't know," Will said. "You have to take my word. Don't blow this one."

"We're safe as a dove. No one's monitoring those cameras. It's all been arranged."

"I told you, there are other things at play," Will insisted.

"Fine, but somebody better call Joe. He's still out there sitting on the trigger."

"Guys, keep it down," said the second person, glancing nervously around at the sound of a car. The group froze and crouched. The headlights turned the corner, stopped, and a night watchman with a flashlight began to sweep the area.

The black-clad group split up and fanned out, silent and shadowy. The watchman peered into the transformer area, illuminating the gray-ghostly metal and casting deep lines of shadow and light up the surrounding slopes. His car idled, the headlights pouring onto the chain-link fence and the humming station.

Zadie glanced over her shoulder . . . the town was a hundred feet of wide-open space away. In the other direction, the thin forest continued to climb the exposed hillside before she could drop out of sight into the side streets and backyards of the neighborhoods.

A hand clamped over her mouth.

"Don't move," Will hissed in her ear.

He said nothing more as they breathlessly watched the night watchman complete his sweep, climb back into the car, and take off. Then Will's grip on her arm relaxed and he ducked his head down to the pine needles with a sigh.

"What are you doing here, Zadie?"

"I heard you on the phone, trying to stop them, so I followed in case I could help."

"How noble of you." Will's sarcasm cut like a knife.

"Look," she hissed back, insulted, "I thought if I came, I could convince them to stop."

"And if not?" Will argued in an undertone, glaring at her in the darkness. "If it didn't work and they blew something up and you got caught at the scene, did you consider how bad that would be, Zadie?"

She bit her lip. She hadn't thought about that.

"We're shadow and light, sweetheart," he muttered. "You shine to the crowds and let me deal with the darkness."

She said nothing.

"Come on, let's get out of here," he said.

"But what about - "

"Leave them. We're getting out. Now."

"But - "

"Argue later. Move now," Will commanded, pulling her to her feet and pushing her into motion as she paused to brush off the pine needles.

They had almost reached the bottom of the slope when the explosion ripped through the silent darkness. The force was strong enough to make them stagger. Will dropped instantly to the ground, pulling Zadie under him as the second explosion boomed.

The emergency back-up generator for the town screamed into action half a mile away. At the far end of Main Street, the police and fire station lights burst on. Vehicles shot out, lights flashing and sirens wailing.

Will didn't waste his breath swearing. The night watchman had already doubled back. He and Zadie were visible and exposed on the hillside that served as a buffer between the town and transformer station.

Will calculated his choices rapidly and coldly. At lightning speed, he weighed their alibis, excuses, and explanations. There was only one plausible way to explain their presence here.

"Zadie," he said, swallowing, "I'm sorry."

"What?" she frowned.

As the people poured out of their houses into the streets and the fire department sirens screamed, Will said a silent prayer to the Devil to have mercy on him - he had no hopes about God - and he pulled Zadie into an embrace and kissed her.

CHAPTER TWENTY-SIX

. . . . .

Sabotaging Love

She shoved him back with a hard pound to the chest he didn't duck or flinch from.

"What are you doing?" she yelled.

"You saw no one. You know nothing. You came out here because I asked you to meet me," Will spat out rapidly.

"What?"

"Repeat that. You saw no one. You know nothing. I asked you to come here tonight."

"But - "

"Zadie, this is going to fall hard and fall fast. But if you trust me, it won't fall on you."

"Trust you?" she hissed with a fury that put cold chills in his marrow.

He steeled his nerves.

"Zadie, you've got ten seconds to save your reputation and the movement. Repeat: you saw no one. You know nothing. You came out here because I asked."

"I heard that," she snapped. "Why?"

The cop cars were surrounding them. Beams of headlights alternated with red and blue flashes.

"Why?" Will repeated in disbelief. What kind of a question was that?

"Why did you ask me to come?" she hissed at him.

Relief flooded him. She'd do it. She'd stick to the alibi line.

"Because I love you, Zadie," he sighed. "That's why."

Truth was always the best lie.

"Quick thinking, Will," the Boss would tell him later. "Couldn't have played that one better if you'd been caught sound asleep in separate beds thirty miles away."

Will did not reply. His mask of inscrutability remained in place, as it had for the entire week of endless interrogations and accusations. The culprits of the explosion had not been caught. The official line of Will Sharp and Zadie Byrd Gray remained unshakable. He had asked her to come. She came. The transformer exploded. She knew nothing about it.

Did he?

He had not expected sabotage to occur that night, he said.

Which was true. When he gave an order to his Roots, he expected it to be followed. But he didn't tell the authorities that.

But he and Zadie were present in that town . . . why?

To try to stop such acts. That has always been the stance of the Dandelion Insurrection.

But why did he go out that night and ask her to come?

Because I love her . . . and I wanted to tell her, Will Sharp informed them.

Did she love him?

That was not a relevant question, the young woman's lawyer interrupted.

But it was. In fact, it surged into nationwide curiosity as *the* most relevant question of the night. The explosion, the culprits, and the temporary inconvenience of power outages throughout the region ended up fanning the flames of the ongoing obsession with Zadie Byrd Gray's love life. The same tabloids that cheered the thrilling story of "the world's most famous revolutionary couple" now trembled in delighted wickedness over the love triangle with Will Sharp.

The question of Zadie's heart outshone the inquiry into the explosion to such a degree that even Friend made little fuss about the investigation. In one of his mercurial bouts of magnanimity, he even stated publicly that his personal opinion was that the poor pair had either been in the wrong place at the wrong time . . . or that they had been framed, which amounted to the same thing. The nation chuckled over his goodwill and his approval rating jumped up.

"It's too bad," he joked, "that we can't have an official inquiry into the real question of national interest: does she love him back?"

Charlie seethed. He had never hated anyone with the sheer venom that he felt at the thought of Will Sharp - not the former tyrants that controlled the country, not the unknown person who had fired the drone, not even the bastard who had abandoned Zadie broke and pregnant long ago. He wished he and Will had met back in the days when he could still pummel him in the schoolyard. But he didn't have that option now. Not as a notorious organizer of a nonviolent movement. As satisfying as it might be to punch Will Sharp, Charlie also knew it would throw oil on gossip's fire, digging them deeper into the quagmire of the sensationalized rumors of this nonexistent love triangle.

Tansy flew out to Kentucky to haul the pair out of legal hot water. When Charlie was finally allowed to speak to Zadie, he asked her to come back to DC.

"We have to talk face-to-face," he told her wearily.

"Yeah, I know," she agreed, sad and subdued.

The police questioning seemed to move at a snail's pace - though Tansy claimed she had never seen an investigation whip along so fast.

"Chuck, there's something funny going on," she commented. "Why are Zadie and Will getting off so easy? It just doesn't make any sense."

Mouse disagreed. The whole pattern fit her theory of Friend's underhanded encouragement of the sabotage as a means of cracking the movement. She studied Charlie's silent fury stalking the house and quietly noted to Tucker that there was more than one way to skin a cat . . . if they didn't watch out, this love triangle disaster would sabotage the movement better than explosions.

Will revealed nothing publicly, letting rumors and gossip do the work for him. It had been a split second choice with no good options. *The Dandelion Insurrection was doomed, regardless,* Will admitted to himself silently as he tried to justify his actions. *They've had a bull's eye pinned on their backs all year.*

In the long hours of incarceration between bouts of police interrogation, he sat in the jail cell forcing himself to examine the truths he hid. He had said he loved her, but the truth was more complicated. He respected Zadie. He appreciated the way she cared so deeply for the country, for the people, and for life. She had loyalty and courage. She worked hard without complaint. She infused life with passion and fanned the embers of the heart. Zadie had matured since the first time they'd met. Back then the sharp edge of her temper had been honed on the whetstone of her raking scrutiny. Unleashed from compassion, her biting truth could slice the heart to shreds. In New York one evening, she had snapped at him to stop skulking at her heels like a feral dog. Then, in a fit of contrition, she slowed her sidewalk-pounding stride and matched paces to apologize.

"I had some rough experiences near here," she confessed suddenly, her face clouded with dark memories.

"Me too," he replied with a scowl.

Then they looked at each other with the startled recognition of fellow survivors, as if their hidden scars were emblazoned on their skin. They started swapping stories with an attitude of jaded one-upmanship, and in the days that followed, looked at each other with somber respect. They shared an unspoken understanding built on seedy experiences and close shaves. It was a bond Charlie could sense, but not comprehend, easily mistaken for other emotions. Zadie and Will related without judgment, whatever stories they hid, the other had seen - or done - worse. They held no shock or shame. The one secret he never mentioned was his mission, which he could never confess to her.

From this common ground, friendship began. At Los Jardineros, it had settled quietly into the ease of working together. In the desert, the core of trust had grown as the drones growled overhead. On the road, he rehashed the debates of the night before and helped generate counterarguments. Will had come to value their friendship. His profession inhibited closeness, but in the past months, he wished he could honor the trust that had grown.

Now, he might have destroyed it.

Will leaned his head against the cold concrete of the holding cell and mourned the loss like a hail-crushed garden of green hope. Without the possibility of friendship, his life stood achingly empty. Zadie undoubtedly seethed in a raging fury at his ploy. At best, she'd chalk it up to a quick attempt at an alibi. At worst, she'd detect the ring of truth in his voice. Or was it the other way around?

Go away, he ordered his treacherous thoughts, desperately attempting to shove his emotions back into the tightly latched box where they were usually imprisoned. Once out, however, his heart cavorted madly through hot flashes and cold chills of frustration and despair. His coolly calculating mind lacked the strength to lasso them and coral them back into submission.

From the way the Boss was congratulating his deviousness, Will knew he was expected to keep up the charade. It was ten times worse than seducing a total stranger to destroy a movement, for now it involved the betrayal of a genuine friend. But, his other option was to turn against his assignment . . . a choice Will coldly assessed that he would not survive.

Zadie arrived back in DC crackling like a live wire, snapping and thundering with pent-up fury. They'd been mobbed by the media from airport security gate to taxicab to the steps of Tansy's house. She'd seen the vitriolic posts of incensed women all across the country snarling that *a slut like her didn't deserve Charlie Rider.* The tabloid racks screamed false headlines along with photos of her and Will.

Charlie opened the door, grimacing at the jostling reporters as Tansy warded them off. There was so much commotion that Will was in the door before Charlie realized it. With an affronted shock, he whirled on Zadie.

"What's he doing here?" Charlie exclaimed.

"Don't start," Zadie snapped back. "I've got death threats in my inbox, angry picketers at the airport, and women threatening to put strychnine in my food and steal your heart. I need a break, not an argument. He's here because I said so."

She stormed up the stairs without looking back. Charlie chased after her, leaving Tansy to deal with Will. When he spun in the door to their room, Zadie tackled him, pinning him to the wall with a long, breathtaking kiss.

Charlie reeled in confusion at the sudden, ferocious change of mood.

"He's up to something, Charlie," she blurted out in a hushed tone, her lips close to his ear. "Those were Roots at the transformer station. They knew Will, and I recognized two of them from guard duty around here."

She'd been waiting all week to tell him. She pulled him over to the edge of the bed, sat down, and related the conversation she had overheard.

"So, why do you think he was trying to stop them?" Charlie asked, confused.

Zadie shook her head with a shrug. It didn't make sense.

"We have to find out what the Roots are up to," she said.

"Well, at the moment, they're guarding the house."

"Better that than blowing up power stations," Zadie pointed out.

"Do you trust him?" Charlie asked, incredulous.

"Will?" Zadie replied, eyes clouded. "I don't know what to make of him. One minute, I suspect he's undermining our every move. The next minute, he's genuinely trying to help us. I don't like having him here, but we have to keep an eye on him. That's the only reason I'm not throwing him out by the scruff of his neck."

She flared with indignation. A slow smile curled across Charlie's face.

"Not because you're - "

Zadie spun toward him.

"No, of course not," she cried.

Charlie sighed in relief.

She stilled, hands on hips, head tilted to one side. Charlie's breath caught in his chest; the ache of longing pulsed in his veins. He loved every inch of her - the wild tangle of black curls, the way her left earlobe stuck out further than the right, the curve of her collarbone, breasts rounding the fabric of her shirt, those endless legs, thighs pressing fullness into the circle of her skirt. The gulf of time and distance sat in the space between them, made treacherous by gossip and rumors. Charlie flushed, suddenly uncertain of the next move. He'd spent hours staring into space, rehearsing this moment - all his words of forgiveness or accusation, hurts, longing - all of it fell away. He loved her. Simple as that. He had loved her for forever and a day, and would love her for all eternity, despite the odds and obstacles.

"Come here," he said, but it was he who crossed the empty distance.

Zadie's grin spread into her cheeks. The familiar smell of his soap brought tears to her eyes. They folded together like a pair of magnets, limb for limb, curve into hollow. Zadie kissed him ferociously, toppling him backwards onto the bed. She'd been taller than him in bare feet until tenth grade when his last burst of height brought his gaze even with hers. In middle school, she'd been able to drag him out of fistfights with other boys, and even now, she suspected she could arm wrestle him to the table.

"I love you, Charlie," she told him.

"Do you?" he asked with such sincere sweetness - as if he truly wondered - that she had to blink back tears again.

"Yes," Zadie replied, "and if I had your gift for words, I could tell you how much."

Charlie grinned at her.

"No, you couldn't," he answered. "Trust me. There aren't any words for this love."

Late that night, when the clock hands suspended at the peak of the unending cycle of time, Charlie woke. The pooling darkness hummed with life. The air slid through the slightly opened window, sweet and sensuous. Zadie curled against his side, breathing in the soft rhythm of sleep. The length of her body rose and fell in silken whispers. The whole night seduced him toward rest, but his mind grumbled awake, roiling with thought. The harsh itch of his curiosity burned. He turned his face toward the window, the angles of his cheekbones forming darker shadows as his brow caught the faint glow of tired streetlights.

Who were the Roots working for? Some unseen hand directed them. He had tried searching records; Tucker caught him at it and told him to cease - he was clumsy as an elephant and twice as obvious. Tucker promised to discretely investigate, but thus far, he had found only dead ends and silence. The records on Will Sharp told them only what they already knew. Tucker warned Charlie against reading too much into them, anyway.

"Records are a lousy measure of a person, Charlie," he reminded the youth. "According to the databases, you're a juvenile delinquent turned domestic terrorist who was accused of treason and crimes against the state before overthrowing the government."

Charlie shot him an appalled glance.

"Records leave out details like love, justice, and a person's reasons for resisting authority," Tucker commented. "Motivations and long stories are reduced to dry lines in official records . . . all the more so if one hasn't written extensively and occupied the national spotlight as you have. For better or for worse, controversy is more revealing than silence when it comes to sleuthing out the arc of a person's life."

Well, Charlie thought, lying wide-awake, *I know one way to find out.*

He slid out from the comfortable tangle of Zadie's limbs, dressed silently and went downstairs. Will was peering out the slats of the blinds and spun at the sound of Charlie's step.

"Sit down, Will," he said. "We need to talk."

Will looked like he'd rather get a root canal, but he circled the couch and sat down.

"Look," he offered, running a hand over his close-cropped hair and leaning his elbows on his knees. "There's nothing between me and Zadie. I just had to come up with an excuse - fast - for being there."

"I know," Charlie answered easily.

"You do?" Will echoed in surprise.

Charlie smiled wryly.

"Yes. If you really loved her, you'd be working a lot harder to win her heart," he pointed out. "Believe me, I know. I spent years at it."

Will hid a smile.

"What I'd really like to know," Charlie continued, fiddling with the fringe on a throw pillow, "is why you were at the transformer station in the first place."

"I was trying to stop the sabotage," he answered with a scowl.

Charlie lifted an eyebrow.

"Stop it? Or set it off?"

Will sighed.

"To stop it. It wasn't strategic. It put Zadie and I at risk."

"Zadie told me those were Roots you were arguing with."

Will tensed.

"Why does she think that?" he asked carefully.

Charlie toyed with the pillow.

"She recognized one of them from around here."

Will swore silently. His mind raced, trying to find a way to protect everyone - Zadie, the Roots, himself - from the danger of Charlie's questions.

"Who do you work for, Will?"

"Curiosity and cats, Charlie. You're treading into dangerous territory," he warned, rising and walking toward the kitchen to signal that the conversation was over.

"Is it the Butcher?" Charlie pressed, following him.

Will spun at him so fast Charlie's back was against the wall before the end of his sentence.

"Stay away from the Butcher," Will growled, an edge of fear lacing his tone. "That man is crazy. Dangerous. We don't work for him."

"You don't work for us, either," Charlie shot back. "Your Roots have become nothing but trouble."

"Nothing but trouble is my middle name, Charlie, and without my *trouble*, you and Zadie would be fertilizing cornfields in Kansas, mowed down by a sniper on a moonlit night."

Charlie stiffened. Until now, he had doubted Will's claims of protection, but he remembered that night. No one had been around except him and Zadie - or so he thought. They had been hidden out at Tucker's house in Kansas, walking at night in the seemingly deserted cornfields, saying goodbye before she left to organize with Inez.

"You were there," he stammered weakly. "I should thank you."

"Don't bother," Will replied gruffly, loosening his pinning grip. "Just leave well enough alone."

He let go of Charlie and stalked into the kitchen, avoiding the other man's eyes. He'd been the only person in that cornfield with a gun. The bullet he had stopped from firing was his own. He reached for a cup of coffee and shivered.

Back then, he hadn't exchanged two words with Zadie. He'd been stopped by the expression on her face that night, a tender intensity that glowed like the moon, shining with all of her gentle compassion and fierce love. As he crouched hidden, it seemed to him that if he destroyed that, he would be the most cowardly, miserable creature ever to exist.

He returned to confront the Boss, and persuasively argued that there was more to be gained by helping Charlie and Zadie succeed than by assassinating them. The Boss surveyed the field of political power and agreed. That was when the Roots had been formed.

"How many times did you save my life?' Charlie asked, holding out a coffee mug for Will to pour the pot into.

"Just once for you," he said, "but without our help, Zadie and Inez would be stuck in prison, and the corporate dictatorship might still be in power."

"I doubt it," Charlie muttered, thinking of the millions of people who had struggled to end the old regime's rule. "Cut one dandelion down and the rest grow back stronger. Nothing can stop people when their hearts are set on change."

"Wish I had your faith," Will sighed, leaning against the counter.

Charlie watched him steadily.

"I think you do," he said slowly, "but you're just scared to admit it."

"Scared?" Will scoffed. "Why would I be scared?"

"Because, if people can create a new world nonviolently, you'd have to figure out who you are without your gun."

Will jolted. His coffee sloshed over the rim of the mug.

"Think about it," Charlie urged softly. "You'd be Will Sharp, the guy who saved my life, the guy who kept Zadie and Inez out of prison; the guy who supported the kids in saving their school, who stood blocking a bridge to protect the water and the earth; the guy who supported Zadie through the fear of the drones, and who tried to prevent an act of sabotage created by his pals."

Will flushed, hearing his actions described that way.

"Careful, Charlie," he joked, "it's starting to sound like you don't hate me."

"I don't hate you," Charlie blurted out then broke off as hard honesty choked him. A flush crept up around his ears.

"Come on," Will mocked, "admit it, you'd love to fight me."

"I am fighting you," Charlie told him softly, "just not with punches. I'm pummeling you with all my strengths: respect, patience, kindness. We all are - Inez, Zadie, Idah - we're all chipping away at the armor over your heart using love and compassion."

"The hell you are," Will grumbled, brushing away roughly and retreating to the living room.

Charlie sipped the lukewarm coffee, thoughtful. If Will was stopping the Roots from doing sabotage and coming up with alibis for Zadie, they weren't just putting up a good fight . . . they were winning.

"When this is all over - " he started to say.

" - it's never over, Charlie," Will interrupted with a pained expression. "There's always someone greedy for more, willing to hurt others to get what they want. And when your back's to the wall, you're going to want all your options on the table."

Charlie sat down quietly.

"My back's been to the wall since I wrote the first essay of the Man From the North," he reminded Will. "I've been threatened, hunted, almost murdered, forced to living in hiding, and nearly killed by a drone, but I never reached for violence. Not once in all that time did I think it would protect me better than the real change we were working for. Justice. Respect. Peace. Democracy. Kindness. Those are what protect us in the long run, Will, and I've never seen them come through violence."

Charlie's smile tugged at the corners of his mouth.

"That's the thing about those moments when you're in a tight corner. When your back's to the wall, your heart has to lead."

Will stared at him for a long moment then shook his head.

"That's what I like about you, Charlie," he grumbled. "You say the craziest things in such a way that I almost believe them."

"Would it be such a bad thing to believe them?" Charlie dared to ask.

Will sighed. He opened his mouth to answer, but he never got the chance.

CHAPTER TWENTY-SEVEN

· · · · ·

Assassins

A thud landed on the roof. They froze. Will dove for the light and turned it off.

"What are you doing? We can't see!"

"Neither can they," Will hissed. "Now shut up."

"Probably a raccoon."

"Too heavy. Those were boots."

"Who - "

"Assassin. Now, stuff it."

They climbed the stairs swiftly, reaching the landing on the same stride. Charlie looked at all the doors - Tucker, Tansy, Zadie - but Will shook his head and pointed to Zadie's door then to the roof. A slight scrape overhead moved toward the east gable. Will motioned for Charlie to stay put and eased toward the door. Charlie's heart raced, churning for solutions. His eyes settled on a glass-paneled fire alarm that must have been installed during the days of multiple roommates and shared housing. He leapt for it, smashed the glass, and hollered at the top of his lungs.

"Get up! Get up! Everybody out of bed!"

"What are you doing?!!" Will yelled.

"Out! Out!" Charlie yelled, banging and pounding doors, gambling that the noise and commotion would send the assassin running while the fire alarm brought the police and emergency responders to their door. "Fire! Call 911. Everybody move. Fire!"

Will didn't bother to try to put out this imaginary fire. He burst into Zadie's room just in time to see a figure lurking in the window with a gun trained on Zadie.

"Drop it!" he yelled, reaching for his weapon automatically and clenching on air.

He cursed. The figure pushed off the window so hard the glass splintered and shards smashed out of the frame. The attacker rappelled to the ground, unlocked in a practiced motion, and darted across the yard toward a waiting car.

Will sprang to the window, swore as he sliced his hand, then dove for the stairs. He slammed out the front door and pelted down the street after the screeching tires of the car.

The fire trucks arrived five minutes later. Police cordoned off the street. Will Sharp was already half a mile away, heading to the headquarters of the man who had sent the assassin.

The house sat in a row of subdued multimillion-dollar mansions masquerading as modest homes, protected by state-of-the-art security systems and private guards. The occupants rotated every election cycle as new faces ousted the old guard of politicians - all of whom found the humble, down-to-earth colonial facades convenient masks to disguise their wealth and ensure the common man's vote. The home he raced toward usually sat empty - its occupants still owned it, but had recently taken up residence in a more prestigious house across town - but Will knew from experience that the man he sought would be here tonight. He liked to retreat to the comfort of his old study when plots were afoot.

Will skidded around the corner and pounded on the door.

"He's awake," Will snarled at the butler, eyeing the light in the study window. "Tell him Will Sharp wants to talk to him. Now."

In minutes, the door opened again and Will was escorted into the private lair of the Boss.

"This is going too far," he fumed, not bothering with greetings, slamming his sweaty palms on the mahogany desk.

"Oh no, I'm afraid it hasn't even come close," the tenor voice chuckled.

The leather chair swiveled around.

John C. Friend eyed Will Sharp.

"You said she wouldn't get hurt," Will reminded him, furious.

"She didn't, did she?"

"You had one of the Butcher's assassins right out the window!"

"Tut tut, Will. He had orders to miss."

Will's chest heaved as his ears rang with disbelief. He knew the Butcher's agents. They were bloodthirsty. Cold-hearted. They couldn't be trusted.

"Where were my Roots? They were supposed to be on guard duty?"

"I gave them the night off," Friend answered cheerfully. "After all, you were there, weren't you? You could have shot the assassin. Isn't that ostensibly why you're hanging around? Protection?"

Will shook his head.

"I had no gun," he admitted. "You ordered me to disarm when Zadie said to, remember?"

He hurled the words back at Friend accusingly.

"Ah yes, that's right. Ironic. Perhaps proves Charlie's theory that this nonviolence stuff works . . . but it undermines the need for the Roots' protection. Maybe we should - "

"Try again and I'll kill the bastard with my bare hands and then come after you," Will threatened impulsively.

"Come, come, be reasonable. I had to do it. How can I move against their enemies if they're never in danger?"

"Their 'enemies' are you and your agents," Will said bluntly.

"That's implausible, dear boy," Friend reminded him smugly. "According to public opinion, their enemies are the various factions of the corporate elite - and since they'll all be sweating bullets trying not to get framed for this while sniffing out who actually did it, I have them all in the palm of my hand."

"They'll catch on at some point," Will warned.

"Oh, I doubt it. People never see beyond their own noses."

Charlie does, Will realized, remembering the midnight conversation. He stayed silent though, mentioning none of that to Friend.

"You look disturbed."

"You could have at least warned me."

"Will," Friend said soothingly, "don't you trust me? Haven't I always said I'd look out for you?"

As long as I remain loyal to you, Will added silently. Friend had gotten him out of trouble, cleared his juvenile delinquency charges, paid for special ops courses after his military training, selected him above others for tasks that required discretion and subtlety, and rewarded him handsomely over the years. Friend had turned him from a charity case into a valued agent.

"Don't worry, Will. I have no intention of killing the Zadie Byrd. I even spent hours talking the Butcher out of killing her. She's the one person who is more valuable alive than dead."

The way he chuckled gave Will shivers.

"Go back and do your job, Will. Don't make me do everything myself."

Shaken and exhausted, Charlie and Zadie blearily drank another cup of nerve-jangling coffee. Tansy paced the kitchen, unable to settle down as she burnt toast and banged into chairs. Alex came over as soon as she heard the news, calling in sick at work. Tucker sprawled on the sofa, staring blankly at his computer screen. Suddenly, he bolted upright. His mouth fell open. Wordlessly, he passed the computer to Charlie.

Rubbing his eyes, it took a moment for the letters to focus properly and even longer before he could comprehend the missive posted on the Alternet from the Roots. He showed Zadie.

"No," she moaned. "Oh, no, no, no."

The Roots had burst fully out of the underground, erupting from hiding and declaring their presence as the *hardcore edge* of the Dandelion Insurrection. They called for armed self-defense by every member of the Dandelion Insurrection. The attempted assassination of Zadie Byrd Gray showed that no haven was safe, no person secure.

Our friends and families are in danger, the post stated. *We cannot wait for the paltry protection of the Interim Government or other authorities. Where were they when the gunman aimed through the window last night? We will not simply remain passive and allow people to die. Be vigilant. Be ready. If they come for us, we will stop them. We will fight our assailants, no matter who they may be - pawns of corporate elites, madmen, or even government agents. We have come to a crossroads where we must question the incompetence and politics of the Interim Government. One has to wonder if John C. Friend is a friend of the people . . . or the friend of the corporate elites?*

Zadie lunged for the phone and left a blistering message for Will, accusing him of writing the piece . . . or if he hadn't, then demanding that he get the Roots under control. The call-to-arms was a dangerous overreaction. Charlie whipped out a counter message, criticizing the Roots' missive, and urging caution, not hysteria. He had just begun a larger essay when the morning news reports began blasting the story of the assassination attempt, fear mongering more than fact-telling.

At eight o'clock in the morning, John C. Friend released an official Interim Government statement and held a press conference. He stated his shock and horror at the assassination attempt on one of the nation's greatest heroines.

"Every effort will be made to find the culprits. We shall leave no stone unturned in the course of the investigation. We have already tragically lost her mother. We will not lose Zadie Byrd Gray."

Charlie snorted and hacked as a burst of coffee splashed up his nose.

"The gall - " he spluttered.

"Shhh, he's not done," Zadie said, urging him to be quiet as Friend studied his notes. He cleared his throat and looked sternly at the camera.

"In regards to the accusations in the recent missive posted by the Roots, I have only one response."

His tone dropped into a growl of a warning.

"Be careful which fights you pick. No matter how beloved by the populace, a movement that cannot discipline its followers to its espoused principles must be held in check by the weight of the government, which holds the responsibility of protecting the safety and security of the nation. You say that I am not your friend . . . but I warn you: you do not want me as your enemy."

Friend switched gears abruptly, smiling reassuringly to the good citizens.

"In light of all of this, the Interim Government has taken decisive action to ensure public safety and national security, reduce the risk of assassinations, minimize the possibilities of violence in our streets, and to protect public infrastructure."

Charlie, Zadie, Tansy, Alex, and Tucker listened in stunned silence as Friend enumerated the points of the new American Protection Act that had been passed unanimously in emergency session early that morning. To protect the cherished right to free speech, only limited protests could be held in designated areas by permit to ensure government protection of citizens from any threat of violence. Large assemblies and public demonstrations were banned. New levels of surveillance were allowed to federal agencies in the hope that they could stop potential assassinations. Friend mentioned several more points, but Charlie buried his head in his hands and stopped listening.

"We're back at square one," he groaned. "Nothing has changed at all."

Zadie lifted his head out of hiding.

"That's not true, Charlie. We've changed. The Dandelion Insurrection has changed. The people have changed. When we started, people were scared and isolated, unwilling to challenge injustice. Now look at us!"

She swept her arm to the nation. In small towns and large cities, thousands boldly stood up on behalf of life, liberty, and love. The streets hummed with actions. Hearts pulsed with passion. The clouds of apathy and fear had been driven off by the determination of the people to end injustice. The Alternet surged with rallying cries and astute warnings; no longer was the Man From the North a lone voice calling out in the thicket of danger and fear. On the heels of Friend's announcement of the Protection Act, organizers across the wide expanse of the country had already leapt into strategizing conference calls and flurries of email exchanges. Few breaths wasted bemoaning the legislation; they cut straight to the chase of how to resist it.

"Let's call the Dandelion Swarm into action," Zadie urged, burning with the fierce indignation of a woman tired of being manipulated by political forces. For the Interim Government to use her life as the rationale for the Protection Act rankled her soul and offended her dignity. Zadie's eyes narrowed with anger. Friend would pay dearly for that. He would learn that she was not a toy, a puppet, or a mechanical doll to be propped up to serve his goals. He could not invoke her mother's death to restrict the very freedoms Ellen had struggled for in life.

"We'll take the streets - our streets - in mass defiance of the law," she vowed. "We'll defy it into the dust of its folly. We'll force them to repeal it."

Tansy nodded in approval, her mind racing into the inevitable landscape of arrests, court cases, and her legal arguments in defense of the First Amendment. She clapped Zadie on the back.

"Give me a dozen arrestees and I'll wrangle this bill all the way up to the Supreme Court. We'll get it overturned no matter how many rodeo circuits of courts I've got to ride it through."

Alex shifted uneasily. Her nose twitched with unspoken concerns. She sensed a trap. This was Friend, after all. If he put out the cheese, there was bound to be a catch. It was too obvious. Defiance and protest were the Dandelion Insurrection's strong suits. Friend had to know the people would rebel against the American Protection Act. He was leading them into a box canyon, a blind alley, a position between rocks and hard places. Alex heard the passion in Zadie's tone and shivered. Friend had provoked them into a bull's charge . . . an approach that made a cautious mouse like Alex nervous. She stayed quiet as the campaign launched, but from the start, trouble showed up.

Outside of Chicago, Idah Robbins led the whole school district in a student-teacher walkout and marched, carrying banners that spanned the street. They made it all the way downtown before they ran into trouble. At the corner of Main and Second Street, the local police department had lined up to stop them. The police chief stared balefully at the students, teachers, and families, and exhaled in a long sigh. He respected Idah Robbins, but she stirred up trouble for justice like a favorite cocktail after work. He sometimes wished she had a normal hobby like crocheting or marathon running. The chief was four years out from retirement and secretly longed to rescue kittens from treetops until the day he turned in his badge. He'd hauled this police department out of the despicable morass of brutality, racism, over-policing, and unaccountability, and had a scar in his guts from routing out the cabal of officers behind the worst of the trouble. He was a legend in the community and didn't appreciate having to arrest the local elementary school students and teachers when he already had his swansong of a retirement speech half-written in his head. All in all, Idah Robbins' restorative justice programs at the school had spared him a solid decade of youth-related migraines and he felt he owed an unspoken debt to the teacher.

He cleared his throat, hoping to find a way out of this collision of justice and law enforcement. As he began speaking to Idah, she caught a flash of movement to her right.

"No!" she shouted, and then threw her body between one of the Solidarity Hotline volunteers and a police officer. A baton cracked down on her shoulder and a punch knocked the wind out of her lungs. She staggered, but remained standing long enough for some fellow teachers to pull the explosively outraged volunteer back from attacking the officers.

That night, icing her shoulder with a bag of frozen peas, she contacted Inez.

"Double your trainings and put your peace teams in place," she warned the New York City organizer. "Tempers are running high, and I'm worried that volunteer was planted just to incite violence."

Inez frowned with concern. She had already scheduled a mass protest. A city street demonstration is an unruly beast compared to the organized community of Los Jardineros. The Roots' call to self-defense - at home and in the street - found fertile ground in a populace battered by police assaults. As the Roots abandoned secrecy and erupted onto the scene with a swagger of toughness, some people began to mimic their all-black styles and militant attitudes. They pushed back when shoved, attacked when insulted, and posted warnings and threats to all who opposed them. Inez argued reason, strategy, morality, and spirituality until she grew lightheaded from wasted breaths. She had no qualms about the people's right to self-defense at home, or on an individual level, but when the people went out protesting with baseball bats, the line between defense and offense blurred. The more protesters readied for battle, the more the police armed up to thwart the attacks. And as the officers brought out the armored cars, the people suited up for war.

The day of Inez' protest arrived. The ire of the masses marched into the streets. The police chief was waiting with tear gas and riot gear. Vans for arrests idled behind him. Thousands of marchers poured out from all corners of the city, and when the tide of people slammed up against the hard shore of police, the tenuous hold on peaceful protest shattered. Coughing on tear gas, Inez found herself struggling to hold back the attacks of her own marchers. She saw shops being ransacked, the wares seized as volleys of projectiles to hurl back at the police - cabbages, used books, sunglasses, football-sized papayas - Inez ducked under a frozen octopus as it sailed overhead. Protesters snatched up sunglasses for eye protection and umbrellas served as shields and sticks. Police chased them down and began beating people into submission. Inez hauled back on the arm of one of her newer organizers - a young man Father Ramon had recommended, though Inez had heard the youth arguing in favor of sabotage. He was twice her size and hauled her off her feet.

"Cop lover," he snarled, shaking free and shouting. "We have a right to protect ourselves!"

In the chaos, his cry fell on desperate ears. Inez' voice calling for discipline was drowned out by the bellow of larger chests. She saw women and elders running in all directions. Her peace teams were overwhelmed, battered and struggling. Police kneed people in the back as they tightened twist-tie handcuffs and shoved faces into concrete.

Something slammed into her. She spun, reeled and saw a glimpse of an officer as she fell. Hours later, she woke with a baseball-sized lump and flashes of light burning in her eyes, a bloody nose drying crusty, and a concerned pack of women hovering over her in the holding cell of a nearby jail.

"Get ahold of Zadie," she tried to say, "tell her to be careful about who comes to actions."

She was certain that organizer who snarled at her was a provocateur.

The next day, Tucker got a call from Gus Reasonover saying the Texas Free Rangers were riding into Dallas carrying guns and ready to swing punches in defense of the First *and* Second Amendment, outraged over police brutality in New York City.

"I'm sorry, Tuck," Gus groaned. "I tried my darnedest, but they threw me out for being a pansy-livered, spineless toadstool. Thought you ought to know they've gone rogue, so Charlie can get out an article denouncing them ahead of the upcoming brawl."

Charlie's denouncement of the Texas Free Ranger Riot, as the headlines called it later, triggered an inflammatory missive in response from the Roots, calling him a coward and a hypocrite. *The people,* they said, *had a right to self-defense and protest. They were not the punching bags of the police.* At demonstrations around the country, the crowds grew rowdier, throwing punches, lighting dumpsters on fire, and breaking car windows. And the Dandelion Insurrection got blamed.

"Control your people," Friend warned.

A melee erupted at a protest in Denver. Hundreds wound up in the hospital.

"The Dandelion Insurrection and the Roots are becoming a menace to public safety," Friend growled on national television, calling for discipline. "I warned you not to make me your enemy. The laws must be upheld."

The Roots and the riot police exchanged bricks and rubber bullets.

"The Dandelion Insurrection has devolved into thugs and criminals," Friend stated publicly, regretful and stern, striking a chord of sympathy among the faction that was irritated over street closures and smashed windows, subway shut downs, and widespread unrest that made them think twice about going out to the store.

Police lost all sympathy for the protesters, swinging away from the favorable stance they had taken during the days of the general strike and march on DC.

"This isn't working," Alex cried. "We have to call off the campaign."

"I'm not sure we can," Charlie admitted worriedly.

People swarmed the streets in formations of boiling fury and frustration, venting outrage over years of injustice, lashing out without strategy. The police fought heated battles with citizens, trying to obey orders to suppress, disperse, and arrest the rioters. The media pounded the movement, striking back at Charlie Rider for his earlier critiques, searing him with a litany of epithets: traitor, coward, terrorist, criminal, weakling. They lambasted him for the violence at the same time that they mocked him for calling for nonviolence. They tore him to shreds and threw the confetti of his public image in the air as they cackled with glee.

In a snit of strategic indignation, Alex snapped at Zadie and Charlie until they conceded to the foolhardiness of large demonstrations and agreed to use a more focused, trained group to challenge the Protection Act in the District of Columbia.

Two days later, the twenty-five activists, along with Charlie and Zadie, converged in front of the White House, golden yellow from head to toe, speaking to the alerted media as they watched the beat cop call in reinforcements and order them to disperse.

"We will not leave," Zadie declared. "We are here to assert our constitutional right to speech and assembly, without which the word *democracy* is nothing more than a hollow mockery of the idea."

They had worked too hard, struggled too long, and sacrificed too much to back down from tyranny under the guise of public safety. Charlie nudged her discretely as a line of police officers assembled. Zadie nodded, but continued talking without missing a beat.

"The Protection Act is just a replay of the same laws that led us down the descent into fear and authoritarian control," she said.

The circle of officers tightened suddenly, cutting Charlie and Zadie off from the rest of the dandelions. From the sounds behind them, Charlie guessed rough-handed arrests were underway. He spoke up, hoping to distract and de-escalate some of the bristling officers.

"Shut up," one said bluntly.

The icy venom in the tone brought him up short. Charlie cursed silently as an officer began badgering Zadie, pushing her backward with the tip of his baton until she bumped into the body armor of another officer. The media jostled for views, riveted by the tension of the scene like flies on a carcass. Charlie caught the eye of the citizen journalists and silently urged them to elbow in closer. If the officer got rough, their images and footage would be essential in making the violence backfire on the government. He couldn't trust the corporate media not to distort or bury the story, but the citizen journalists would plaster the Alternet with outrage, using Zadie's courageous vulnerable stand to galvanize people into action. He turned his focus back to Zadie as she locked eyes with the aggressive officer. Charlie saw the snake's coil of the man's muscles tense.

"No!" Charlie cried. Burly arms reached out from the wall of uniforms and choked him from behind, hauling him up onto his toe tips.

The officer backhanded Zadie across the jaw, sending her stumbling to the side.

"You don't have to do this," she told him between gasps, rising to her full height again. The media zoomed in on the blood streaming from her split lip and the rising red of her cheek.

The officer slammed his baton across Zadie's ribs. She cried out and doubled. Charlie felt the choking grip lighten. Hands shoved Charlie forward. He whirled. The officer's face was unreadable.

It's a trap, he heard Alex's voice echo in his thoughts. *Be careful.*

Zadie staggered to her feet, hands on ribs, eyes squeezing and blinking back tears of pain. The officer raised his club. Charlie darted forward.

CRACK!

The blow meant for Zadie hit his back. Stars electrocuted in his eyes. He arched.

CRACK!

The officer hit him again as he threw his arm out over Zadie.

"Stop."

Her voice shot through the cries of the protesters as they peered, handcuffed, through legs and shoulders of officers. Zadie rose to stand over Charlie, neither pleading nor threatening, but firmly defying the violence with every ounce of courage in her body. A surreal calm settled on her. Her mother whispered in her heart.

"If you beat us down, we will rise up," she told him softly. "If you strike one of us, our beloveds will come to shield us from the blow. There are millions of us. Your arms will tire before we cease resisting. Stop this, now."

The officer stared at her, incredulous at her defiance. His scowl darkened. One of his officers called out to just arrest them. He shook his head in tight dismissal, rage in his eyes. He raised his arm to strike. Zadie did not flinch. The man's hand heaved on the fury of his breath. She refused to turn her head. His grip tightened.

Zadie's eyes softened. Just as she had done in the desert when she lit the spark in Frank Novaro and catalyzed people nationwide, she called up in her heart the Love that cracked reality and defied the limits of possibility. She gathered it inside her, magnificent and wild. She let it build, blossom, and rise towering over the street, higher than the day it had walked, electric, in the bodies of the people under the shadows of the drones; more massive than the night it had gathered like the breath of a tsunami, carving out the space to enter the earth through this young midwife to the coming world.

This great Love stared into the eyes of the officer, poured into the angry and fearful corners of his mind, reached deep under his armored heart, and touched the vein of common humanity.

He breathed.

She breathed.

No one spoke.

Her eyes forgave him, told him she knew his challenges, his orders, his worries about his job, his frustrations with the protestors, his concerns for his country, the pain in his lower back, the hidden loneliness in his soul, his drinking problem, his dying mother - everything and more.

He lowered his hand a fraction of an inch.

Breaths began to release in the crowd of people.

"No, you bastard!" The words exploded with a snarl of motion as someone leapt through the circle and punched the officer, once in the balls, doubling him over, then under the jaw, sending him staggering back. Charlie ducked as bodies crashed into the circle of police and spotted Will pummeling the officer.

The Roots were fighting back.

"Stop!" he shouted, but his voice was lost in the eruption of roars. Limbs flung every direction. Bodies barreled left and right.

"Get moving. Now!" Will hurled the words at them as an officer to the side. "Take Zadie and go! This is going to get ugly and there's nothing you can do."

Will skidded over to Charlie's side, hauled him to his feet, seized Zadie by the arm, and thrust them through the madness, pulling them into a flat-out run then shoving them forward down the street. He wheeled and returned to the fray.

Charlie and Zadie stumble to a halt. Tears welled in Zadie's eyes as she clutched her ribs. Charlie's shoulder screamed louder than the wailing sirens approaching.

"Go! Go!" a voice cried.

A yellow-clad dandelion came hurtling toward them.

"But we have to - " Zadie gasped out.

"Get out of here, like we agreed," the man reminded her, seizing their shoulders, spinning them into motion, and propelling them toward one of their strategized escape routes. They had agreed to scatter if the situation turned violent or fatally dangerous.

As they ran, cries of pain chased their heels.

CHAPTER TWENTY-EIGHT

. . . . .

Dare To Love

Sharp Saves Zadie; Roots Rescue Revolutionary Duo
Every headline in the nation blared the news of "The White
House Fight". The Roots rocketed to stardom, and Will Sharp
was featured on the five o'clock news.

"I just did what any man would have done," he shrugged,
his face carefully expressionless, a black eye bruising his socket,
a seam of blood running down his eyebrow as the cops shoved
him toward the station.

"Anyone except Charlie Rider," one newscaster joked
maliciously to the other. "He just stood there, the wimp. I'd
have punched the cop."

"Me too, Al," the other man agreed. "The president is
expected to make a public statement on the attack at six o'clock.
Stay tuned. Meanwhile, groups across the country are signing
up for self-defense courses. *If the cops attack,* they say, *we'll fight
back.*"

Charlie buried his face in his hands, clenching his hair in
frustration. Zadie paced the length of Tansy's living room, icing
her ribs and cheek. Tansy's voice pounded like a jackhammer in
the study as she alternately cursed the Roots to hell and back,
and finagled legal support for the eighteen dandelions that had
been arrested.

"Should have let him rot," her voice snarled.

She popped her head out the door to update the others.

"Someone posted bail for Will. He's getting released soon."

"Who's picking him up?" Zadie asked wearily.

283

"Not us," Tansy retorted firmly. "He can go back to whatever demon hell he came from, so far's I'm concerned."

"He was trying to help," Zadie pointed out.

"Bull cockle. He's an agent provocateur - all the Roots are, I swear on the Pope."

"Tansy has a point," Charlie put in. "He's been nothing but trouble."

"He stopped the cop," Zadie said, trying to be fair.

"He hamstrung the rest of us, Zadie," Charlie snapped back. "He turned our action into a street brawl and our team took the blows."

"Charlie - "

"Stop defending him!" he bellowed, his frayed temper snapping. "That's all you do, no matter what trouble he causes, you keep sticking up for him!"

"What were you going to do? Let the officer beat me bloody?"

"You were handling him. He was backing down," Charlie protested.

"And if he hadn't?" she challenged.

"I'd have tried to block him - "

"But you wouldn't have fought back - "

"No!" he snapped. He took a deep breath and tried to slow the hot burn of his frustration. "This is a movement, Zadie, and you've said it over and over: we have more power unarmed and beaten than we do through violence. When we go into the streets to take action, we're using our nonviolence for a purpose. You know that."

Zadie looked up at the ceiling, tears brimming in her eyes. She knew the dynamics of struggle as well as he did. She knew the Roots' attack would trigger harsher repression on everyone else. She knew Will's punch had thwarted her effort to de-escalate the danger and actually shoved more people into harm's way. She knew all these things intellectually, but a shaken part of her also remembered the times she'd been beaten senseless by an abusive man. Every terror of those days was still throbbing, toxic, in her veins.

Courage had surged through her in the heat of the moment, but now, as the adrenaline fled from her limbs, the pain of her injuries evoked old fears. Long-buried uncertainties rose up. Stinging barbs of criticisms jabbed at her, including the memory of a sanctimonious nurse at a religious hospital telling her that the beating was punishment for the sin of her wild ways. The vitriol of the hate mail she had received in the past months scorched her. *A slut like you doesn't deserve Charlie Rider,* women across the country had screeched at her. The poison of hate sinks into people in strange ways, and a vulnerable, scarred part of her believed the gossips that deemed her unworthy.

Zadie's lips trembled as she looked at Charlie. Underneath their talk of movements and strategy, a deeper strand of worry had gnawed at her for months, haunting the unspoken words beneath their arguments over Will Sharp, the Roots, protection, and dangers. She listened to Charlie reject Will's protection over and over, and wondered if he took the dangers seriously . . . and a very quiet, hidden part of her worried that he didn't care if she got hurt.

"I guess," she confessed quietly, "part of me wanted you to stop that cop, Charlie. I - I guess I wanted to know you cared more about me than about the movement . . . and that you loved me more than your principles."

Charlie's mouth fell open, speechless. His anger dissipated like steam off a cooling pot. Of course he loved her . . . how could she doubt that? He loved her the way heroes of ancient stories loved: he would do the impossible for her. He would rearrange the stars for her; he would traverse the underworld and challenge death for her; he would make the sun and moon dance across the sky for her. And, in a way, he had. As a mere mortal, a man who not-so-very-long ago had been nothing more than a boy working at a small town newspaper, he had already accomplished miracles.

But that was the catch; his love demanded more than that. It wasn't enough for her to be held secure and safe behind his strength. Heroes of today had harder tasks than rescuing damsels in distress or defending princesses in towers. The days of strong-arm heroes, of Odysseus and Hercules, were done. Zadie was no Penelope to stay at home, waiting for him to return victorious. No, she was an adventurer, a creator, a heroine in her own right. She deserved a whole world of freedom, safety, respect, and dignity. And such a world was best forged through nonviolent action - the entire weight of history, studies, and statistics demonstrated that. It was built from the kind of courage that breaks the cycles of violence and domination even as it ends systems of oppression and injustice.

Charlie stared at Zadie as an encyclopedia of words pounded through him, trying to find a way to explain why he couldn't throw a punch - not because he *didn't* love her, but because he *did*. He could have fought off that cop - he'd lobbed plenty of punches in her defense back in high school - but the world in the wake of that fight wouldn't be any safer. The cop would come back harder and meaner, and while he could stand up for her over and over, what about everyone else? It wasn't enough to keep her protected if it meant her friends - Inez, Tansy, Tucker, Idah, Alex, Kinap - weren't also equally safe, able to protest injustice, stand up for their rights, and exercise their freedoms.

Love demanded this of him. Love demanded this of everyone. To care, not just about one person, but about the whole world. To work for justice, not just for those we know, but for everyone we don't. To keep not just our loved ones safe, but also keep the beloveds of strangers safe. To treat others with as much dignity and respect as we ourselves wish to be treated.

This was an idea that many people believed would never come to pass. It was the world of dreamers and idealists, an impossible vision, but this was the world Zadie deserved, the only kind of world worthy of her. And so, though the journey from here to there would make the greatest heroes blanch, he was willing to strive in that direction. That's how much he loved her.

Charlie gazed at Zadie as the long moment stretched until it brushed up against the eternal and the infinite. He held her eyes as the forms of body and time fell away. Love opens the gateway of a single person onto the limitless, if only we will dare to cross the threshold. For the love of one person, we can find the strength to love the whole world. Charlie dared to love Zadie without limits, without the blindfold of delusions. His love forced him to see the truth: there was no line where she stopped and the rest of the world began. It was all tied together, weaving through her breath into the trees, across the atmosphere, around the earth, touching every single human being, growing in the green and leafy plants, leaping in the animals, falling in the rain, running in the rivers, crashing in the ocean waves, rising into clouds, swirling across continents back into she and he as they stood with locked eyes searching for the words to say, *I love you.*

Charlie breathed in the whole vast being that was she and he, woven through their love, and dared to stumble over mortal words in search of truth.

"I love you, Zadie," he said simply, "but that love demands that I care about everyone else, too. I have to care about all the women - and the children - and the elderly - anyone standing defenseless. I have to care enough to let us risk getting hurt so we can create a world where everyone's rights are respected. I have to care enough to risk our lives so anyone - not just the strong - can protest in public spaces."

Charlie felt tears rolling down his cheeks, but he didn't stop.

"I could have fought off that officer, like Will did, but if the size of my shoulders determines your safety, what kind of freedom is that? Your rights shouldn't stop at the end of my fist. That's not right. You deserve a better world than that.

"And, if I love you, I have to find the courage to let you stare down hate and violence. I have to find the strength not to usurp your power with my fists. I have to muster the faith in our people that they will rise into action even if we fall, knowing that the beatings and arrests are wrong."

That was love, as far as he could see it, and he had to trust that her love was as vast and deep as his. He refused to believe that she could live with anything less than that. He knew her. And the Zadie Byrd Gray who had held his heart from the first moment that they met would never be able to live inside anyone's cage, let alone the false protection of Will Sharp's violence. Outside, the world howled about men and manhood, strength and power. The winds of opinion screamed against him, labeling him a pussy, a weakling, a coward. But violence is no measure of love, and even though he might not throw punches, he would leap in front of bullets for her, challenge tyrannical regimes, stand up for the beauty of the Earth, wage struggle with every breath in his body . . . and dare to love the whole world as deeply as he loved her.

Charlie opened his arms, inviting her to sense the depth of what he felt. Zadie embraced him back, but beneath the rise and fall of their chests, he could hear her heart still pounding, its rhythm syncopated uneasily with his own. He sighed. Her long exhale echoed the sentiment, neither quite certain that the other understood, each willing to stand on the fragile limb of trust, and try to balance in the buffeting winds of the world.

"I love you," he whispered, hoping she heard, hoping it would be enough, hoping that it would ease their hearts . . . at least for now.

By morning, the Roots had posted a fresh missive announcing a *Day of Demonstration* in the District of Columbia, a confrontation between authorities and people who were prepared to defend their rights . . . by any means necessary. The Roots called on everyone to show up for this act of mass defiance.

Charlie groaned.

"This mass bloodbath, they mean."

"We've got to stop it," Alex warned, sensing a disaster brewing. "I swear if we let this Day of Demonstration happen, it will be the movement's death knell. Friend will use the violent clash as an excuse to arrest all of us and crush the resistance once and for all."

Charlie agreed. For weeks, they'd noticed the demonstrations growing smaller and smaller as violence increased. The mothers and children stayed home. The elderly and frail avoided the protests. People offered excuses and evasions. Public sentiment soured on the Dandelion Insurrection, complaining about the destruction and violence. Meanwhile, the police and authorities used every outbreak of violence, every destruction of property, as an excuse to crackdown on the actions. If the Day of Demonstration devolved into a massive fight, the Dandelion Insurrection would suffer. Charlie whipped out an essay denouncing the Day of Demonstration, warning that violent tactics were likely to backfire on the movement.

The movement fractured like a cracked egg, divided between those who howled that Charlie Rider was a traitor, and those who railed against the Roots as the problem. The Day of Demonstration erupted into an internal battleground of ideologies, violence versus nonviolence, tearing open a rift that split the movement. Critics furiously accused Charlie of selling out to the Interim Government, betraying them for a bribe, being in league with Friend, the military, the rich, the corporations, even the Devil himself. The corporate media tore at him like starving vultures swooping down on a limping creature.

The Dandelion Insurrection has failed, they proclaimed.

Dandelions Falter, Roots Surge, the headlines declared.

The Roots tied the discussion of tactics into a knot, scorning the voices arguing for other approaches.

If you're not with us, you're against us, they claimed. *You're traitors to our rights and freedoms, no better than the tyrants we oppose.*

Tansy hollered until she turned purple that mass defiance of an unjust - and unconstitutional - law was as effective as levers and pulleys. It was as pragmatic as nuts and bolts. It worked according to the principles of movement mechanics!

"Just give me a dozen clean civil disobedience arrests," she swore, "and I'll win this case faster than Gandhi made salt."

But every case coming her way was sullied by the violence. Protesters were being charged with assault, not civil disobedience of the American Protection Act.

Charlie churned out essays trying to sway people into using other types of actions, including walk-outs, sit-ins, flash mobs, street theater, protest strikes and more. *We have better ways to 'fight back'*, he told them.

The Roots shot down every suggestion of alternate tactics, refusing to consider dispersed actions like boycotts or strikes, calling civil disobedience a charade.

Those unwilling to take a courageous stand, the Roots replied in their next missive, *should serve on the medic line and support those doing the dangerous work.*

Courage, Charlie retorted in a seething response, *comes in all shapes and sizes. Respecting the humanity of our opposition – who are our fellow citizens whether we approve of their actions or not – requires a depth of fearlessness far beyond the tactics of dehumanization and attacking.*

The Roots howled with derisive laughter.

We face pigs of police and soulless corporate stooges who only listen to the language of violence. We speak in ways they understand, showing through our tough stance that we refuse to be bullied and abused. Get to the medic line, Charlie Rider. If you won't swing a bat, serve the movement in other ways.

Charlie seethed. He suspected Will Sharp was penning the cleverly worded arguments. The man hadn't been seen since he threw that punch at the White House - though Charlie attempted to draw him out in his writings.

Come out of hiding, Will Sharp, he wrote. *Come discuss this face-to-face.*

The next missive slapped him with a counter-challenge.

Come down to the Day of Demonstration and we'll settle it there.

The rumor that Charlie Rider and Will Sharp were going to confront each other at the protest whipped across the country so fast that truth blurred into a streak of nonsense blazing against the dark sky of rumors. When people announced that they were going to the Day of Demonstration just to watch the spectacle, Charlie gritted his teeth and prepared to debunk the rumors.

When your back's to the wall, Charlie thought grimly, *your heart has to lead.*

He lifted his pen and signed the death sentence of his popularity, sacrificed his sway on the movement, and answered to the demands of his conscience. Surrendering to the inevitability of insults, he told the nation he had no intention of fighting Will Sharp.

I will not fight him, not with fists or baseball bats, not in a street brawl, not for control of the movement, not over Zadie, not over anything. Since the beginning of the Dandelion Insurrection, I've been working for a world of peace, justice, dignity, and democracy. This world won't be won by those who throw punches, but by those who have the restraint not to. This world does not grow from violent roots. It flowers from the seeds of love and respect planted in our hearts. It arises in people who hold the dignity of others in equal measure to their determination for justice. It emerges in the hearts of those who remember that the greatest courage is to move from love instead of hate.

He wrote that he would not go to the Day of Demonstration; he couldn't support it, not by a thousand miles, not while the Roots proclaimed that might made right and the righteousness of their goals justified their use of violent might. He refused to serve on the medic line of an emerging civil war, patching people up to go out and fight again. He had hundreds of tools for making change and he would use them until he drew his last breath, but he could not - would not - condone violence as a method of resisting the American Protection Act.

Charlie sent out the essay and closed his computer. He sat silently. His heart called out to the countless souls around the world who had challenged injustice with committed nonviolence. He whispered the names he knew: Gandhi, Dr. Martin Luther King, Jr., Thich Nhat Hanh, Badshah Khan, Fannie Lou Hamer, Bayard Rustin, Dorothy Day, Sophie Scholl, Leymah Gbowee, and so many more. On their heels came the images of thousands - millions - more, people whose names he did not know, courageous souls who poured their lives into movements for change. A tide of history swelled and crashed over him. Around the world and throughout time, Charlie could envision the billions of lives illuminating a rising story of humanity. Uncounted and unrealized, generations of people were, for reasons both pragmatic and principled, turning away from violence and toward nonviolence as a way of working for change. In the darkness of his current moment, he invoked them all. He saw them marching in one of the largest mass movements of human history. They came to stand with Charlie, lifting up their lives and examples, people of all races, genders, ages, creeds, nationalities, faiths, and classes. The lineage of nonviolence surrounded him, quietly embodying the greatest achievement of humanity: creating a way of transforming injustice and oppression without causing violence to their fellow human beings.

Stand by me now, he called to them.

For his people might soon turn against him.

CHAPTER TWENTY-NINE

. . . . .

Day of Demonstration

When the blow came, it caught him by surprise. His essay unleashed the expected round of howling. His critics tore him apart limb-by-limb, sentence-by-sentence. The Roots mocked him. The Offshoots scorned him. Friend praised him and made everything worse.

But he didn't expect Zadie to disagree.

She caught him as he was packing his bag - when he said he couldn't support the demonstration by a thousand miles, he meant it. He was heading north in an act of protest against the violence. An essay calling on others to boycott the Day of Demonstration was ready to be posted. A longing had welled up in him for the land, the wide fields of honest potatoes, and the shockingly cold clarity of the lakes of Northern Maine. He thought of his vast, extended French-Acadian family with the desperation of a person who senses the doors of the world slamming shut around him. His compass still pointed north, but his critics claimed up was down, and south was north, and he was wrong, wrong, wrong.

He was digging through the bureau searching for matching socks when Zadie stormed in and slammed the door so hard it knocked a painting off the wall.

"Where are you going?" Zadie asked, standing with her hands on her hips, eyes narrowed at the half-packed duffel bag.

"North," he retorted, hanging the painting back on the nail.

"Are you joking?" she replied, incredulous.

"No. I haven't visited my grand-père in a long time," he remarked, shoving socks in his backpack. "You ought to visit your father, too."

Zadie stared at him in exasperated disbelief.

"Now?"

"Yes, now!" he exclaimed. "So no one goes to that cursed demonstration expecting us to show up and work miracles."

"We can't just leave, Charlie!" Zadie reacted in horror.

"Yes, we can. And I'm going to," he answered, digging out a spare pair of blue jeans. "It's not the Dandelion Insurrection, Zadie. It's a mob and state thugs having a street fight. Inez refuses to go. Idah told her students not to organize in solidarity. I've made my views clear."

"But - "

"Do you want to go and get massacred? Beaten? Tear gassed? Because that's all that will happen. There are no strategic objectives to this. If there's one more protestor than police officer left standing in the carnage, it's not going to overturn the law. It's going to justify the severity of the law."

He started pulling his tee shirts from the second drawer.

"We can't run, Charlie."

"I'm not running."

"I'm not going north," she stated flatly.

They stared at each other.

"What are you going to do, hurl bricks?" he asked caustically, his patience shredded into barbed-edged remnants by the slice of constant arguments.

Her eyes flashed in anger.

"There's a medic team," she pointed out. "We could help them."

"They've bullied you into being Florence Nightingale in support of their war when you ought to be Dorothy Day opposing it," he shot back. "The best way to *do no harm* is to stop the brutality and slaughter on all sides."

"It's going to happen, Charlie," she argued. "There's also a group going who are committed to nonviolence."

He snorted in disgust. He knew that group. They showed up at protests and hid behind the violent flank. The Roots and Offshoots used them to justify their punches by claiming that they were *protecting* the peaceful protesters. They were like princesses in towers, wringing their hands through the Dark Ages as the soldiers and knights slaughtered each other in the name of chivalry. The only ethical option he could see was to boycott the whole fiasco. He shoved a sweatshirt in his bag.

"Zadie, I love you . . . but I can't support this."

She sighed and crossed her arms over her chest as he shouldered the bag.

"I can't leave, Charlie."

"Don't go to the demonstration," he pleaded, though his heart sank. He already saw the stubborn fire rising in her eyes.

"I can't promise you that," she replied.

"Be careful," he said sadly.

She put her hand on his chest. He covered it with his and held it tight. They leaned together, heart to heart, blood throbbing with the twin surges of love and longing, promising each other with every wordless breath that they would make it through this disagreement and come out the other side of this hard moment. They kissed, each hoping silently and secretly that this wouldn't be the last time.

A sudden calm descended on Charlie as he drove north. The hours stretched along with the miles. He breathed again and again, rolling open his window and gulping the air. He pulled off, bought gas, found himself weeping at the pump, shook off the sorrow, and kept driving. North of New York, he curled up on the back seat and slept, waking in the predawn darkness. Alert and refreshed, he got back on the empty freeway and beat the rush hour bottleneck in and out of Boston. The sun rose on the Portsmouth Bridge and his heart lifted as he entered the tall pines that bordered the highways of Maine. He stopped in Portland and made a phone call.

It rang twice.

"*Bonjour?*"

"Ma?" he said, breaking into a smile at the sound of Natalie's voice.

"Charlie? What's wrong?!"

Everything, he thought.

"Nothing, Ma," he assured her. "Just thought I'd tell you I'll be home for dinner."

"Don't joke with me. I'm too old."

"You're not that old, and I'm serious."

"What happened? What's going on?" Natalie demanded, savvy to her son's ways.

"Nothing," Charlie insisted. "I'm fine. Everything's . . . well, you know how everything is - it's a mess. I'm just coming home for a bit. I'm tired."

And there it was: the truth. Every last bone in his body was weary of the fight, the struggle, the accusations, the arguing with Zadie, the danger, the hate. His mind focused on the quiet pine forests of the valley like a homing beacon and he let it draw him northward infallibly over the eight-hour journey.

The air changed, cleared, and entered him good and fresh. When he turned into the valley, he couldn't stop crying, thinking of the distances he'd traveled and the dangers he'd survived since he left the cupped hands of its hills. The strain of the past weeks suddenly collided with the contrasting quiet of a valley so familiar he could see the ghosts of his great, great, grandparents as he passed the old Acadian farmsteads.

He drove slowly through the outer edges of the small town, crawling down Main Street, catching glimpses of startled looks and wild craning necks as friends and relatives spotted him headed homeward. His mother's house gleamed in the evening light, compact and humble, every inch scoured from spring cleaning and each light blazing in the window to welcome him. His mother and grand-père were waiting anxiously on the front stoop. Both burst into tears at the sight of him.

"I'm alright, Ma," he lied over and over.

"Leave him alone, Natalie," Valier told his daughter as she fussed, "or he'll go to hell for lying to his mother."

Valier winked at Charlie.

"Tell us when you are ready. If I die tonight, well, I'll hear all about it on the other side, God help me."

Natalie smacked her father's arm.

"*Bah, voyons.* You're not going to die."

"No," Valier assured her gently, nodding at Charlie, "and neither is he."

Charlie slept like a rock in a bed still carved in the bowl of his younger self, stretched from boy to adolescent to youth. The same twist of a palm leaf *rameau* was pinned to the headboard with a thumbtack; it had guarded him through his recuperation after he nearly drowned in the river when he jumped off the bridge on a dare. A picture of Zadie in ninth grade was stuck into the side of his bureau, reminding him of the hopeless lovesickness of his teenage days. The stub of the candle he'd lit for her safety after she ran away was stuck between the wall and the back of his battered desk. On the shelf, the rows of books - Gandhi, King, Gene Sharp, Thoreau - that had offered him knowledge had collected a layer of dust as he lived their wisdom in action.

Natalie checked on him once, rolling her eyes at her sprawled, sleeping son and stroking his sandy hair affectionately. Charlie Rider might have brought down a hidden corporate dictatorship, but Natalie Beaulier still saw the echoes of her scrappy little boy hiding under the serious lines of her son's face.

Mon Dieu, she told her memories of her younger self, *had we known what he would grow up to do, we'd have quit worrying and started praying.*

Since that shocking day he'd revealed he was writing the inflammatory essays of the Man From the North, she'd woken in cold sweats over the threats of assassination, arrest, indefinite detention, torture, beatings, and drone strikes that chased his heels. She thought of Ellen, dead, and Pilar, burying her youngest daughter.

God, she cried, *thank you for watching over him despite his lack of faith. Just keep him alive and help him succeed so no other mother has to worry like I do.*

Then she crossed herself and quietly backed out of the room.

On the Day of Demonstration, Charlie drove up to his grand-père's cabin by the lake. He stood for a while, looking out across the hills and into the shaded solitude of the woods. His hands shook with concern for Zadie, the nation, the Dandelion Insurrection; his treacherous mind roiled with the critics' accusations that he was a traitor and a coward. He circled through strategies and challenges until he was dizzy then lay down on the cot in the spare bedroom and simply gave up.

He didn't have all the answers. He couldn't solve the world's problems. He certainly didn't see a way out of this mess.

Charlie lay on the cot, facing the wall, feeling empty inside. Every word he had written, every warning he had issued was coming true now. The violence held no shock for him: he had seen it brewing in the undercurrent of the movement for months. He saw how the Roots fed the strands of anger and righteousness; how fear put weapons into peoples' hands; how the divisions and arguments between insurrectionists allowed the movement to falter and fragment. The nation was a pile of dynamite exploding . . . this eruption held no surprises for Charlie.

And that - the wary cynicism, the disillusionment, and his inability to avert this moment - made him turn his face to the wall in a blank slate of emotion. He felt nothing as the nation tore itself into shreds.

As the sun slanted toward evening, he heard the sound of a muffled voice. Then silence.

Valier tapped on the door.

"Tucker just called," Valier commented.

Charlie hadn't even noticed the phone ringing.

"He wanted to talk to you."

"I have nothing to say."

Charlie realized it was true: he'd wrung himself out. No more daring, bold phrases. No more sentiments of love. No more hotheaded scathing remarks. He felt he could be silent for the rest of his life as the world shrieked into insanity.

"*Charles-Valier! Lève-toi!* Get up!" Valier commanded, hauling off the scratchy wool blanket and sending Charlie half-tumbling out onto the floor.

"*Voyons! Pepère! Arrête-ça!*" he automatically snapped back in the Acadian French of his *tantes* and *oncles*.

"Get up! You're either too old or too young to be napping. Come with me."

The short old man turned and gestured imperiously with his weathered, sun-browned hand. He limped slightly on his aching knee and reached for his walking stick leaning beside the door.

Charlie groaned and followed. He knew from experience that if he didn't get up, Valier would return with a bucket of well water and douse him and the bed, leaving him with a damp mattress and a foul temper.

He blinked in the golden sunshine and the pulse of spring heat. Valier strode up the long meadow slope, out toward the fields and the forest. He shoved his hands in his blue jean pockets and trudged after his grandfather. The old man saved his breath for walking, but from time to time, he reached out and patted Charlie's shoulder. Once, on a steep incline, his grip tightened and the youth felt his grand-père lean into him for support. Valier pushed eighty years of age, and still tended a vegetable plot each summer large enough to keep his children and cousins and siblings complaining about too many *les fèves* and *eshallots*.

"Let's catch our breath," Valier suggested as they crested the top of the hill.

They turned. The land fell away past the house, down toward the shining blue of the cold lake. It was hard to remember that beyond the shores, far past the wind-swaying glossy boughs of the pine forests, hundreds of millions of human beings struggled desperately in political turmoil. Charlie's head bowed toward his chest. By his feet, the beautiful star moss pressed up against the dark shale rocks that broke the surface of the hill's loam and meadow grasses.

"Charlie, Charlie," Valier sighed, watching the wind ripple the green fields. "Someday, I'm going to be lying under this earth, not standing on top of it."

"Don't say that, *Pepère*," he objected.

"*Eh, voyons*," Valier retorted, "I didn't say soon. Now, *tu m'écoutes!* Listen: I'm proud of you."

"It's all falling apart," Charlie moaned, shaking his head.

"*Mon Dieu!* It's always falling apart. Everything. My chicken shed. The roof. The tractor. My body. That doesn't matter as much as how you pick up the pieces and put them back together."

"I don't know if I can," Charlie admitted quietly.

"*Oui, c'est vrai*," Valier conceded. "That's how I feel each morning. Someday, I won't be able to pull this body back together and it will be time to let it lie under the grasses, eh? But until then, Charlie, you got to keep trying."

Charlie didn't reply right away. He watched the ants crawl up to investigate his sneakers.

"When I said, I am proud of you," Valier commented, "it is because you try. You wake people up. You make courage possible. You have done so much."

He paused and squinted at the sunset.

"But, Charlie, you cannot do it all. At some point, you have to let go. You have to let people stumble on the way to walking. *Mon Dieu*," he chuckled, "I did it for my boys and your mamma, and I did it for you."

Valier remembered his grandson as little Charles-Valier, his namesake, always pushing the edge of trouble, driving the tractor into the lake by accident, shoving his cousin into the manure on purpose, sneaking out at night to try to catch a pet raccoon and running into skunks instead. Charlie's daredevil rebelliousness had brought Valier's heart into his throat dozens of times. *That boy will be the death of me,* he'd said more than once, snatching Charlie out of the path of tractors, or grabbing the wheel just in the knick of time as he careened through the driving lessons Valier claimed turned his hair gray. In quiet moments, late at night, after his heart ceased thundering in his chest, Valier would chuckle and confess to God that despite the frights, he loved Charlie best of all.

"Love takes more courage than hate," he muttered, thinking of all the breathless scares the boy had given him.

Charlie looked up sharply. His eyes narrowed as the blue sky burned in his eyes.

"You know, *Pepère,*" he said slowly, "I think you're right."

And for the first time in weeks, he started to grin.

Charlie spun around the doorframe of the cabin and dialed Tucker, his heart heaving in his chest. He breathed and leaned against the wall as the phone rang in the distance.

"Hello?" Tucker said.

"It's me," he answered. "Sorry I missed your call. Zadie?"

"She's fine," Tucker replied quickly, knowing his worry.

"Did she go down to the demonstration?"

"No, uh," Tucker hesitated, sounding torn between laughter and choking, "Will held her hostage the whole day."

"He what?" Charlie exclaimed, both jubilant and shocked at the tactic, grinning despite himself and glad no one could see him.

"She's madder than a snake tied in a knot and somehow blames it all on you," Tucker warned him in the aggrieved tone of someone who has tried to reason with a raging fury all day.

"Me?" Charlie exclaimed.

"She said you called Will," Tucker said.

"Sure, I called him on the way north and left a message chewing him out for this whole mess, and telling him if Zadie got hurt, it'd be all his fault, and I'd skewer him in writing for the rest of our miserable lives."

"Oh," Tucker groaned. "That must have been quite a message because Will showed up at five a.m. and locked her bedroom door from the outside. Once the report of the Demonstration started, she stopped shrieking and got real quiet."

A silence fell around Charlie as Tucker told him about the news. Reports had cracked faster than lightning, one after another, relentless. Dozens of acts of sabotage, large and small scale, struck across the United States, including a ransacking of government offices in Virginia, smashed equipment at an extraction company headquarters in Texas, and an Interim Government member's personal car set on fire in DC. In Chicago, police shut down half the city during a tense standoff with the perpetrators of a bomb explosion.

"Coordinated mayhem," Alex had surmised in a growl. "Wouldn't be surprised if Friend's behind half of it."

Tucker refused to believe her, but she'd read about the tactic of using incited chaos to provoke riots in CIA handbooks. She checked the time, betting that by noon, Friend would declare a state of emergency.

At quarter to twelve, Friend delivered a public address, calling for order and safety.

"Violence, destruction, terror: we cannot bow to these forces. No matter the demands, these actions cannot be condoned, and must be stopped."

Then, he did the unthinkable.

He suspended the upcoming elections.

"I have conferred with the state governors, and we are in agreement: under threat of violence, no citizen can fairly vote. Under fear of retaliation through attacks on homes or businesses, no voter can safely exercise his or her democratic rights. By the power vested in us, the Governors and I have suspended all elections until order and safety can be assured in every precinct."

Hopelessness combusted into hate. People poured into the streets burning with fury, striking out in desperation and despair. The Oath Guardians, a group of fanatic patriots in the military who had once formed a tenuous relationship with the Dandelion Insurrection, decided to take a stand in barracks and bases nationwide, declaring the suspension of the elections unconstitutional and refusing to serve. Had they stopped at noncooperation, they might have succeeded. But, armed and uncontrollable by anyone - not commanders, citizens, conscience, or government - their seizure of the military bases triggered counteraction by other branches of the military. The two factions started to exchange fire as ranking commanders sought to suppress the mutiny.

In DC, there had been no attempt at peaceful protest. The swelling ranks of Roots and Offshoots came in swinging, charging into the designated demonstration area hurling bricks. The police responded with a volley of rubber bullets. Hundreds of black-clad protesters clashed with police in body armor. Tear gas choked the streets. Tucker forced himself to watch the footage, hour after hour, reeling from the brutality, the wanton violence, the hatred and fear.

When Will had barricaded Zadie in her room, she had let loose a stream of justified outrage, pounding on the locked door. Will had stoically leaned on the landing banister, agreeing that it was unfair, unjust, probably against the law, humiliating, demeaning, and everything else she said, but he was not going to let her out until she promised not to go down to the demonstration. It was a trap, a ploy, a trick to justify cracking down on the movement, everything Charlie suspected.

"Then why did you write those missives?" Zadie demanded, kicking the door in frustration.

"I didn't," he said, quietly and honestly, not expecting her to believe him as he explained that the other Roots had written them.

"So, why aren't you down at the Demonstration with them?" she asked.

Will sighed and studied the ceiling.

"I - we've had a difference of opinion lately and," he paused to chose words carefully, "my loyalty has been questioned."

"Your loyalty to the Roots?" Zadie pried, her voice muffled by the door.

Will winced.

"Zadie, can we just leave it at: I'm here. Charlie chewed my ears off, twisted my conscience, and I'm going to be in a helluva lot of trouble with the Roots later."

"Charlie?" she snapped. "What's he got to do with this?"

Will squirmed. Sighed. Wrestled with secrets. He couldn't tell her that the night he had been arrested for fighting off the cops at the White House, he had come back to Tansy's house after the Boss had anonymously posted his bail. As he approached, he had heard Zadie and Charlie arguing.

If the size of my shoulders determines your safety, what kind of freedom is that?

Something cracked in him that night, as if the foundation of his existence split, leaving him reeling on shaky ground. He had pulled back from everything, ignoring the Boss' insistent calls and avoiding the Roots. Friend had even sent his henchmen out to find out what was going on with him. Will had shrugged and said he was sick - and he was: sick of his mission, sick of the Roots, sick of his lies, sick of deception, sick of it all.

"Open the door," Zadie said.

He took a deep breath and slid back the deadbolt.

Zadie flung the door open, eyes flashing, furious with him. Color rose in her cheeks. Her bare feet tapped in pent-up irritation. Her strong arms crossed over her chest. He eyed the distance between them in case she decide to make an exception to her nonviolence commitment.

Zadie studied him and finally spoke.

"This is going to be a very long day."

And it was. Tucker told Charlie they had watched the news reports and live feeds all day, including Friend's press conference just an hour ago.

"Did you see it?" Tucker asked Charlie.

"No, I missed it," Charlie answered.

"So, you don't know?"

"Know what?" he asked, his heart dropping lower than ever.

Tucker cleared his throat.

"Friend called for the Dandelion Insurrection to disband."

CHAPTER THIRTY

. . . . .

Disband? Never!

We won't, Charlie vowed.

We might have to, Tucker warned.

Friend refused to set new election dates until the movement disbanded.

"But we're the only force keeping the elections honest," Charlie growled.

"That's why he needs us gone," Tucker pointed out.

Charlie's head reeled.

"We need to figure out what to do. Let me talk to Zadie."

"I'm afraid that's not possible - "

"Tell her I don't care if she wants to scorch my ears off. I still want to talk to her."

"She'll scorch more than your ears, Charlie," the mild man commented drolly. "She left a couple hours ago. She's coming north to ream you out in person."

CHAPTER THIRTY-ONE

. . . . .

The Spyder and the Fly

Late that night, long after Zadie had left and Tansy went to bed, Tucker settled his jangling nerves by working on an obscure bit of programming as the house grew still and silent. The intensity of the violence and the images from the news reports replayed through his ragged mind. Will was still slouched downstairs on the couch, avoiding the Roots and delaying his inevitable confrontation with them.

Tucker immersed his tired consciousness into the sea of comforting ones and zeros. He was propped up on his bed, dozing off over the keyboard when the Mouse popped online and sent Cybermonk a message:

Spyder caught your Fly.

See attached encrypted file. Wouldn't even let me peek at it!

Don't stay up all night.

– The Mouse

He grinned at her disgruntled tone as his heart notched up a pace. Months ago, they'd set out to discover everything they could about Will Sharp and the Roots - which wasn't much. Nervously tiptoeing around the alerts the group had set up on searches related to their identities, Alex decided to ask Spyder to apply the delicate touch for which the hacker was known. Tucker had shivered.

"We can't afford to hire Spyder," he told Alex.

"Spyder owes me," she answered, refusing to say anything more.

He reread the message from the Mouse and then rose. On the pretense of crossing the hall to use the bathroom, he peered over the railing on the landing. Beyond the stairs, he could just barely see Will's legs propped up on the coffee table in the living room. He listened, but couldn't detect if the young man had fallen asleep or sat wide-awake, reading reports from the Day of Demonstration.

Tucker frowned thoughtfully and returned to his room. He sat on the edge of the bed, jiggling his knee impatiently as he downloaded and decoded the file. The first thing that popped up was a message from Spyder:

Bullet-in-back material. Be careful.
Don't share unless necessary. I don't want Mouse hurt.

- Spyder

The file contained only a few records. Tucker's eyebrows furrowed. He had expected more. He began reading. He choked. His muscles clenched right down to his fingertips. A shudder ran through his spine.

"It can't be."

Everything made sense. Nothing made sense. He reeled in confusion. As fast as one thought came into clarity, a dozen more contradictions sprang to mind. Tucker wiped his sweaty hands on the bedspread as he wondered what to do about this information. He didn't have enough evidence to blow the whistle on the Roots. He needed time he didn't have. There was one way . . . but it was risky. He could get killed. It was dangerous.

Tucker had thought his push-come-shove moment had arrived when Charlie and Zadie had showed up in his town needing a place to hide. He counted the rise of the Alternet as bonus points on his karmic record, but all of that paled compared to the risk before him now. The dangers stretched

312

astronomical, but if he played this card right, he could save everyone - maybe even himself.

Tucker searched his soul. Once, in the heat of an argument with Charlie, he had snatched up a silvery dandelion head and shaken it in the young man's face, demanding that Charlie accept a dangerous risk in order to help the whole movement. In that moment, he had wished he could be standing in his friend's shoes, able to lay down the sacrifice of his life if necessary, and risk all to gain all.

Do you know why the dandelion is invincible? he had asked Charlie. *Because it offers a promise to every man, woman, and child: make a wish, the dandelion says, and this lowly weed will do its best to carry your seed-borne hope to fertile ground.*

Tucker's resolve cemented in his chest. He sent a message to the Mouse, signing off at the end before she peppered him with questions.

Wish me luck. And, if things go wrong,
scatter this file like dandelions seeds.
- Cybermonk

He meditated for a moment, clearing his mind and calming his nerves. He brought courage into his veins and compassion into his heart. Then he quietly walked downstairs to confront Will Sharp.

"What's up, Tucker?" Will asked in a gravely, weary tone. "You look like you swallowed a spider."

"It was a fly, actually," he replied in a mild tone, struggling to keep his voice from shaking.

Will's smile twitched in the corners of his mouth. He ran a hand over his face. He looked so troubled and worn out that Tucker hesitated for a moment.

"Will, I appreciate what you did for Zadie today. It took courage and . . . " he faltered.

"She's my friend, Tucker. I owe her," Will said softly. "I've done her some wrong turns lately, and needed to make amends."

"Yes," Tucker agreed, "and because of that, I'm going to give you a chance."

Will frowned in confusion.

"Walk out that door, now," Tucker ordered, pointing with a trembling finger, "and don't come back. Disappear. Go underground."

"What?!"

"If you kill me - "

" - I'm not going to kill you," Will objected, wondering what in hell's name had gotten into the quiet man.

" - everyone will know about your father."

"My father?" he repeated, confused. "What's he got to do with anything? I don't even know who he is."

"You - what?" Tucker broke off, alarmed. Will had to be lying. "You don't know who your father is?"

Will shook his head. His eyebrows drew together in a ferocious scowl.

"Bastard abandoned my mom when she got pregnant. She never spoke about him."

"But surely there were records for child support - "

"She never took a dime from him. Said it'd be like taking money from the Devil."

"But you never got a paternity test?" Tucker's voice squeaked in disbelief.

Will shrugged.

"Thought about it," he commented with a half grin to hide how nervous the idea made him. He'd lived his whole life without the man, why open a can of worms now? "I'd like to punch the guy at least once."

Tucker exhaled in a whoosh. He had not expected this. A shocked realization cracked over Will.

"You know who my father is," he choked out.

Will wasn't lying, Tucker thought wildly. *He really didn't know.* He backpedaled frantically. This changed everything.

"Who? How did you find out?" Will exploded furiously.

Tucker pointed to the youth's hand.

"Remember when you cut yourself on shattered glass the night of the assassination attempt? I took a sample," he confessed.

Will frowned.

"I ran a test, Will, on your DNA."

Will shook his head.

"Bullshit," he said. "I'd know it if you did. We have alerts for the Roots. Can't get caught just because some cop runs a piece of our skin or hair."

"I know about the alerts," Tucker answered, trying to think faster than the racing speed of this conversation. "That's why I ran it at a paternity lab with strong privacy and security practices."

Will sat back with a thud, startled. Then he shot off the couch and grabbed Tucker by the shirt.

"Who is he?" Will snarled as his fist leapt up.

Tucker braced himself for a punch that never came. When he opened one eye from his reflexive flinch, Will looked like the one who had been hit.

"I won't tell you if you don't want to know," Tucker said softly. "I just thought you *had* to know, given . . . "

"Given what?" Will demanded when Tucker fell silent.

"Given the Roots . . . and Zadie . . . and the Dandelion Insurrection," Tucker stammered.

"What does that have to do with my father?"

Tucker looked at the young man with mournful compassion.

"Friend," he said. "Your father is John C. Friend."

CHAPTER THIRTY-TWO

· · · · ·

The Devil's Friend

The Devil's friend. The Devil's friend. Will wept in the rain as his lungs burned fire. Anger coursed through his veins as he ran.

Her dying words. She was trying to tell him, to spill the secret she had kept hidden as she felt her life slipping away.

The Devil is Friend. The Devil is Friend. Will's body pounded the concrete sidewalks as he hurtled down the dark and deserted streets. The rain lashed his skin.

Does he know? Will had practically screamed at Tucker, lifting the little man by the shirt collar.

He knew, Tucker confirmed. Spyder had hacked the back end of the lab's records and found that John C. Friend had also run a report. All these years, Friend had known who Will was and had not once said a word. Spyder had dug deeper into the archives of history and found a trail of data connecting Will's mother and Friend. The trail abruptly stopped six months before Will Sharp's birth certificate recorded his father as the Devil.

"Don't tell anyone," he had begged Tucker, shaking from limb to limb. "Please. Please."

"That depends, Will," the older man had answered, still willing to blackmail Will Sharp to protect the movement. "Who are the Roots working for?"

"Not for Friend," Will had replied vehemently, lying automatically, covering his trail, retreating into his habitual secrecy to buy time.

"Then your secret is safe with me," Tucker promised.

Will had muttered about needing air, dashed out of the house, and raced down the street. He skidded to a stop as a taxi threw a cold dose of water onto him. Soaked, he paced backward and slammed his back hard against the brick wall of a building, sliding to the ground.

John C. Friend was the Devil.

And he was Devil's spawn. Devil's pawn.

Used, abused, abandoned, deceived.

Friend had a wife, no children. She was blonde, wealthy, and well connected. Will had met her. Stood in their house. His father's house.

Will rolled and retched into the sewer grate.

Gutter rat. Ghetto boy. Trained killer. Devil's pawn.

Friend had snatched him out of the jaws of juvenile incarceration and sent him to military academy. *Just a random act of goodwill, m'boy,* he had claimed. Not so random.

Friend had paid for his private security training program. Will had learned to hide and hunt, shoot and kill, manipulate, lie and deceive. Friend had asked Will to serve him privately.

What kind of father does that to his son? Will cried silently, clenching his fists in rage and pain. *He used me. Used me like he used my mother.*

I want to punch the guy at least once, he had joked to Tucker.

He wanted to tear him apart piece by piece and drown him in his own blood. Will got up and started slogging down the flooding streets. He couldn't see where he was going through the downpour. He didn't care.

The Devil is Friend, his mother had said. *The Devil is Friend.*

318

CHAPTER THIRTY-THREE

· · · · ·

Revolutionary Tractor

Bill Gray paused as he tromped through the fresh-tilled field of the vegetable plot, thinking he had heard a car turn in the drive. He shaded his eyes against the sun and for one heart-lurching, painful moment, he thought the woman who unfolded from the vehicle, long and slender as a birch tree, was Ellen.

The next moment, his knees buckled and his face crumbled. Ellen would not ever rise with her long graceful beauty. Bill crouched down on the soft earth of the land and put his hand to it for steadiness. He still saw her in the stand of white-barked birches swaying on the hill above the farmhouse. She had painted them, over and over, until she became part of the copse of trees to Bill's eyes. That was where he would scatter her ashes someday when Zadie came home.

His head jerked up, breaking through the fog of grief that blinded him.

Zadie.

That's who had stepped out of the vehicle looking like her mother at a distance. Same build, minus a foot of height.

"Dad?" he heard her call, cupping her hands to amplify the sound and swiveling to find him.

"Coming!" he hollered, breaking into a loping jog down the slope, happier than he had felt in months.

"To what do I owe the pleasure of this visit?" Bill pried after a long bear hug and the obligatory scan to check that her limbs were still attached.

"Maybe I just came to see you, Dad," she answered with grin.

He threw her a knowing look.

"It's a long drive to visit your short-tempered old man," Bill drawled, lifting an eyebrow and nodding in the direction of Valier's cabin by the lake. "Saw him drive past a day or so ago."

Zadie cleared her throat.

"Yes, well, I have a few choice words for Charlie Rider."

"How about, 'I love you'," Bill suggested wryly, nudging Zadie. "Everything else is wasted breath, sweetheart. I'd trade all my years of ranting and raving for the chance to say it to your mother again."

"You miss her," Zadie stated as their footsteps instinctively turned out to the fields and forests. Bill had much on his chest and too many years of old lectures at the kitchen table to want to risk saying it all indoors. Besides, his girl never got enough time on the land. Too much city air was hard on the soul, and he could tell she needed to feel the soft forgiveness of the soil and the eternal patience of the pines whispering in the winds.

"Of course, I do, Zadie. I ache for her like ice water on the bones. She's gone and there's nothing that'll bring her back."

Zadie made a sob of a sound.

"Dad, I'm sorry."

"Nothing for you to be sorry for," Bill said. "Ellen knew the dangers. So did I."

"But it's all my fault - the Dandelion Insurrection, the march, the deaths."

Bill grunted.

"Don't be so full of yourself, Zadie. You get it from me and it's a terrible trait."

She turned her teary eyes on him, hurt. Bill swore silently and wished she wouldn't do that.

"Just because it seems like we're all in the palm of your hand or wrapped around your little finger, doesn't mean you're in control."

"I don't think that – "

"You do, and as your father, I have the dubious distinction of being the first person who had to learn to resist your charms. Your mother never fell for them, thank god, otherwise you'd have been an unbearable brat. As it is, you think everything's your fault, but it's not. Ellen and Natalie started that march. They knew what they were doing."

"No one knew about the drones – "

"Not even you, so quit beating yourself up about it."

"But I made the call to stand – "

Bill snorted.

"There wasn't anywhere to run, so that was just putting a good face on a hard situation. You just gave us the jolt of courage and love to carry us through."

Zadie said nothing to that. They kept walking.

"So . . . you don't blame me?"

"No, and I never have."

They fell silent at that, letting gentle thud of footsteps falling on the earth speak volumes.

Zadie scanned the hills and slopes of her parents' farm, a bit wilder and weedier than she remembered, with all the remnant signs of the Dandelion Insurrectionists who had worked and studied resistance until the government raids had cleared them out. The land stood lonely and majestic, a quiet tribute to the absence of Ellen, and gently patient with Bill's long recuperation of body and heart.

Suddenly, Bill straightened up and shaded his eyes.

"Now," he began in a lecturing tone, "remember, when you see Charlie, you're going to tell him . . . "

"I love you . . . and a bunch of other things," Zadie replied shortly.

Bill tsk-tsked.

"You'd best straighten out your heart where Charlie's concerned," Bill muttered with a far-off look.

"Dad, there's no question - " Zadie's exasperated tone broke off at the sight of his broad grin.

"That's good," Bill chuckled. "Because that looks like him climbing up the hill."

Zadie turned. A lone figure strode through the green grasses, hands shoved in pockets, sandy hair turned bright in the sunlight. Bill clapped her on the back and gave her a nudge before stalking off in the other direction mumbling about checking on the apple seedlings over the other side of the hill.

For all that this valley had born and raised that half-Acadian man, Zadie thought wryly, *Charlie had certainly outgrown its cradle.* She watched him skirt a patch of stinging nettles. He would never slide back into the landscape quite the same way he'd left it. Then, he had been jammed in by familiarity and habit, pushing the edges and growing red-faced in his itching rebellion to get out. Now, he had grown beyond the contours of the valley, stretching into the vast terrain of the nation.

Zadie broke into a smile and met him halfway up the rise.

"How'd you know I was here?" she asked breathlessly.

"The usual way," Charlie answered with a glint of mischief in his grin. "Ma's cousin's hairdresser saw you as she drove to the post office, told half the town, then called my ma, who told *Pepère*, who hollered out the window loud enough for the rest of the town to hear, including me."

Zadie laughed brightly.

"You're not still mad at me?" Charlie asked, ducking his head sheepishly and looking up at her.

She brushed his hair out of his eyes.

"No. I stewed all the way up to the Portsmouth Bridge, then crossed over and - "

"It all fell away," he finished knowingly.

He nodded at the dark sheen of the pines. It did something, the land. It was mineral, marrow, cellular, and mysterious. He could feel it humming in his bones. His body recognized the land that raised him, even if he'd been gone too long.

They began to walk through the grasses, meandering, drifting apart to step around a tangled cluster of purple vetch, pausing to inhale the sweet scent of sheer life rising from the earth. Their fingers entwined, released, and reached across the soft winds for one another as they spoke.

"You were right to come up here, Charlie," she said, gesturing expansively, "to get out of the stench and fear and lies, and remember what's real."

They broke out of the wild grasses onto an old farm road, the dirt packed down in the tracks of hundreds of years of use that spanned from horses and wagons to diesel tractors to biofuel. A glint of faded red metal shone at the top of the next rise.

Ellen's tractor.

They turned toward it, leaving the farm road to tromp over the uneven remains of the rows that had never been harvested. Charlie shaded his eyes. The old potatoes had sprouted again, struggling against weeds. Ellen left the tractor there before the march and it had become a memorial of sorts. Charlie's mother had told him that people had taken to coming by to lay out flowers and sit quietly.

They drew close. Small bouquets leaned against the wheels, dried and toppling. Stacks of pebbles and a few candle stubs sat on the hood of the engine. A faded photo of Ellen in a plastic covering had been pinned to the grill. They circled the machine. Zadie gripped the massive rubber wheel and climbed up. Charlie followed, perching on the metal covering of the wheel as Zadie slid into the seat.

"Nice view from up here," Charlie commented.

In a landscape of dense forests and rolling hills, an extra six feet of height lent perspective to the world. The grasses rippled in long sweeping patterns. The valley tumbled down into the river bordering Canada in a sea of green.

"We've got some tough decisions to make, Charlie," Zadie said quietly, running the tip of her finger around the steering wheel. They had come full circle in a long arcing revolution of change. Another day, another tyrant, another turn of the struggle lay before them. Friend threatened mass arrests and warned that the new election date would not be set until the Dandelion Insurrection disbanded. He had forced them into the position of blocking democracy by their very existence.

Charlie swallowed down his bitterness. He didn't have the numbers, but he *knew* in his heart and through common sense, that more of the Dandelion Insurrection held true to nonviolence than not. The Roots and Offshoots were flashy, loud, media grabbing, incendiary, and divisive, but they were not the whole of the movement. They were not even the bulk of it.

"Maybe it is time to disband," Charlie murmured, simply to say the words out loud even as his heart rebelled against the notion. "Maybe the Dandelion Insurrection should go dormant, dig deep, and connect to our real roots, the origins of where we began. Then we could regroup and start again."

He sighed, wondering if he and Zadie would be resisting tyrants and dictators forever, popping up each season to challenge the new face of injustice until they were older than his grandfather. He snorted. They wouldn't be allowed to live that long.

Clouds of troubled thoughts stormed across Zadie's face. She leaned back in the tractor seat, eyes distant. Silence thickened as she pondered his words.

"Maybe we have to sacrifice the movement to get the elections," she murmured.

Charlie's jaw tightened. It was unfair to all of the indomitable, golden dandelions that a small group of people - the Roots and Offshoots - could sabotage and undermine their collective efforts. It galled him that John C. Friend, one man, could point the sword of political power at their throats and hold democracy hostage. *As if Friend cared about democracy!* Charlie thought. The man had no intention of supporting fair elections. He had allowed the corruption of the Elections Commission and turned a blind eye to the uneven playing field that favored corporate candidates over popular ones. If the Dandelion Insurrection disbanded, the people wouldn't get democracy; they'd get the illusion of elections without a shred of actual change.

His blood turned sharp with disappointment. A slow poison of despair seeped into his heart. He twisted northward and looked at the river and the other slope of the valley. A mad idea popped into his head.

"Zadie," he blurted out, "what if we ran away to Canada, eloped, and let the Dandelion Insurrection sort itself out?"

She jolted as if stung. She drew breath to berate him - then stopped as another thought hit her. Her eyes widened and she burst out laughing in a peal that echoed off the hillsides.

"No ... maybe ... and yes," she answered to his three ideas, turning sideways on the tractor seat to look him in the eye. "I'm not running away to Canada."

"Okay, scratch that part," Charlie said hastily, turning red around his ears. He knew they wouldn't jump ship, no matter how tantalizing it might seem. "What's the maybe? Maybe you'll marry me?"

"If you ask real nice someday . . ."

"Someday?" he choked, his heart pounding. "Is this because of Will?"

Uh-oh. Her glare split him in two.

"Charlie Rider, only you could be so dense. There . . . is . . . nothing . . . between me and Will."

"What if he's in love with you?" he blurted out.

"That's his problem," Zadie retorted.

Heartbreaker, Charlie thought happily as his heart surged with relief.

"What about the yes?" he asked. "Yes, let the Dandelion Insurrection sort itself out?"

Zadie grinned.

"Exactly. Friend wants us to disband, ostensibly to stop the violence," Zadie pointed out. "Instead, we could put the question of tactics to a vote, and - "

"Disarm, not disband," Charlie concluded with a shock of understanding. He leaned over and kissed her. "Zadie, you're brilliant! We can use Tucker's verifiable online voting system and let the dandelions decide: go with the Roots and fight; surrender to Friend and disband; or disarm and continue like true dandelions!"

"And if they're not true dandelions, Charlie, ask me again about Canada. But if they are, if they want to pick up the tools of nonviolence and wage struggle with all of their crazy, wild hearts, then - "

"I want to marry you no matter what the outcome is," Charlie stated a bit wildly, grinning like a fool. "If you'll have me, that is."

Zadie smiled to herself.

"I've already got you, Charlie, always have."

"Always will," he promised breathlessly.

She kissed him, murmuring, "You're such a romantic."

"Hopeless, I know," he answered.

He slid forward to embrace her and knocked his knee hard against the steering column.

"Ouch," he groaned, rubbing the tender spot between the bones. The keys still sat in the ignition, threatening to rust in place.

"Wonder if it still works," Zadie murmured, reaching for the keys. Before she twisted them, she glanced at Charlie. "Wanna bet it runs?"

"I doubt it'll even turn on," he replied pragmatically.

"Let's see," she said with a daring tone.

"But isn't this a memorial to your mother?" Charlie hesitated, pointing to the candle stubs and remnants of flowers.

Zadie shrugged. She could feel Ellen in her veins; hear her voice in her ears. There was a time to plant and time to sow. *And these times will change*, Zadie thought fiercely, blinking back sudden tears. Times would change and the gardens and fields would be planted once again. They would not live all of their lives in the crisis of political upheaval. *We will heal*, Zadie vowed, *we will heal our broken hearts, our mangled bodies, our crippled democracy*. Times will change and people will be free to live a little more fully, plant vegetables and live to harvest them, love with less of the fear and more of the passion she felt rising in her veins. This tractor, the farm, the world, the movement had been clenched in the shadow of sorrow long enough. It was time to break with the past and lunge for the future. The wheel of revolution turned yet again. It was time to grasp it and steer in a new direction.

Her fingers turned on the key.

The engine roared into life.

CHAPTER THIRTY-FOUR

. . . . .

The True Roots of Resistance

The Man From the North put pen to page with a lion's roar of defiance. He wrote with the renewed passion of one who has dug deep into the dark night of the soul. He had curled into his core, searching for truth. When his essay burst forth, it challenged the very notion and meaning of roots.

Roots, he wrote, *symbolize more than underground strong-arms. Roots are also origins, the tendrils of a sprouting seed that give rise to life. Zadie and I have been here since the beginning of this movement. We know, deeply, where the true roots of this resistance emerged.*

Will Sharp and his self-proclaimed Roots were not the origins of the Dandelion Insurrection. They were parasitic plants, attaching themselves to the movement as it grew. Their seeds of secrecy, arms, and sabotage had developed into danger, violence, and division, threatening to strangle the once-flourishing movement.

The true roots of the Dandelion Insurrection were the stories he and Zadie had tracked down of people driven by love to use nonviolent action to stand up to injustice and organize for change. These were the anchoring structures that had weathered the storms of dangers. These were the nourishing roots that fed a nation hungry for change. They reached down into the fertile soil of history and pulled up the essential minerals of inspiration from the lineage of people all around the world who proved nonviolence worked. The true roots of the Dandelion Insurrection's bold resistance gave rise to the golden blossoms of creative, joyful, indomitable action. Love was the acorn, the oak, and the forest of the world they longed to create.

But, they were at a crossroads. They had to act, and boldly.

Friend wants us to disband, Charlie wrote, *but instead, we could disarm, and return to the true roots of our resistance.*

He invited the country to put it to a vote in two weeks, posing a three-way choice for the movement:

Disband as Friend says.

Fight back like the Roots

Disarm and Resist like Dandelions

We must hear from everyone, he wrote, *every person who has ever taken action with the Dandelion Insurrection.* The Man From the North called forward the voices of the movement, lifting the conversation on tactics out of the bullhorns of the few and into the hearts of the many. For too long, the loudest voices had dominated the discussion. Many people had been shoved into silence; now was the time to speak out. He stepped down off his platform, quieted the roar in his throat, and beckoned to the timid, the shy, the tired, the weak. The choice was not a decision for one voice alone. In a leaderful movement, everyone had to step forward, each person had to choose to embody the world they longed to create.

We need to hear from those courageous early resisters that gave us sparks of hope in the midst of despair. We need to hear from the determined, silent messengers who spread the essays of the Man From the North. Let the votes of those who banged on pots and pans for the Cacerolazo Countdown make some noise. Let the opinions of the parents and children in the Suburban Renaissance be spoken. We must weigh the perspectives of those who organized the evacuation of the cities and the March of the Gray Riders. The views of the participants in the community governance projects must be counted. Those who stalled and stopped fossil fuel expansion during Operation

American Extraction, and those who resist the plunder monkeys today, come forward!

From the margins and sidelines he called the underestimated, ignored, and forgotten. He opened the space for these voices to be heard. He asked each dandelion to come forward and join in the debate. The fate of the movement lay in their hearts.

He called out to the loners in the mountains, the mothers on the plains, the students in the playgrounds, the elders with their walkers. The world that they longed for lay down the path of their footsteps; young and old, large and small, bold and gentle. But they stood at a crossroads, caught in precarious choice, and without every person, the road they were making vanished.

There is a place between passivity and violence, Charlie wrote to the movement, *I'll meet you there . . . come find me at the spot where our roots of resistance emerged, in the fertile ground that gave rise to the Dandelion Insurrection, at the place where courage crosses paths with compassion, and the seeds of change spring to life.*

Charlie flung his heart out on the sleeve of his words. Then he sat quietly in the place where the movement had begun, and waited for the dandelions to emerge.

From all directions and corners of the country, they came. The Man From the North was joined by the Woman in the Southwest, the Kid on the Coast, the Guy in the Bible Belt, the Schoolteacher by the Lake. The answer to Charlie's passionate cry flew across the landscape of controversy with a golden clarity of heart. Letters and essays flooded the Alternet from the Mechanic in the Rust Belt, the Pastor Up Country, the Emancipator Down South, the Free Ranger in Texas, the Fisherman in Maine, and many more. These were the voices silenced by the angry vitriol and furious arguments. These were the people who couldn't - wouldn't - throw bricks. These were the mothers and fathers who could not bring their children into a street fight. These were the original dandelions that had chosen nonviolence in dangerous times.

We are the true roots of resistance, they declared, *and the scraggly leaves, golden flowers, and windborne seeds.*

They remembered the days when reading an essay was treason. They remembered the courage it took to speak truth out loud at the dinner table. They remembered the times when to *be kind, be connected, and be unafraid* was a dangerous and revolutionary act. They remembered how the Dandelion Insurrection emerged from the smallest stories of resistance: mothers who told the truth; children who shared their lunches; men who stood together in times of distress; people who turned back the tide of fear in their hearts; communities that burst forth with love.

We are the Dandelions, the insurrection against hate, the flowers bursting through concrete and the grip of control. We stand enduring, indomitable, and eternal. We are the body of the people, immortal. We'll out last the dangers. We'll rise to the challenges. We'll live to see the dawn of our changes arrive with the sun.

For anyone teetering on the brink of despair, on the edge of darkness, on the cliff of violence, they wrote messages and shared hope:

We, too, have been hurt. We, too, have lost faith. We, too, have been flooded with rage. We've been where you are, and we've thought as you do. Our fists have been ready to strike. We've longed to smash windows. We've burned to ignite cars. But we found better ways to fight back.

I organized an occupation, wrote the schoolteacher.

I coordinated the boycott of plunder monkey businesses, said the librarian.

I was at the resistance camp in the desert, declared the student.
I was the one who won housing for all.
I taught resistance in schools.

Dandelions are humble plants, close to the ground. Dandelions are medicinal, healing to the core. Every part of the plant is a remedy for what ails us. Not one part - flowers, leaves, or roots - does harm. Dandelions grow in every field, back lot, and sidewalk crack in the nation.

We began as a nonviolent movement, they wrote. *Let us finish what we started as such.*

In the sweltering sidewalks of the intense spring heat, a flutter of gray caught the eye of Inez Hernandez. As if waking from a long nightmare, she saw the flags of atonement hanging from storefronts and apartment windowsills. Gray, gray, gray, everywhere she looked. A false act of contrition coopting the memory of Ellen Byrd, chaining the sorrow of her loss to the proper shades of mourning, stripping the world of color.

"*Basta!*" spat Inez.

Shaking with sudden realization, she called Zadie far up north.

"We are dandelions, not cold-hearted concrete," Inez told her with the bite of bracing truth. "It's time, Zadie. Let her revive and blossom in us."

Inez shared her idea.

"I want to circulate Ellen's Pledge . . . remember? She used a nonviolence pledge on the march. There are millions of signers. Many still hold their early commitment. And there are many more that could not go to the march, but could now sign online. It would help everyone boldly proclaim their beliefs, not just later at the vote, but right now, when it matters most."

Zadie's eyes turned watery. What better way to honor Ellen Byrd's life than by embodying her integrity? Zadie thought about all the gray atonement flags hung in store windows. Time had proven them to be empty gestures. Zadie stared out the window of the old farmhouse. The verdant exuberance of spring resurrected life across the land. Fields that had turned gray in autumn were now erupting into swaths of green. Seeds emerged from dormancy. Dandelions blossomed again. Zadie's eyes fixed on the barn at the other end of the driveway.

"You know," Zadie told Inez, "if Mom were alive today, she would not only haul down those gray flags, she'd paint the city as yellow as our barn."

Ellen's last mural gleamed in the sunlight, blazing the French translation of the Dandelion Insurrection's rallying cry: *Pour la vie, liberte, et l'amour!*

Inez burst out laughing. Zadie's comment gave her a brilliant idea!

When Inez Hernandez moved into action, mountains didn't just move. They danced with the thunder and earthquakes of two-stepping continents. The five-foot tall powerhouse organized with the conviction that she had finally found a lever long enough to move the world . . . and all she had to do was throw every ounce of her ninety pounds onto this idea.

"You know me," Inez told the movement in a video calling them to sign the pledge. "I am in your streets and at your rallies. I have cradled your children in my arms and wept with you in sorrow. For me, there has never been any question about the Dandelion Insurrection. It grew from love and nonviolence. I don't know who these Roots are . . . but they aren't ours. Dandelion roots are deep and strong, healing, and resilient. We have to decide: life, liberty, and love . . . or violence, destruction, and death? If you choose the Roots' way, you may as well wear the black of mourning. And if you choose to disband, wear the disgraceful gray of the Interim Government - they'll be the ones running your lives. But . . . if you choose the true roots of the Dandelion Insurrection, and believe in our nonviolent beginnings, wear yellow, take down the gray flags, and let our golden banners fly!"

It was as if spring blossomed anew. As millions of people signed Ellen's Pledge, the gray disappeared. Flag by flag, golden blossoms popped up the flagpoles and hung out the windows. Schoolchildren drew pictures and taped them to doors. The sidewalks turned into meadows of gold. Blossoms of dresses and scarfs, jackets and hats, bobbed down the streets between the typical grays and blacks of the cities, challenging convention and neutrality by redefining the meaning of colors. Inez couldn't stop laughing - or crying - and took photos to send to Zadie.

Everywhere the yellow flowers appeared, Inez saw Ellen Byrd and her sister Lupe revived in the hearts of the people. She saw Charlie's cousin Matt and everyone lost on the day of the drone attack. They lived again in the return of support for the Dandelion Insurrection. Tansy and Alex reported that the Interim Government was quietly taking down the gray banners. Inez had successfully exposed their symbolism as a shallow gesture of cooption and control. Inez turned every person who signed Ellen's Pledge into an organizer to reach out to five more people. Supporters of the Dandelion Insurrection's commitment to nonviolence popped out of the woodwork as silence gave way to courage.

The other factions fought back, in some cases vandalizing the gold flags and harassing those who wore yellow, mocking them as weaklings, idealists, fools. Murals were defaced with black slashes of paint. Interim Government forces tore down posters with dandelions. The downtown merchants and financial districts stuck to the gray guns of Interim Government support. They pumped an arsenal of money into advertisements and propaganda, but the dandelions kept blossoming in workplaces and schools, on subways and in supermarkets. Every attempt to crush the dandelions sent a surge of conviction through yet another person's heart.

We should have the right to speak our views in safety, they proclaimed. We should be able to stand up for our ideals and not get struck down. We should be able to protest in our streets without the need for armed protection. A world of life, liberty, and love should be allowed to blossom in our towns and cities. And, if the powerful outlaw life; if they ban love, if they constrict liberty with unjust laws . . . then the dandelions must leap up in defiance, in numbers too vast to suppress, with persistence too determined to stop. And why should they wait for violent means to achieve such a goal, when they could embody that world today?

Hassled and harassed by both the Interim Government and the supporters of the Roots, the dandelions remained resolute. They used Ellen's Pledge to network and organize, and met all opposition with unshakeable nonviolent discipline. They gave Tansy Beaulisle dozens of clear civil disobedience cases with which to challenge the American Protection Act in court. When the Interim Government objected; when the police came to scatter them like seeds, the dandelions returned in other places, lifting up the scraggly leaves of their ordinariness and showing the golden blossoms of their hearts boldly. They popped up in the lawns of public parks. They cracked the concrete of control on the street corners. The supporters of the Roots chased them and mocked them, argued with them at every turn, but as the videos circulated of dandelions standing up for the right to nonviolently protest, such aggression stood in stark contrast to the gentle firmness of the yellow-clad dandelions, who spoke their message simply and clearly:

They were not being passive and silent.

They were not waiting for violence to set them free.

They were daring to be the change they sought, to jump-start the engine of freedom, to embody their goals here and now, and walk the new world into existence through the doorway of their bodies and hearts. With the vote looming closer by the day, the dandelions demonstrated that the dreams of tomorrow could spring to life in this moment. For them, the vote shifted from a nail-biting decision over their fate to a chance to make a declaration of their truth:

They were dandelions . . . and they could not be stopped.

CHAPTER THIRTY-FIVE

· · · · ·

The Vote

On the day of the vote, dawn rose with a shiver. Charlie and Zadie sat on the porch of her parents' old farmhouse. When Bill rose and the online voting opened, they would cast their votes and then the three would climb the hill to the birch grove and lay Ellen's ashes to rest. They'd exhausted all arguments. With a sense of surrender, they stepped into the unknown of the day like a small boat without oars. The tide of the people would carry them to whatever shore awaited.

South of them, Kinap stood on the banks of her ancestral homeland, prayer reverberating from her heart like a stone tossed into the river of the world. The rising sun lanced the thick mist. Water and light poured around Kinap as the sentinel of her ceremony formed a gateway for the day. As light streamed from the Dawnland across the curves of the continent, the sun illuminated millions of dew beads and plucked the harp strings of spider webs. Her vote would be cast for nonviolence; the alternatives had already filled too many tragic and brutal chapters of human history. The path forward required a different way of walking through change than using violence to control and dominate others. That belonged to the era of conquest and Kinap's challenge was to end those times and to help initiate the new. One human action after another, the ways of violent conquest had to be buried until the day finally came when the sun rose on a landscape growing toward healing and peace.

The great body of the earth rolled eastward. Sunlight ran its fingers through the skyscrapers of New York. Inez Hernandez' hand moved from head to heart, shoulder to shoulder, in the ritual gesture that closed her prayer. As the soft light crept in the empty church, the votive candles turned shy and pale. *Por el amor de Dios, let the dandelions stand strong,* she pleaded. That was all. Inez Hernandez had toiled in the grace of her faith for decades. She persevered for justice whether God lent his omnipotent hand or not. She stood in for overbooked guardian angels and saved lives when the divine turned its back. She had slept in the church pews and broken the concrete of the old parking lot open to plant gardens that fed whole neighborhoods. Her faith prayed on its feet. Her tithe to the church came in hard work and sweat. She was a parishioner of action, seen more often shaking the world than kneeling on Sunday. Inez would spend the day pounding the streets, reminding people to vote. She asked everyone, equally, without regard for their stance on the issue. The voices of the neighborhoods had to be heard from the smallest child to the strongest youth to the *abuelas* and *abuelos* who needed help navigating the online voting. Inez had hundreds of volunteers arriving at the church just before the polls opened. She turned on the coffeemaker and prepared for the day.

At eight o'clock precisely, Tansy Beaulisle's fire engine red fingernail cast her vote with her lips pursed in satisfied anticipation of being the first vote ... *or one of them,* she amended as the counter registered a hundred votes along with hers. Before the system churned out the results, she clicked off the screen and laced up her dusty hot-pink running shoes. Tansy couldn't sit around heart-in-mouth, stressing her nerves all day. She swigged the last of her coffee and bolted out the door toward the nearest park.

Tucker Jones watched her leave with the seemingly implacable calm of a meditating buddha. The entire Alternet team had been stationed on watchdog alert to thwart hackers from tampering with the results. An all-out virtual siege erupted as the votes leapt up by the thousands. Tucker watched the counter as the three options swung wildly by the second and wished they hadn't programmed it for real-time results.

Hour by hour, the stream of votes grew into a deluge. Idah Robbins and the school resistance network taught hundreds of thousands of school children how to cast their vote. Community centers let the Dandelion Insurrection organizers host open polling places for those who needed access to a computer. In Northern Maine, the entire valley, everyone who was related by blood and distant cousinship to Charlie, added their votes. Gus Reasonover cast his choice to disarm, not disband - and discovered - to everyone's surprise - that many of the other Texas Free Rangers did the same, declaring that they would uphold their early promise to the Dandelion Insurrection.

But, as Tucker watched, the other opinions rolled in, too. The counter swung between Roots and Dandelions with only a small faction choosing to disband.

He eyed the totals as the clock ticked toward noon. As massive as it seemed, three million votes was a mere fraction of the nation's hundreds of millions of potential voters from kindergarteners to great-grandparents. Where was everyone? Waiting to see which way the winds blew?

Something's got to give, Tucker thought, watching the tallies inch upward, neck and neck for Roots and Dandelions. Those bystanders needed to move. He tried calling Charlie. No answer. Zadie's phone went to voice message. Inez told him she was already pestering the whole world. Tucker hung up and stared at the screen.

Come on, he urged. *This matters to our futures, our lives. Our fates are tied to the Dandelion Insurrection. The hopes and dreams of our children depend on this moment's choice.*

At noon, everything stalled. Tucker checked the system, but nothing was wrong. Voting slowed to a trickle with the Roots' violent tactics slightly in the lead. The flicker of hope in Tucker's heart began to smolder with the acrid smoke of bitterness. A scorching sensation of betrayal burned in his chest. His eyes watered.

The front door flew open with a bang. Tansy hurtled in, wild-eyed and shouting.

"Turn it on! Turn it on!"

Her fingers reached for the computer.

"Heard the news at the corner store . . . he's going to stab us in the back, the crooked weasel."

"Who is - " Tucker's question broke off mid-sentence as Tansy opened a live feed.

Will Sharp's face appeared on the screen.

CHAPTER THIRTY-SIX

· · · · ·

Will's Turn

The lines of his face drew shadows into their creases. He sat, carved in contrast to the cream of the flat wall behind him, lips twisted in a mocking smile. Tansy wanted to throttle him.

"Trace that signal, Tucker. I could run over and drag him off the air," she growled, hands on her hips and jogging shoes kicking the carpet in fury.

Tucker doubted that Will Sharp would be foolish enough to use an easily traceable signal, but he got to work, his gut twisting in a fit of nerves. He'd never told the others what he knew about Will's father; the young man had been so shockingly appalled that Tucker had offered the promise of his discretion. He regretted that now. A sinking feeling dragged his heart down into dismay, wondering if Will would backstab them all to curry favor with his father. He had seemed furious when he learned who it was, but blood ran thicker than the waters of other loyalties.

"About Will," he began, turning to Tansy.

"Shhh, wait. He's starting," she hushed him.

Will stared coolly at the screen, arrogant and composed.

"I can see by the numbers that millions of you are dragging your feet on voting. Why? This is, perhaps, the most important vote of your whole life, a vote not about which candidate you'll give your political power to, but how *you* will grasp power in your own two hands. This vote is poised to shape the course of events that will affect every aspect of your life . . . and you're hanging back?"

His voice rose, incredulous.

"I expected more from a movement that swells into the millions and claims to be leaderful. You're not leaders," he accused with a look of scorn, "you're chickens. You're looking over your shoulder to see what everyone else is doing. You're trying to play it safe, to be on the winning side of this coin toss."

He looked away for a moment then stung the listeners with his next words.

"There is no winning side to this argument. There's no truth inside this vote. You're voting on lies, deception, and hidden agendas."

Tansy broke into a milk-curdling tirade ignoring Tucker's shushes. When the phone rang, she lunged for it.

"Yeah, Chuck, we heard. We're watching that contemptible lump of lies right now."

Tucker frowned at the young man on the screen. Will waited. His eyes flicked to the corner of the computer, noting the rising number of viewers on his channel. Tucker knew he'd stall to give people more time to log on. Every second he delayed gave Tucker another chance to catch his signal, decode the scramble, and shut him down.

"A friend of mine once said that every non-action counts. This decision today is cast as much by those who stand aside as by those who move into action," Will commented, looking off to the side as if remembering the friend.

A thousand miles away, Idah Robbins felt tears come to her eyes. She had followed the rise of the Roots and the choices of Will Sharp. *Don't betray us,* she pleaded in her aching heart; *think of the children, Will.* Participation matters, she had told him, and the youth stood at the pivot point of everything. His next move would determine the course of the future for years to come. The children's lives would be shaped by his next breath. Idah's eyes brimmed as she envisioned the kids hanging by the thin thread of his principles. If he crushed hope in the grip of his actions, Idah Robbins felt she would have failed as a teacher. *Please,* she urged Will, *let the countless hours of knowledge I shared with you not be in vain. Let my efforts as a teacher take root as deeply in your heart as they did in your mind.*

"Before you cast your vote," he said, stalling and delaying as millions of people connected to his channel, "I want you to search your heart. Think of everything you know about the Dandelions. Consider all the actions pulled off by the Roots. Weigh in your vision of the world we're working for. Account for the dangers and challenges we face."

Kinap ran into her house, breathless at the news that Will Sharp was about to speak out against the Dandelion Insurrection on the live feed. As she listened, a sense of failure weighed heavily on her. Despite all her efforts, she had not been able to get this young man to truly understand the concept of *kinap.*

You could have chosen nonviolence, she accused him. *You had – and still have – the power in your hands to steer an entire culture away from cycles of violence. Were all my teachings for nothing?* Kinap closed her eyes against despair and called on the spirits to guide him back to his heart.

"Charlie asked me once," Will said, "whose Roots are you? He said we weren't the roots of the Dandelion Insurrection, that violence could never be the seed and the structure of a movement growing toward love, kindness, and connection. The Dandelions were the insurrection of love against hate, he said, courage against fear, kindness against cruelty . . . and nonviolence against violence and destruction. *These* were the roots of the Dandelion Insurrection, he said, embodied by

345

children and mothers, elders and families; ordinary, everyday people who planted the seed of the future in their actions today, letting the world we longed for grow in each moment, each footstep, each breath. Our means were our ends in the making, he said."

Far up north, in Bill's farmhouse, Zadie stared at the screen, remembering what Will was forgetting: that *she* had spoken those words to him, quoting Charlie's writing from memory, ferocious as a mother protecting her baby, blistering Will in a voicemail he never returned, scorching him for the missive that called people to pick up arms. He was betraying all of her trust, every moment of forgiveness, every second of friendship she'd ever extended to him.

I trusted you, she told him silently, *don't do this.*

Will licked his lips, nervous. A band of sweat broke out across his forehead. He took a deep breath and looked skyward for a long moment. This was it. The moment of truth. The breath that would change everything for millions of people, and for him, Will Sharp, bastard son of John C. Friend, founder of the covert group called the Roots, ex-military special ops agent, armed fighter, delinquent, street rat, troublemaker.

"My name is Will Sharp," he said.

. . . defender of children, protector of the weak . . .

"I am the founder of the Roots."

. . . he had stopped assassins - including himself - he had stood on a bridge called by the water; he had held Zadie in her terror, kept Inez out of jail, protected Charlie Rider from the cruelties of the Butcher. He was a liar, a spy, an infiltrator, and provocateur. He was staked like a martyr on the crossroads of change, his heart burned with truths that could kill him. He was splintering and cracking between fear and hope. He was a coin being tossed by the world . . .

"And I am the son of John C. Friend."

John C. Friend bolted upright in the Oval Office. Fury swept the man's expression. A strangled half-smile formed under his bulging eyes. He dialed a number and told the Roots to find him, stop him, break his livestream connection, kill him if they had to . . . then he hung up and watched the screen like a battered boxer awaiting the next blow.

"The Roots work for Friend," Will confessed. He swallowed nervously, though his safe house was well concealed. "In the beginning, our mission was to help the Dandelion Insurrection succeed. We made sure that the cradle would rock and the old regime would fall. Once Friend assumed the presidency, our job changed. We were instructed to crush the Dandelion Insurrection, leaving Friend unchallenged as he put his people in power. The acts of sabotage, the pipeline explosion, the assassination attempt, the violence at the protests, and the Day of Demonstration were all planned by Friend to weaken the Dandelion Insurrection. As the elections approached and it became obvious his people couldn't win fairly, we were also instructed to foment violence, riots, and upheaval, allowing him to suspend the elections."

In all his years of secrecy, hidden actions, and silence, Will had never felt so alone. He could not know that, far beyond the walls of his safe house, Idah Robbins burst out in sobs, waving her hand and trying to explain how proud she was of Will Sharp. He could not know that Tansy Beaulisle stood speechless for the first time in her life, then bent over and kissed his forehead on the screen. He did not hear Pilar Maria and Inez Hernandez' stream of Spanish thanking God for this miracle. He did not hear Kinap's blessing in her native tongue, honoring him for being, at long last, *kinap*. He did not see Zadie's glory of a smile breaking through the storm of her tears.

He did not hear the murmured words of Charlie Rider, though they would have meant more to him than anything else.

"You are a true dandelion, after all," he said.

On the screen, the young man shook his head in incredulous disbelief. A small breath of laughter escaped his lips as he thought of how hard the Roots had tried to sabotage the Dandelion Insurrection. Nothing had worked. Just when the movement teetered on the edge of self-destruction, the seeds of trust, friendship, and compassion had broken through the hard shell of his heart, calling on him to step up and tell the truth.

"You can't stop the dandelions," Will said. "We couldn't. We tried every trick in the book. We tried to kill them, break them, crush, coopt, and corrupt them, but they're still here, still rising up, still bursting out of all corners of the country, standing up for crazy things like kindness, respect, and love."

The Roots claimed that they had ensured the early success of the movement, but looking back, he could see that nothing could have stopped the Dandelion Insurrection. It had even triumphed despite their best attempts to thwart it. He smiled slightly, remember Idah Robbins' audacious claim that nonviolent movements succeeded *in spite of* violent flanks, not because of them.

Add us to the statistics, he thought.

Suddenly, the livestream faltered. The furious Roots had intercepted the signal.

"Oh no, you don't," Tucker Jones vowed, hot on their heels.

The image abruptly stabilized.

"So, now it's up to you," Will told the millions of listeners, reminding them of the vote. "It always is. It is our choices, day in and day out, which make the difference. It is our hearts, voices, actions that swing the fate of the world toward hope or despair, life or death, destruction or resurrection."

Will reached for the keyboard.

"I'm casting my vote now," he said, eyes flicking across the screen. "I choose to disarm, not disband."

His mouse moved. He clicked once.

A sense of peace passed over his face.

He smiled and the screen went dark.

CHAPTER THIRTY-SEVEN

. . . . .

Operation Full Stop

Tucker Jones stared at the empty screen in stunned silence. Then, as the full impact of Will's whistleblowing sank in, the hairs on his neck rose. A message popped onto his computer:

Here's the proof about the Roots and Friend.
Thanks for telling me the truth about my father.
- W. S.

Attached was full documentation backing up his claims. Tucker took a deep breath. Then he typed two words to the Mouse.

It's time.

In her crowded cubicle in the government IT support office, Alex Kelley read the message and looked up, scanning the shocked expressions of her coworkers. She checked to make sure no one was watching then she quietly hit the send button on an interdepartmental email.

It's time, it said. *Launch O. F. S.*

Alex held her breath.

Ten seconds. Thirty seconds. One minute.

At two minutes and thirty seconds, Operation Full Stop began.

One by one, computer after computer locked.

"It's happening!" her coworker hollered, leaping up and shouting over the cubicle dividers. "The call for Operation Full Stop just went out! Shut them down!"

Alex nearly burst into tears of relief as her coworkers jolted into action, dashing for keyboards and computers, hollering

351

explanations to the new interns who stood confused. Alex's heart swelled with affection for her fellow techies as they implemented the plan of civilian-based defense, locking down the government according to a strategy she and Tucker had designed months ago. They had quietly spread the plan from one department to the next as a simple suggestion that *when in the course of human events, it becomes necessary* to defend against yet another tyrant - and no one breathed a word of suspicion about Friend - the government workers would know how to withhold their support and deny access to their departments' files, resources, and workers.

Because Operation Full Stop made no mention of the Interim Government or Friend, there was little anyone could do to stop people from talking about such a theoretical strategy.

You can't kill an idea, Alex chuckled to herself, and the more anyone tried to stop it, the faster the gossip about Operation Full Stop seemed to spread from coffee dispensers to water coolers to break rooms.

Her only real concern was whether or not anyone would actually do it. Mouse and Cybermonk could have programmed the lockdown into a single-source code set-up by Tucker's inventive fingertips, but Alex's ethics stopped them. No one - not even she or Tucker - should be able to push a button and lockdown the government. So, they pushed Operation Full Stop into the dangerous and uncertain territory of the human conscience, and required mass, collective action on the part of hundreds of thousands of government workers to pull the strategy off. It was a terrible risk, requiring a level of faith Alex wasn't certain she had for her irascible, ornery, fractious fellow human beings. Yet, here was her obnoxious coworker - of all people! - putting the protocol into action. She beamed a smile as he leaned over the divider.

"Come on, Alex, get moving. The call for Operation Full Stop just went out."

She must have blinked because he groaned at her slowness and scurried around to her desk.

"Operation . . . Full . . . Stop," he informed her through gritted teeth, hunching over her keyboard, "is a lockdown of government offices against rising tyrants or in the event of an attempted coup."

"I know what it is," she snapped, slapping his sweaty fingers off her board.

"Then hurry up!" he urged excitedly, straightening and starting to hustle the gawking interns at the end of the row. "We've got him! Friend'll resign by the end of the day. Shut it down!" he bellowed to the office. "You know the protocol! Computers locked, passwords changed, and staff gone. No sense in hanging around waiting for security to arm-twist us."

Alex shook her head in surprise. You just never knew what scraggly weed of a coworker would blossom into a genuine dandelion under the right conditions.

"Look!" hollered her coworker from the window.

Alex shoved her rolling chair back so fast she nearly crashed into her supervisor. She leapt to get a glimpse and squirmed through the taller interns to the front. The government workers were walking out. From every doorway, a stream of suits and white-collared shirts, clicking heels and skirts exited the building. Some hollered up at the faces in the windows, gesturing for them to come down. The tide of people ran toward the White House. Alex could hear the chant rising: *resign, resign, resign!*

"Shall we?" her coworker suggested with a grin.

Alex nodded. Their work here was done.

CHAPTER THIRTY-EIGHT

· · · · ·

In The End

Dusk slipped down with a satisfied sigh of relief. Zadie climbed the footpath between the tall grasses toward the birch grove, her skin tingling with the reverberations of the day, blood pulsing in the rhythm of hope.

"Can you feel it, Mom?" she murmured as the birches whispered through their leafy hands. Across the nation, the suspended heartbeat of celebration surged back to life. The cheer truncated by the drone strike and stifled by sobs erupted in millions of throats. Love walked like a giant across the landscape of change, scattering the storm clouds of despair.

Friend had resigned. With the government workers on strike and the system locked against him, he had wisely stepped down from the presidency. As cops armed with arrest warrants circled political doorsteps, Congress found it prudent to swiftly repeal the American Protection Act and restore the suspended elections.

Zadie's smile trembled in a surge of emotion. She tipped her head back to catch the tears escaping her eyes. The fluttering canopy overhead shimmered as the wind danced between the leaves. In the end, everything hinged on the pivot point of a single human heart. Will's choice to be a dandelion of the soul had turned the tide of darkness. In a strange way, Will Sharp had become a true root of resistance, holding firm to the principles of honesty, love, kindness, and connection, taking a tremendous risk to do what was right, and inspiring millions of people to cast their votes to disarm, but not disband.

355

"They came through," Zadie whispered in a prayer of a voice, speaking to her mother's soul.

All across the country, the real victory was won when the people stood up for their hearts. The Dandelion Insurrection had passed through its moment of truth on its own feet, leaderful, replete with people standing shoulder-to-shoulder on common ground. From Alex and the government workers to Tucker Jones and the Alternet crew to Idah Robbins and the school resistance, and so many more, the people were organizing and leading themselves. The Dandelion Insurrection had grown beyond she and Charlie and taken root in millions of people. When the crisis of tactics shook them, the movement came through not because she or Charlie had ordered them into line, but because the people had followed their hearts. This was the ground of democracy, the fertile soil of shared governance, the first foundational step toward the world of their hopes and dreams.

Ellen Byrd's gentleness, her strong stance, conviction and principles had not died under the blast of the drone. Her body fell, but the seeds of her spirit took root and endured in the lives of thousands. When the Dandelion Insurrection laid down their votes, they laid bare their hearts, and in them the long lineage of nonviolence rose immortal.

Through long stretches of time and countless chapters of human history, this lineage has risen to confront injustice: Egyptian pyramid craftsmen striking for bread wages; Roman plebeians refusing to work for patricians; pagans veiling the sacred in secrecy to escape death on the pyre; Gandhi's pinch of salt multiplied in millions of Indian hands; African-American children facing fire hoses and attack dogs; Estonians singing for independence; miles of Baltic hands joining to end occupation; striking millworkers and miners walking out by the thousands;

Danish families saving the Jews; the Madres de la Plaza crying out for their disappeared children until regimes toppled at their feet ... across the globe and throughout time, the roots of resistance run deep, broad, and thick through the story of humanity's struggles.

They show up when a mother teaches her child to love, when embittered enemies wage peace, and when the person who caused harm speaks out to right wrongs. Resistance is more than a battle; it is the indomitable presence of life against forces of destruction. It is laughter when fear is mandated, respect when hate is demanded, compassion when cruelty is ordered, and generosity when greed is expected. Resistance is singing your grandmother's songs so the next generation will know them. Resistance is loving the humble honesty of origins. Resistance is weeping when rivers run oily and vowing to redress the harm. Resistance is listening to the stories untold. Resistance is standing up for a stranger.

Zadie stood quietly among the slender grace of the birches, sensing her mother's spirit running like a river through the world, eternal, enduring, never lost, always living, revived through the actions of the people. Lupe, Matt, and all of the dandelions struck down shone brightly as the torch of love marched onward toward change. Great challenges remained; the wheel of revolution turned with the Earth, the power-hungry still scrambled for control. The poor neighborhoods continued to struggle for survival. The plunder monkeys still snatched at anything they could grab. But Zadie knew with utter certainty that the challenges could be met, because the people remained true to their hearts.

The grasses swayed. The light dipped. A flash of silver caught her eye. Zadie bent and picked the dandelion, turning the orb of its seeds in her fingers. The last brush of sun flooded the leaves overhead. The birch grove blazed golden. Zadie breathed in the hopes of the people. She closed her eyes and made a wish on the seeds: when night falls and day breaks and the world spins around, she wished that our roots of resistance hold strong; that the ground of our hearts stays true to great Love; that we rise to the challenges with courage; that the lineage of nonviolence revives in the living; that her mother's life inspires our own.

Zadie blew without looking, and then opened her eyes, smiling as the seeds rose on the wind and took flight.

The End.

If you enjoyed *The Roots of Resistance* . . .
you can connect others to the novel
in the following ways:

Spread the word about the book.
Tell your friends.
Post about it on social media.
Review the book on your favorite online bookstore.
Recommend it to your book group.
Suggest it to teachers and students.

Thank you!

Author's Note

· · · · ·

Four years ago, I began to write *The Dandelion Insurrection*, a story about a "time that looms around the corner of today" and a "place on the edge of our nation". Since then, we have seen the rise of greater levels of greed, bigotry, climate denialism . . . and also the eruptions of widespread resistance. The fate of humanity appears tied to the swinging pendulum of each moment - one minute brings hope, the next heralds disaster. The closing chapter of each day leaves us suspended in the breathless uncertainty of an eternal cliffhanger.

These are times for courage, and times for love. The trappings of normalcy have no business in our current world - indeed, they are often the causes of the very dangers we seek to avert. *The Dandelion Insurrection* and *The Roots of Resistance* were born from and in these times as stories to inspire and instruct. The world of Charlie and Zadie, Inez and Tansy, is not exactly ours. It lives one step outside our reality, just far enough for fresh possibilities to emerge, yet close enough for us to glean ideas and inspiration.

If the characters loom both larger than life and intimately familiar, it is because I have encountered real people like Tucker, Alex, Kinap, and Will, all across this country. I have also seen Friend, Devanne, and the Butcher. Ultimately, I think each of us is a Frank Novaro, poised at a moment of truth, ready for the hard shell of our hearts to crack open, about to throw the weight of our love into the struggle for justice. We are also Will Sharp, conflicted, soul-searching, and growing. His struggle over tactics and loyalties stirs up the same questions we are facing in our lives today. There are few easy answers.

The Roots of Resistance portrays the dynamics of different methods of struggle. As much as possible, I have tried to follow the identified patterns noted by researchers who are looking at hundreds of conflicts. The novel also draws inspiration from many real life examples of nonviolent struggle, including the theories of civilian-based defense, Denmark's resistance to Nazi occupation, Sherri Mitchell - Wena'hamu'gwasit's teachings on *kinap* and conquest ideology, the nation's first nonviolent public elementary school in Rhode Island, Standing Rock and many other fossil fuel and water extraction resistance campaigns, and much more.

The novel also highlights another important trend: our opposition is studying the ropes of nonviolent struggle - not to use it, but to stop us - and they are often learning faster than we are. If we wish to see our efforts succeed, we need to prioritize widespread education about the strategy and dynamics of nonviolent struggle. The opponents of today's movements are becoming more and more skillful at infiltration, disruption, and division. They intentionally provoke activists to violence and sabotage, knowing exactly how to defeat such tactics and use them to discredit movements.

The discussion of violence vs. nonviolence needs to grow beyond the current argument around the moral right to self-defense into an informed analysis of the dynamics of collective struggle and organized resistance. The statistics that Idah Robbins quotes are real: nonviolent action succeeds twice as often as violent means, in a third of the amount of time, and with a fraction of the casualties. Violent flanks have no demonstrated effect on the success of nonviolent movements, which are succeeding *in spite of* (not because of) the presence of violent flanks.

The knowledge and study of nonviolent struggle has advanced far enough that advocates of the method need not be naive idealists. In fact, they shouldn't be! Over thousands of years, especially in the last two centuries, hundreds of millions of your fellow human beings have picked up the tools of nonviolent action to dismantle oppressive structures and build a new world of respect and justice. All of us who yearn for change should honor their sacrifices and courage by studying the stories of this remarkable lineage and applying the hard won lessons.

This knowledge, which is woven into the pages of this novel, determines more than the plot twists of the Dandelion Trilogy. It contains the hope of humanity as we wage struggle for survival. If we choose to learn from our past, we have the chance to alter the swing of the world's uncertain pendulums. The knowledge of nonviolent struggle can change the landscape of our lives, especially on the coming day when the "time that looms around the corner of today" arrives in the heartbeat of the present.

With love,
Rivera Sun

Glossary of Techniques

. . . . .

Introduction

Years ago, as I began to research for *The Dandelion Insurrection* (the prequel to *The Roots of Resistance*), I stumbled onto the vast and ever-growing field of nonviolent struggle. More than just protests and marches, the world of courageous change-making involves strategy and dynamics, techniques and philosophies, studies and experiments. My nonviolent struggle library now takes up a whole wall of my house and threatens to pile up in stacks in my writing corner. *The Roots of Resistance* is written on the building blocks of this knowledge. Much of the novel's plot was crafted by applying my understanding of strategy for nonviolent movements to the situations the characters faced. This glossary of techniques offers insights into a few of the concepts that appear within the pages of this novel. Each definition also includes examples from the book and some have suggestions for further study. I encourage all of my readers to learn more. This knowledge will change our world. Indeed, it already has.

If you are reading the print book version, please note that this glossary can also be found on my website, where further resources on each concept are hyperlinked to leading organizations in the field of nonviolent struggle. Find it at: www.riverasun.com/roots-glossary/

You can also find over one hundred essays on nonviolent struggle on my website, plus the essays of *The Man From the North*, inspired by Charlie Rider's writings in the novels.

Another useful resource is *The Dandelion Insurrection Study Guide to Making Change Through Nonviolent Action*, which uses the novel as a fun and engaging way to learn some very practical knowledge about nonviolent struggle. This glossary references the study guide, connecting you to further study and group exercises on certain topics.

· · · · ·

Affinity group: a small group of people who train for and participate in nonviolent actions together. *Example: the Dandelion Swarms could be viewed as affinity groups.* Learn more on War Resisters' International website: www.nonviolence.wri-irg.org

Agent Provocateur: a person hired by one's opponents to intentionally instigate or commit violent acts during a nonviolent struggle in order to provoke and/or justify repression, or to discredit the movement. *Example: the Roots act as agent provocateurs during the latter chapters of the novel.* Learn more at: www.theantimedia.org

Alternative & Parallel Institutions: organizations and systems aimed at partially or fully replacing institutions controlled by or in support of the oppressor group. These can be economic, political, social, transportation, educational, or communications systems. *Examples: the Alternet, and the Penny Elementary.* Learn more at www.mettacenter.org

Assassination: Murder for political purposes.

Backfire/Backlash (also called political ju-jitsu, aikido effect): an effect that occurs when an opponent's use of violent repression is met by disciplined nonviolent resistance, and backfires against the opponent, showing the opponent in the worst possible light. Opinions and power relationships shift in favor of the nonviolent group, weakening the opponent's strength and contributing to their defeat. For this to occur, nonviolent resisters must remain steadfast in the use of nonviolent tactics. If the nonviolent resisters adopt violence, it is likely to undermine their position rather than their opponent's. (Adapted from Sharp's Dictionary of Power and Struggle) *Example: this dynamic occurs at the bridge in the desert, when the violent repression of the police and private security agents causes Frank Novaro to blockade the road with his truck. The violence of the security agents also plays a role in catalyzing nationwide actions against extraction companies.* Find a study exercise on managing repression in *The Dandelion Insurrection Study Guide,* pg 18-20.

Boycott: an organized refusal to continue social, economic, or political participation with an injustice or opponent. The word comes from Irish resistance to exploitive landlords. In 1886, tenants in Mayo County refused to speak or do business with Captain Boycott, a land agent, in protest of his evictions in the region. *Examples: Charlie's corporate media boycott, the boycott of businesses opposing the Relief Bill, the boycott of businesses using prison labor during the Debt Prison Strike.*

Burnout: to tire due to overwork or stress; to reach a point of collapse due to overwork. *Example: Charlie reaches this point several times in the book, and uses a variety of restorative practices to keep going, including support of friends and taking a break.* See also: self-care

Casualties: deaths. Despite occasional massacres and the unarmed nature of nonviolent protesters, nonviolent struggle has a 1:10 casualty rate compared to civil wars. (Chenoweth and Stephan, *Why Civil Resistance Works*) *Example: pg 8, as Charlie walks to the funeral of the people killed in the drone strike, he also notes the comparable casualty rate had they chosen to start a violent civil war.*

Citizen Media: journalism by persons who are not professional journalists. The term is related to participatory media and democratic media. *Example: Charlie mobilizes citizen media teams to support the efforts of the Dandelion Insurrection when the corporate media presents their work in a negative light.* Learn more: en.wikipedia.org/wiki/Citizen_media

Civilian-Based Defense: a plan of nonviolent action through which it is possible to deter and defeat foreign military invasions, occupations, and internal coups through noncooperation and defiance by society. *Example: Idah Robbins references this concept, later Tucker Jones and Alex Kelley implement a plan of civilian-based defense in the context of Operation Full Stop.* Learn more at the Albert Einstein Institution website (www.aeinstein.org) through the work of Gene Sharp.

Civil Disobedience: the active refusal to comply with specific laws that are considered unjust, or breaking laws to achieve objectives considered crucial enough that breaking the law is justified. *Example: the Freedom of Speech marches and demonstrations attempt to use civil disobedience of the recently passed American Protection Act to overturn the law in the courts and make it unenforceable through mass noncompliance.* Learn more at the Metta Center for Nonviolence: www.mettacenter.org

Civil Resistance: widespread nonviolent resistance by the civilian population. The means of action and dynamics are those of nonviolent action. Learn more at the International Center On Nonviolent Conflict: www.nonviolent-conflict.org

Concentration and Dispersion: refers to methods of nonviolent action that assemble or disperse bodies in a physical space. Examples of concentrated actions include marches, rallies, blockades, and sit-ins. Examples of dispersed actions include stay-at-home strikes, call-in-sick strikes, and boycotts. When dealing with violent repression, shifting from concentrated to dispersed actions can protect people while maintaining pressure on one's opponents. *Example: the blockade on the bridge, the marches for the Freedom of Speech, and the anti-eviction squads are examples of concentrated actions. The debt strike and the boycotts of the company's blocking the Relief Bill are dispersed actions.* Learn more in *The Dandelion Insurrection Study Guide*, pg 35.

Constructive Program: "Constructive program is a term coined by Gandhi. It describes nonviolent action taken within a community to build structures, systems, processes or resources that are positive alternatives to oppression. It can be seen as self-improvement of both community and individual. Constructive program often works along side obstructive program, or Civil Disobedience, which usually involves direct confrontation to, or non-co-operation with, oppression. Constructive program is doing what one can to imaginatively and positively create justice within one's own community." (From the Metta Center Glossary) *Example: the community conflict resolution teams, peace teams, and restorative justice circles are constructive programs dealing with the lack of trust of police in certain neighborhoods. They are also examples of alternative* *institutions. Idah Robbins' Nonviolent School is also a constructive program.* Learn more about planning constructive programs in *The Dandelion Insurrection Study Guide* pg 61-66 or at www.mettacenter.org

Co-optation (also co-option): has two meanings. The first refers to awarding individuals from an opposition group with a degree of privilege or power in order to control them. The second refers to when a larger (or more powerful) group takes over some of a smaller group's related interests without adopting the full program or ideal, often undercutting the need for deeper change. *Examples: pg 1-39, Friend tries this with the Gray Atonement Flags; pg 165, the Butcher tries to get Charlie and Tansy to sell-out on some movement goals in exchange for others.*

Counterrevolution: action taken to undermine or reverse a revolution. This occurs when the previous government has been removed from power but the usurping group has not fully consolidated its own control. *Example: many of the Dandelion Insurrection's challenges in The Roots of Resistance are related to attempted counterrevolutionary measures by the rich and formerly powerful.*

Cultural Resistance: has two meanings. The first refers to holding to one's own way of life, language, customs, and beliefs despite pressures from another culture. The second is the use of arts, literature, and traditional practices to resist oppressive systems or policies. *Examples: the Acadians and the tintamarre; Kinap and the Indigenous nation's style of organizing.* Learn more at New Tactics In Human Rights: www.newtactics.org

Cumulative Campaigns: a series of campaigns toward movement goals that build cumulatively upon the success of the previous campaign. *Examples: The school resistance campaigns build cumulatively from the catalyzing model of Los Jardineros into dozens of similar school struggles nationwide. These, in turn, inspire parallel resistance campaigns to stop the seizure of other public assets by plunder monkeys.* Learn more in *The Dandelion Insurrection Study Guide*, pg 53-59.

De-escalation: using skills and tactics to diminish the intensity, size, or likelihood of violent conflict. *Examples: Many characters apply these skills at different points throughout the story, on both small and large scales. They are used during street actions by Idah, Inez, and various peace teams. Zadie's speeches and Charlie's writings calling for nonviolent discipline could also be considered de-escalation tactics for the broader movement.* Learn more at www.metapeaceteam.org

Debt Strike/Debt Resistance: refusal to pay some or all of a debt and its interest as a method of economic boycott. This tactic has been used in opposition to debtors' policies, and also as a method of denying resources to opponents. *Example: the Debt Strike in solidarity with the Debt Prison strike.* Learn more at Strike Debt: www.strikedebt.org

Demands: a set of goals or objectives, generally defined in tangible points, that the movement wishes the opposition to concede or meet. *Examples: pg 67, the movement expanded its initial demands to include another list of economic justice and human rights issues outlined in the People's Demands that formed the basis for the new Relief Bill.*

Direct Action: social, economic, or political action taken by people to intervene directly in an injustice. Direct action is contrasted with indirect action, such as getting someone to act in favor of one's group (i.e. lobbying politicians to get a new law passed), or by leaders or public figures (as by negotiations). This term has been used in both violent and nonviolent contexts. *Examples: Let's Be Frank campaign's vehicle blockades of roads, the children of Los Jardineros marching to reclaim their school, the Freedom of Speech marches and demonstrations.* Learn more at Beautiful Trouble: www.beautifultrouble.org

Disruption: a theory of social change that argues that *disruption* of the current system is necessary for propelling change. It was articulated by Frances Fox Piven and Richard Cloward who felt that poor people gain leverage only by causing "commotion among bureaucrats, excitement in the media, dismay among influential segments of the community, and strain for political leaders." *Examples: the tintamarre, murmurations, Dandelion Swarms, Los Jardineros, Begging for Change campaign.* Learn more in Piven and Cloward's book, *Poor Peoples' Movements.*

Escalation: in the context of nonviolent movements, escalation refers to increasing the intensity of a campaign either through frequency of actions, types of actions, pressures upon targets, or shifting to more confrontational strategies in which the stakes to all parties heighten. *Example: the campaign for the new Relief Bill follows stages of escalation from awareness-raising murmurations, to Not One Penny More's boycotts, to rent strikes and anti-eviction efforts, to the debt prison strike, to the solidarity debt strike.* Learn more at War Resisters' International: www.wri-irg.org or in *The Dandelion Insurrection Study Guide,* pg 16-17.

Flash Actions: a flash action is a rapid convergence of people into action, generally unrehearsed or pre-organized. The concept originated with flash mobs as a form of participatory performance art, with groups of people using online communications to arrange to show up in a public location to do some kind of playful protest activity. In later years, the spontaneity of flash mobs gave rise to a wide variety of flash actions characterized by their rapid organization on short notice. *Examples: the Dandelion Insurrection implements flash mob-type actions with many variations. They also utilize tactics that have elements of spontaneity within a more choreographed structure. They call these murmurations, which is further defined below.* Learn more at Beautiful Trouble: www.beautifultrouble.org

Hacking: to break into or alter a computer program or system. *Example: the Spyder hacked into the paternity lab's computers to get DNA results on Will Sharp's identity.*

Humanizing Effect: unlike violence, which relies on dehumanizing the enemy, nonviolent struggle gains strategic and practical advantages by humanizing the opposition, the movement, and the bystanders. It cuts through the illusion of the opponent's infallibility, helps maintain nonviolent discipline, reduces the likelihood of violent repression in some cases, builds empathy particularly among ally groups, and increases willingness to participate in the movement. *Examples: the desert resisters frequently humanized themselves to the extraction company workers, and also to the security agents; also the Man From the North humanizes the Dandelion Insurrection by calling upon the many voices in the movement in an attempt to build nonviolent discipline.* Learn more in *The Dandelion Insurrection Study Guide* pg 12-14.

Infiltration: the process of deliberate, usually covert, entry of agents into an organization or movement in order to influence its actions or goals, disrupt the organization, or discredit the movement. Approaches and tactics used by infiltrators include seduction, surveillance, insertion into command and communications structure, spreading misinformation, provoking violence or sabotage, stalling and obstructing movement activities, and more. *Examples: pg 231-233, the Roots report on their progress infiltrating different groups within the Dandelion Insurrection. Later in the book, they leverage their positions to disrupt and discredit the movement.* Learn more about the widespread infiltration of social justice movements through these articles by Kevin Zeese and Margaret Flowers of Popular Resistance: *Infiltration to Divide, Disrupt and Mis-direct are Widespread in Occupy* and *Infiltration of Political Movements is the Norm, Not the Exception, in the United States.* www.popularresistance.org

Interposition: in third party nonviolent intervention, interposition is the act of physically getting in between conflicting parties to deter them from using violence against one another. *Examples: Idah Robbins uses interpositioning during the Freedom of Speech march when one of the Roots, undercover as a Solidarity Center volunteer, attempts an act of provocation toward a cop.* Learn more in the Metta Center Glossary at: www.mettacenter.org

Kinap: a Wabanaki word that means "warrior" or "helper", and describes someone who dedicates themselves in service of the community. *Example: the character Kinap is named for this quality.* Learn more in *Sacred Instructions: Indigenous Wisdom for*

Living Spirit-Based Change by Sherri Mitchell - Weh'na Ha'mu' Kwasset (She Who Brings the Light).

Leaderful: a style of leadership which stands in contrast to "leaderless" by empowering shared leadership and actively cultivating the ability of many to hold responsibilities, skills, and decision-making capacities. *Examples: the Dandelion Insurrection uses a leaderful structure paired with trainings and communication to manage its multi-nodal, dispersed nature.* Learn more in *The Dandelion Insurrection Study Guide,* pg 83.

Leaderless: an organizational style popularized by the 2011 Occupy Protests which eschews hierarchical leadership and charismatic leaders.

Leaked Information: knowledge or data that is disclosed to an unauthorized person. *Examples: the Mouse leaks several pieces of information to the Dandelion Insurrection, including the secret version of the Relief Bill, the businesses lobbying against the Peoples' Demands, and the threat of plunder monkeys. These actions allow the movement to adapt their strategies effectively.*

Movement of Movements: a description of many movements occurring simultaneously and working toward shared or overlapping goals of systemic change. Learn more through two essays: *We Are A Movement of Movements* at www.riverasun.com and *Awakening the Movement of Movements* at www.popularresistance.org

Multi-nodal: similar actions or campaigns coordinated in multiple locations at the same time. *Example: during the Let's Be*

Frank campaign, people all over the country parked their cars across the roads to block extraction companies.

Murmuration: an act of flocking by a group of birds, generally to evade a predator, used as a category of nonviolent action in the Dandelion Insurrection wherein the simple rules are known to the participants, allowing cohesive, yet flexible, action. *Examples: during the Relief Bill campaign, streets are blocked, social functions disrupted, and politicians swarmed using murmuration style actions.* Learn more in *The Dandelion Insurrection Study Guide,* pg 83.

Nonviolent Action: a method of working for change that does not use physical violence, but rather engages a broad range of nonviolent tactics of protest and persuasion, noncooperation, and intervention. In 1973, scholar Gene Sharp catalogued 198 Methods of Nonviolent Action. Find them at the Albert Einstein Institution: www.aeinstein.org

Nonviolence Commitments: an agreement, often written and signed, that outlines expectations of behavior during a nonviolent action, and helps to maintain both discipline and accountability. Check out Dr. King's Nonviolence Commitment Card on the Teaching American History website: www.teachingamericanhistory.org

Nonviolent Discipline: sticking to the agreed-upon course of a nonviolent action, both with the predetermined strategy, tactics, and methods of action; and with the maintenance of persistent nonviolent behavior even in the face of repression. *Examples: the Dandelion Insurrection has varying success maintaining nonviolent discipline throughout The Roots of Resistance. The school resistance* *and Relief Bill campaigns show widespread discipline and commitment. Later campaigns, such as the extraction resistance and the effort to repeal the American Protection Act, struggled with agent provocateurs, violent flanks, and mixed perspectives on the need for nonviolent discipline.*

Nonviolent Intervention: directly interfering in a situation using nonviolent action. The intervention usually - but not always - involves physically disrupting the system or structure of injustice, or the activities of the targeted power holder(s). Nonviolent intervention is distinguished from both symbolic protest and noncooperation. *Examples: the blockade at the bridge, the car blockades, Dandelion Swarms, Will Sharp's whistleblowing, Operation Full Stop's shutdown of systems, the Mouse's shutdown of the former president's access to funds, occupying toll booths in protest of plunder monkey takeovers, and the Grapes of Wrath filibuster speak-in.*

Nonviolent Noncooperation: "Ending, restricting, or withdrawing social, economic, or political cooperation with opponent individuals, activities, institutions, or a government." (From Sharp's Dictionary of Power and Struggle) *Examples: Los Jardineros' school walkout, boycotts of businesses that were blocking the Relief Bill, Operation Full Stop's walkout, the Little League strike for Stolen Bases, debt strike, rent strike.*

Nonviolent Protest and Persuasion: a broad range of nonviolent actions that either protest an injustice or attempt to persuade individuals or groups to take action on an issue. Some of these methods include: protests, demonstrations, rallies, banners, posters, colors and symbols, marches, walkouts, renouncing honors, protest letters, and more. *Examples: Charlie's essays, the* *yellow shirts before the Dandelion Insurrection vote, the tintamarre, marches, the Begging for Change cans and coins shaking.*

Participation: one of the key dynamics for successful nonviolent struggle, identified by Chenoweth and Stephan in *Why Civil Resistance Works*. This study found that any nonviolent movement that successfully mobilized 3.5% of the population into acts of noncooperation and intervention always won their struggle. Learn more in Erica Chenoweth and Maria J. Stephan's book, *Why Civil Resistance Works* and also in *The Dandelion Insurrection Study Guide*.

Peace Teams: "A Peace Team is a group of local people trained in peaceful conflict resolution methods who promote friendship, solidarity, social justice, and alternatives to violence in the local community. Peace teams, when requested, can provide service outside their local communities. Peace teams have been developed as responses to war and conflict much the same as that of the localized Gandhian Shanti Sena in India. Many times they are a response to potential violence in a community supported by training committed volunteers in the principles of nonviolence strategies and mediation skills." (From the Metta Center Glossary) *Example: the Dandelion Insurrection engaged peace teams in two contexts, using them as an alternative institution to police in local neighborhoods, and also using them to help maintain nonviolent discipline at demonstrations and marches.* Learn more at Meta Peace Team: www.metapeaceteam.org

Pillars of Support: the institutions and sections of a society that supply a given government (or opposition group) with its needed sources of political power to maintain and expand its power capacity. By undermining or eroding these pillars, it is possible to weaken the power of the opponent to a point where desired change is possible. The term was introduced by Robert L. Helvey. (Adapted from Sharp's Dictionary of Power and Struggle) Find an in-depth strategic analysis tool for Pillars of Support in *The Dandelion Insurrection Study Guide*, pg 40-45.

Plunder Monkeys: a term invented by author Stephen King, who referred to Donald Trump's cabinet choices as "a motley crew of plunder monkeys".

Power Vacuum: as it relates to nonviolent struggle, this describes a situation when one regime has vacated the power structure, but the incoming regime (movement or otherwise) has not yet taken over. Unexpected power grabs can occur during a power vacuum, thwarting or supplanting the nonviolent movement that ousted the previous regime. *Example: when one third of the elected officials resigned or fled, a power vacuum was opened. Without a clear plan from the Dandelion Insurrection, the remaining politicians were able to mobilize quickly to form the "Interim Government" and use the transitional period for their personal gain.*

Principled Nonviolence: a group of belief systems which include rejection of violence on grounds of a principle. "Principled nonviolence is not merely a strategy nor the recourse of the weak, it is a positive force that does not manifest its full potential until it is adopted on principle. Often its practitioners feel that it expresses something fundamental about human nature, and who they wish to become as individuals." (From the Metta Center Glossary) *Examples: several characters reference personal commitments to principled nonviolence, including Idah Robbins who draws from Dr. King's legacy, Zadie who draws from* *her beliefs about love and human nature, and Kinap whose understanding comes from her Indigenous beliefs.* Learn more at the Metta Center for Nonviolence: www.mettacenter.org

Pragmatic Nonviolence: adoption of nonviolent tactics for pragmatic reasons of effectiveness, or because violence is not a realistic option in the particular socio-political situation. *Example: the Texas Free Rangers agreed to use nonviolent tactics for their efforts with the Dandelion Insurrection. They did not adopt the principles or philosophy of nonviolence.* Learn more at the ICNC website: www.nonviolent-conflict.org

Propaganda: messaging (written, oral, or pictorial) intended to influence the attitudes, opinions, and beliefs of those to whom they are directed.

Property Damage/Destruction: physical damage or destruction to property. This is an often-contested area of tactics and has been interpreted as both violent and nonviolent, depending on situation and those defining it. Nonviolent struggle researcher Gene Sharp defines destruction of *one's own* property as a nonviolent action, but not destruction of others' property. *Examples: the Roots use property damage toward the extraction companies, as do the Offshoots during public demonstrations.* Learn more through this historical and strategic analysis piece by George Lakey, *'Suffragette' raises question of property destruction's effectiveness* which can be found on Waging Nonviolence's website at: www.wagingnonviolence.org

Repression: violent or hostile actions threatened or applied by an opponent to stifle, punish, crush, or destroy movement opposition. *Examples: private security, police, and military forces at*

the bridge during the Desert Resistance; the police at Inez' protest march; the assassination attempt on Zadie; the smear and slander campaign aimed at Charlie and Zadie. Find an exercise on managing repression in *The Dandelion Insurrection Study Guide,* pg 18-20.

Resistance Camp: a tactic of building an encampment to support resistance action, sometimes in the direct path of an opponent's intended goals. *Example: the Desert Resistance Camp.*

Restorative Justice: "Restorative justice is the nonviolent replacement for the present model of retributive justice, whose aim is punishment. Restorative justice aims to transform the harm done by a crime, which is considered a breach of relationships, into restored relationships among all parties." (From the Metta Center Glossary) *Example: restorative justice is mentioned as an alternative community conflict program used by neighborhoods struggling with lack of trust of established channels such as the police and justice system.* Learn more at the Metta Center for Nonviolence: www.mettacenter.org

Sabotage: acts intended to immobilize, dismantle, damage, or destroy equipment, machinery, communications, facilities, means of transportation and so on, carried out by persons or groups in conflict with the owner, operator, or beneficiary of the goods or services (including the state or occupation regime). *Examples: the pipeline explosion and the transformer station explosion.*

Self-Care: practices that nourish the physical, mental, emotional, and spiritual well-being of activists with the intention of building resilience for the long-haul of social change. *Examples: Tansy Beaulisle's jogging practice, Alex Kelley or Tucker Jones' meditation practice.*

Self-Defense: defense of one's self when physically attacked. In the context of nonviolent actions, the forms of self-defense used at protests or demonstrations should remain non-violent if the group seeks to make repression backfire on the oppressor.

Smear Campaign: an effort to damage or call into question someone's reputation through negative propaganda. *Examples: pg 209, onward, Charlie and Zadie are both the subjects of smear campaigns.*

Slogans: short and memorable written or spoken messages, opinions, or views. *Examples: "Be kind, be connected, be unafraid" is a slogan of the Dandelion Insurrection, as is "For life, liberty, and love!"*

Spectrum of Allies: a strategy tool used by nonviolent movement organizers to identify ally/opposition stances and analyze how to shift people and groups into more favorable positions in relation to the goals of the movement. Learn more at Training for Change: www.trainingforchange.org or in *The Dandelion Insurrection Study Guide,* pg 46-48.

Spiritual Activism: a style of activism rooted in one's spirituality; or conversely, a socially-engaged spirituality. *Example: Kinap's approach to spirit-based activism.* Learn more at: www.spiritualprogressives.org or in *Sacred Instructions: Indigenous Wisdom for Living Spirit-Based Change* by Sherri Mitchell - Weh'na Ha'mu' Kwasset (She Who Brings the Light).

Strategy: a plan of action that shows how to achieve desired goals and objectives. *Example: pg 91, Alex Kelley works on strategic analysis and planning in relation to stopping the plunder monkeys.* Learn more about developing strategy for nonviolent campaigns in *The Dandelion Insurrection Study Guide.*

Strike: an organized halt or slow-down of labor during a conflict, intended to pressure employers or others for a particular goal or set of goals. This is a broad category of nonviolent action that includes many variations based on participants, duration, intention, and application. *Examples: the Towing Union strike in support of the car blockades, the Little League strike against "stolen bases" in protest of plunder monkeys; the Debt Prison strike. Note: though the broader Debt Strike and earlier rent strikes used the term "strike", they are technically not strikes, but other forms of nonviolent action involving withholding of payments.*

Swarming: a collective behavior of animals moving en masse, including swarms of hornets or bees, schools of fish, flocks of migrating birds, and murmurations of starlings or swallows. Swarming is used for group protection, hunting, and travelling. As a concept, it is applied to human group movement and strategies for mass action. It has been used in small groups (as in some flash actions) and also in complex systems analysis for the movement of movements (see definition, above). *Examples: the Dandelion Swarms, pg 68, use swarming and murmurations to create flexible, but unified, mobile street actions capable of pressuring politicians and others.* Learn more on Wikipedia under "Swarm Behavior". See also, *Swarming: That's How the Movement of Movement Rolls* at www.riverasun.com

Targets: the focus of a nonviolent action, campaign, or movement. Targets may be individuals, groups, corporate entities, government bodies, and more. A target may be a primary target (capable of making a direct decision or action on the issue), or a secondary target (capable of applying pressure to the primary target), or even a tertiary target like a potential ally group the movement is attempting to mobilize into action. *Examples: during the Relief Bill campaign, the primary targets were the Congresspersons, the secondary targets were their donors and businesses trying to block the bill, and the tertiary targets were several groups of citizens, including those who opposed the bill.* Learn more about planning strategic campaigns and choosing targets on the War Resisters' International Website: www.wri-irg.org

Tintamarre: an Acadian pots-and-pans, bells-and-whistles demonstration named after the sound of birds rising to wing and settling down again. It is used as a celebration of culture and survival, as well as overcoming cultural repression. *Example: pg 71, Valier suggests adding an element of the tintamarre to the Relief Bill actions.* Learn more about the tintamarre on Wikipedia.

Transparency/Openness: an operational principle in nonviolent action that states that the organizations and individuals involved in the nonviolent movement will act publicly and without secrecy, that the leaders will be known to the public and opponents, that activities will be announced and responsibility for them will be taken by the movement without deceit or hiding. *Examples: the Dandelion Insurrection operates largely on transparency and openness in The Roots of Resistance, unlike in the* *first novel. This stands in contrast to the actions of the Roots, who operate covertly and secretly.*

Violent Flanks: an armed and violent group existing either within or independently of a nonviolent movement. *Examples: the Roots and the Offshoots are both violent flanks in relation to the Dandelion Insurrection.* For further research of the dynamics and effects, see Chenoweth and Schock's study, *Do Contemporaneous Armed Challenges Affect the Outcomes of Mass Nonviolent Campaigns?*

Whistleblowing: action by individuals to expose harmful or dangerous policies, corruption, or falsehoods of a company or government agency. *Examples: the Mouse blows the whistle on the hidden version of the Relief Bill. Will Sharp blows the whistle on the true identity and purpose of the Roots.* Learn more at Wikipedia: en.wikipedia.org/wiki/Whistleblower

Resources for Further Study

. . . . .

Books:

The Dandelion Insurrection Study Guide: Making Change Through Nonviolent Action by Rivera Sun

Sharp's Dictionary of Power and Struggle by Gene Sharp

Why Civil Resistance Works by Erica Chenoweth and Maria J. Stephan

Sacred Instructions: Indigenous Wisdom for Living Spirit-Based Change by Sherri Mitchell - Weh'na Ha'mu' Kwasset

The Handbook for Nonviolent Campaigns by War Resisters' International

Websites/Online Resources:

Albert Einstein Institution: www.aeinstein.org

Backbone Campaign: www.backbonecampaign.org

Beautiful Trouble: www.beautifultrouble.org

International Center On Nonviolent Conflict: www.nonviolent-conflict.org

Metta Center for Nonviolence: www.mettacenter.org

Meta Peace Team: www.metapeaceteam.org

New Tactics in Human Rights: www.newtactics.org

Pace e Bene/Campaign Nonviolence: www.paceebene.org

Popular Resistance: www.popularresistance.org

Rivera Sun: www.riverasun.com

Training for Change: www.trainingforchange.org

Waging Nonviolence: www.wagingnonviolence.org

War Resisters' International www.wri-irg.org

ACKNOWLEDGMENTS

This novel is something of a miracle, and would not have been possible without the support of hundreds of people. I would like to thank all of the readers who supported the Community Publishing Campaign. Your enthusiasm means the world to me and is the essential ingredient in bringing this novel to life.

I would also like to thank Maja Bengston, Robert Simonds, Leslie Cottrell Simonds, and DeLores Cook for your support this year as I healed from cancer. Another surge of gratitude goes out to my doctors and healers, particularly Dr. Lilly-Marie Blecher, Dr. Joanna Hooper, and Dr. Elizabeth Lokich. Without your loving care, I would not be here today, and neither would this book.

Many thanks to my early readers: Cindy Reinhardt, Jenny Bird, Tom Hastings, and Dariel Garner for your invaluable feedback and perspectives. Also, thank you to civil resistance researchers Erica Chenoweth, Kurt Schock, Maria J. Stephan, and many more, for your information about the dynamics of violent flanks in the context of largely nonviolent movements. I would also like to thank Stephanie N. Van Hook for the idea to include a glossary of techniques in the novel.

Special thanks to Veronica Pelicaric for help with Spanish translations, and to Andre Roy, Luc Roy, Dave Wylie, Debbie Gendreau, and Leah Cook for assistance with French translations and Acadian culture. All mistakes and errors are my own. I would also like to thank Sherri Mitchell - Wena'hamu'gwasit for the inspiration and input on the character of Kinap. It was an honor to include this wisdom.

Lastly, my gratitude goes out to all the people around the world and throughout time that have walked with the lineage of nonviolence and made the rising tide of movements one of the most remarkable set of stories humanity has ever told.

About the Author

Rivera Sun is the author of *The Way Between, Billionaire Buddha, The Dandelion Insurrection* and *Steam Drills, Treadmills, and Shooting Stars,* as well as nine plays, a study guide to nonviolent action, a book of poetry, and numerous articles. She has red hair, a twin sister, and a fondness for esoteric mystics. She went to Bennington College to study writing as a Harcourt Scholar and graduated with a degree in dance. She lives in an earthship house in New Mexico, where she writes essays and novels. She is the cohost of a weekly radio program, a nonviolence trainer, and an activist. She writes several essays each week for peace and justice journals. Rivera has been an aerial dancer, a bike messenger, and a gung-fu style tea server. Everything else about her - except her writing - is perfectly ordinary.

Rivera Sun also loves hearing from her readers.
Email: info@riverasun.com
Facebook: Rivera Sun
Twitter: @RiveraSunAuthor
Website: www.riverasun.com

Praise for Rivera Sun's
The Dandelion Insurrection

A rare gem of a book, a must read, it charts the way forward in this time of turmoil and transformation." - Velcrow Ripper, director Occupy Love, Genie Award Winner

"When fear is used to control us, love is how we rebel!" Under a
 gathering storm of tyranny, Zadie Byrd Gray whirls into the life of Charlie Rider and asks him to become the voice of the Dandelion Insurrection. With the rallying cry of life, liberty, and love, Zadie and Charlie fly across America leaving a wake of revolution in their path. Passion erupts. Danger abounds. The lives of millions hang by a thin thread of courage, but in the midst of the madness, the golden soul of humanity blossoms . . . and miracles start to unfold!

"This novel will not only make you want to change the world, it will remind you that you can." - Gayle Brandeis, author of *The Book of Dead Birds*, winner of the Bellwether Prize for Socially Engaged Fiction

"Close your eyes and imagine the force of the people and the power of love overcoming the force of greed and the love of power. Then read *The Dandelion Insurrection*. In a world where despair has deep roots, *The Dandelion Insurrection* bursts forth with joyful abandon." - Medea Benjamin, Co-founder of CodePink

"THE handbook for the coming revolution!" - Lo Daniels, Editor of Dandelion Salad

Also Available!
The Dandelion Insurrection Study Guide
to Making Change Through Nonviolent Action

The Way Between
by Rivera Sun

Between flight and fight lies a mysterious third path called *The Way Between,* and young shepherdess and orphan Ari Ara must  master it . . . before war destroys everything she loves! She begins training as the apprentice of the great warrior Shulen, and enters a world of warriors and secrets, swords and magic, friendship and mystery. She uncovers forbidden prophecies, searches for the lost heir to two thrones, and chases the elusive forest-dwelling Fanten to unravel their hidden knowledge. Full of twists and turns and surprises, *The Way Between* is bound to carve out a niche on your bookshelves and a place in your heart!

"This novel should be read aloud to everyone, by everyone, from childhood onward. Rivera Sun writes in a style as magical as Tolkien and as authentic as Twain."
- Tom Hastings, Director of PeaceVoice

"Rivera Sun has, once again, used her passion for nonviolence and her talent for putting thoughts into powerful words."
-Robin Wildman, Fifth Grade Teacher, Nonviolent Schools Movement, and Nonviolence Trainer

"A wonderful book! It is so rare to find exciting fiction for young people and adults that shows creative solutions to conflict, and challenges violence with active nonviolence and peace. Ari Ara is a delightful character and this story is a gem."
- Heart Phoenix, River Phoenix Center for Peacebuilding

Reader Praise for Rivera Sun's
Steam Drills, Treadmills, and Shooting Stars

Steam Drills, Treadmills, and Shooting Stars is a story about people just like you, filled with the audacity of hope and fueled by the passion of unstoppable love. The ghost of folk hero John Henry haunts Jack Dalton, a corporate lawyer for Standard Coal as Henrietta Owens, activist and mother, wakes up the nation with some tough-loving truth about the environment, the economy, justice, and hope. Pressures mount as John Henry challenges Jack to stand up to the steam drills of contemporary America . . . before it's too late.

"This book is a gem and I'm going to put it in my jewelry box!"

"It 'dips your head in a bucket of truth'."

"This is not a page turner . . . it stops you in your tracks and makes you revel in the beauty of the written word."

"Epic, mythic . . .it's like going to church and praying for the salvation of yourself and your people and your country."

"Controversial, political, and so full of love."

"Partway through reading, I realized I was participating in a historical event. This book has changed me and will change everyone who reads it."

"I am sixty-two years old, and I cried for myself, my neighbors, our country and the earth. I cried and am so much better for it. I would recommend this book to everyone."

Praise for Rivera Sun's *Billionaire Buddha*

From fabulous wealth to unlimited blessings, the price of enlightenment may bankrupt billionaire Dave Grant. Emotionally destitute in the prime of his career, he searches for love and collides with Joan Hathaway. The encounter rattles his soul and unravels his world. Capitalism, property, wealth, mansions: his notions of success crumble into dust. From toasting champagne on top of the world to swigging whiskey with bums in the gutter, Dave Grant's journey is an unforgettable ride that leaves you cheering!

". . . inspirational and transformational! An enjoyable read for one's heart and soul."
-Chuck Collins, senior scholar, Institute for Policy Studies; co-author with Bill Gates Sr. of 'Wealth and Our Commonwealth'

". . . inspiring a skeptic is no easy task and Rivera Sun manages to do so, gracefully, convincingly, and admirably."
- Casey Dorman, Editor-in-Chief, Lost Coast Review

"People, if you haven't gotten your copy of *Billionaire Buddha* yet, you are letting a rare opportunity slip through your fingers. It's that good."
- Burt Kempner, screenwriter, producer and author of children's books

"This is the kind of book that hits you in the gut and makes you stop and think about what you just read."
- Rob Garvey, reader

"A clear and conscious look at our times and the dire need for a real change to heart based living."
- Carol Ranellone, reader

Made in the USA
San Bernardino, CA
06 March 2018